Poetry and Contemporary Culture

Poetry and Contemporary Culture

The Question of Value

Edited by Andrew Michael Roberts and Jonathan Allison

Edinburgh University Press

© Andrew Michael Roberts and Jonathan Allison, 2002

Edinburgh University Press Ltd
22 George Square, Edinburgh

Typeset in 10pt Sabon
by Bibliocraft Ltd, Dundee, and
printed and bound in Great Britain by
MPG Books Ltd, Bodmin, Cornwall

A CIP record for this book is available from the British Library

ISBN 0 7486 1137 1 (hardback)

Contents

Acknowledgements

The editors would like to thank Jackie Jones and Robert Crawford for valuable advice, Jim Stewart for his work on the index and the staff at Edinburgh University Press for their patient support.

The sources of copyright materials quoted in this volume are acknowledged in detail in the endnotes to each chapter, which should be seen, like this page, as an extension of the copyright page of the present volume. Grateful acknowledgement is made to the following sources for permission to reproduce material previously published elsewhere. Every effort has been made to trace the copyright holders, but if any have been inadvertently overlooked, the publisher will be pleased to make the necessary arrangements at the first opportunity.

Kenneth Goldsmith, excerpts from *Fidget* (1999), including pages from web version (http://www.chbooks.com/online/fidget/text.html) and excerpts from *No. 111 2.7.93–10.20.96* (1997). Reprinted by permission of the author.

Kenneth Goldsmith and Clem Paulsen, still image from Java Applet version of *Fidget* (http://www.chbooks.com/online/fidget/text.html), by permission of Kenneth Goldsmith.

Paula Court, photograph of *Fidget*, performed at the Whitney Museum of American Art at Philip Morris, New York, by Kenneth Goldsmith and Theo Beckmann. Reproduced by permission of the Whitney Museum.

John Kinsella, excerpts from *Kangaroo Virus* (1998). Reprinted by permission of the author.

Ron Sims, photographs from *Kangaroo Virus* (1998). Reproduced by permission of the photographer.

Jackie Kay, excerpt from *Twice Through the Heart*, BBC 2, 19 June 1992. Quoted by permission of the BBC and Peters, Fraser & Dunlop on behalf of Jackie Kay.

Simon Armitage, excerpts from *Killing Time* (1999). Reprinted by permission of Faber and Faber and David Godwin Associates.

Edwin Morgan, excerpt from 'Pleasures of a Technological University', from *Collected Poems* (1990). Reprinted by permission of the author and Carcanet Press Ltd.

David Marriott, excerpts from 'Names of the Fathers' and 'the "secret" of this form itself', from *Angel Exhaust* (1997). Reprinted by permission of the author.

Robin Becker, excerpt from 'Why We Fear the Amish', from *The Horse Fair*, © 2000. Reprinted by permission of the University of Pittsburgh Press.

Robert Pinsky, excerpt from 'The Night Game', from *The Want Bone*, 1991. Reprinted by permission of HarperCollins Publishers.

Edwin Morgan, excerpt from 'The Second Life', from *Collected Poems* (1990). Reprinted by permission of the author and Carcanet Press Ltd.

Liz Lochhead, excerpts from, 'Letter from New England' and 'In the Cutting Room' from *Dreaming Frankenstein and Collected Poems* (2000). Reprinted by permission of Polygon.

John Montague, excerpts from 'A Muddy Cup', 'A Flowering Absence', 'A Grafted Tongue', 'A New Siege', from *Collected Poems* (1995). Reprinted by kind permission of the author, the Gallery Press, Loughcrew, Oldcastle, Co Meath, Ireland, and Wake Forest University Press.

William Carlos Williams, excerpt from 'This is Just to Say', from *Collected Poems: 1909–1939*, Volume I, copyright © 1938 by New Directions Publishing Corp. (1987). Reprinted by permission of the estate of the author, Carcanet Press Ltd and New Directions Publishing Corp.

Ted Hughes, excerpts from 'Ghost Crabs', 'Out', 'Scapegoats and Rabies', from *Wodwo* (1967); 'Dust as We Are', 'For the Duration', from *Wolfwatching* (1989); 'Tiger Psalm', from *New Selected Poems* (1995). Reprinted by permission of Faber and Faber.

Philip Larkin, excerpts from 'MCMXIV', *Collected Poems* (1988). Reprinted by permission of Faber and Faberand Farrar, Straus and Giroux, Inc.

Michael Longley, excerpt from unpublished draft of 'Wounds'. Reprinted by permission of Emory University, Atlanta and the author.

Michael Longley, excerpt from 'In Memoriam', from *Selected Poems* (1998). Reprinted by permission of The Random House Group Ltd and Wake Forest University Press.

Michael Longley, excerpts from 'Wounds' from *Selected Poems* (1998). Reprinted by permission of The Random House Group Ltd and Wake Forest University Press.

Michael Longley, excerpts from 'The War Graves' from *The Weather in Japan* (2000), published by Jonathan Cape and Wake Forest University Press. Reprinted by permission of The Random House Group Ltd and Wake Forest University Press.

Michael Longley, excerpts from 'Ceasefire', from *The Ghost Orchid* (1995), published by Martin Secker and Warburg and Wake Forest University Press. Reprinted by permission of The Random House Group Ltd and Wake Forest University Press.

Gwendolyn Brooks, 'We Real Cool', from *Blacks* (1987). Reprinted by permission of Third World Press.

Stevie Smith, excerpt from 'Tenuous and Precarious', from *Collected Poems* (1975). Reprinted by permission of Penguin Books.

Roger McGough, excerpt from *Poet's News* (1993). Reprinted by permission of the BBC and Peters, Fraser and Dunlop.

Simon Armitage, excerpt from *Drinking for England* (1998). Reprinted by permission of the BBC and David Godwin Associates.

Kathleen Jamie, excerpt from 'Mr and Mrs Scotland are Dead', from *The Queen of Sheba* (1994). Reprinted by permission of the author.

W. N. Herbert, excerpt from 'The Anthropological Museum', from *Other Tongues* (1990). Reprinted by permission of the author.

Tom Leonard, excerpt from 'Just ti Let Yi No', from *Intimate Voices: Selected Work 1965–1983* (1984). Reprinted by permission of Galloping Dog Press.

Robert Lowell, excerpts from 'Words for Hart Crane', from *Life Studies* (1972) and 'For the Union Dead', from *For the Union Dead* (1965). Reprinted by permission of Faber and Faber and Farrar, Straus and Giroux, Inc.

Seamus Heaney, excerpts from 'From the Land of the Unspoken' from *The Haw Lantern* (1987) and 'Beyond Sargasso Sea' ('A Lough Neagh Sequence'), from *Door Into the Dark* (1969). Reprinted by permission of Faber and Faber and Farrar, Straus and Giroux, Inc.

Douglas Dunn, excerpts from 'Renfrewshire Traveller, 'The Wealth' and 'Stranger's Grief', from *Selected Poems 1964–83* (1986) and 'Jig of the Week no. 21', from *Northlight* (1988). Reprinted by permission of Faber and Faber and Peters, Fraser and Dunlop.

Paul Muldoon, excerpts from '7 Middagh Street', from *Meeting the British* (1987) and from 'The Briefcase', 'Campanella', 'Rutherford', 'Franklin', 'Pascal' and 'Hobbes', from *Madoc: A Mystery* (1990). Reprinted by permission of Faber and Faber and Farrar, Straus and Giroux.

Louis Simpson, excerpt from 'Walt Whitman at Bear Mountain', from *At the End of the Open Road* (1963). Reprinted by permission of Wesleyan University Press.

Hugh MacDiarmid, 'A Drunk Man Looks at the Thistle', from *Selected Poems* (1992). Reprinted by permission of Carcanet Press Ltd.

Introduction

I Contemporary Poetry and the Question of Value
Andrew Michael Roberts

Poetry occupies an ambivalent place in contemporary British and American culture, where it is viewed simultaneously and paradoxically as a specialist, abstruse intellectual discipline and as the most accessible and personal of expressive media. On the one hand poetry is still perceived by many as a 'high' art form, of interest to a small minority: even students of literature often regard it as relatively difficult and inaccessible. These perceptions are conditioned both by the Romantic image of the poet as unique, inspired prophet and by the Modernist/ avant-garde stress on difficulty, complexity and allusion. On the other hand, poetry is often seen as a 'natural' medium for the recounting and examining of personal experience: this is apparent in the large number of people who write poetry, the huge entries for poetry competitions and the popularity of poetry in creative writing classes on both sides of the Atlantic. In the US a large volume of poetry (often written under the guidance of a resident or tenured poet) is continually published in small magazines, produced by the English departments of many colleges and universities throughout the country. There is also a growing subculture of open mike sessions in 'poetry bars', especially in the larger metropolitan areas like New York and Chicago, and of 'poetry slams', described by one critic as 'an indigenous if belated populist revolt against the complacencies and etiquette of poetry's public venues'.[1] Such phenomena, all occurring in the shadow of major cuts in National Endowment for the

---

[1] Jed Rasula, *The American Poetry Wax Museum: Reality Effects, 1940–1990* (Urbana, IL: NCTE, 1996), p. 366n. John K. Walters notes that '[p]oetry slams are becoming a national phenomenon. These competitions probably originated in 1985 in Chicago, IL, and spread to Boston, New York, and other areas. In a poetry slam, each poet performs one poem, without props or costumes, in three minutes and ten seconds. Judges are selected from the audience at random and award each poem a score from 0 to 10. In the National Slam Championships poets compete in teams; the 1999 national slam had about 200 poets in 45 teams and an audience of more than 1300. Abstract, John K. Walters, 'Slam-Bang Poetry', *Biblio*, 4.4 (April 1999), p. 30. For a history of slams, see Kurt Heintz, 'An Incomplete History of Slam: A Biography of an Evolving Poetry Movement', retrieved 19 October 2000, from the World Wide Web at http://www.e-poets.net/library/slam.

Arts (NEA) funding for the creative arts, point to the continuing popularity of poetry as an expressive medium. Poetry readings, poetry workshops and traditions of performance poetry give the form accessibility in
both Britain and the US, while in Britain a wide variety of promotional
methods have been deployed by poets and publishers, including the 1994
'New Generation' promotion, which led to much-derided claims that
poetry was 'the new rock and roll' and, briefly, to a high level of exposure
on television and other media.[2] Some forms of poetry are strongly
associated with the academy, and thus tend to be positioned as part of
contemporary theoretical debates; yet poetry is closely allied to song
lyrics, one of the most popular forms of post-war Western culture and
often associated with youth and 'alternative' cultures.

How do we assess the value of poetry in the context of these competing
representations? Discussions of contemporary poetry are pervaded by the
tension between singular and multiple values, and the related, though not
identical, binary of absolute and relative value. Is there ultimately only
one form of poetic value, a gold standard against which all poetry can be
assessed? Or are different poems and different sorts of poetry valuable in
incommensurable ways, so that, in assessing their value, one must first
ask, valuable for what? Both the critique of essentialism in contemporary
theory and the evident multiplicity of contemporary poetic practice
militate against the belief in a single form of poetic value. On the other
hand, the idea of poetic value being contingent upon the particular
context and the particular needs of the reader or group of readers comes
up against a continuing resistance to an instrumental valuation of poetry,
a form of valuation which would seem to subordinate poetry to the
tyranny of local purposes.

If such considerations seem abstract and remote from the ordinary
conversations which go on about poems and poets, this is an illusion.
Poetry and, more especially, its value or lack of value arouse strong
feelings and strong opinions. Questions of singular versus multiple value,
and absolute versus relative value, are raised implicitly or explicitly
whenever such feelings and opinions are expressed, whether in the context
of sophisticated academic debate or conversational expression of personal
preference. So, for example, whenever a reviewer or broadcaster describes
a poet as 'amongst the three or four finest poets of his or her generation',
or as 'perhaps the greatest poet writing in English today', a singular scale
of value is evoked. Literary prizes, unless for a specific form of poetry, also
assume the possibility of ranking on a single scale of value. There is a
curious convention operative in some blurbs and reviews that to praise a
poet one must denigrate other poets. An example would be the comment
by James Fenton in the *Sunday Times* which adorns the front of Tony

---

[2] See *Poetry Review*, 84.1 (Spring 1994), 'New Generation Poets' special issue.

Harrison's *Selected Poems*: 'one of the few modern poets who actually has the gift of composing poetry' (one wonders what gift other contemporary poets possess).[3] Less extreme but in the same vein is the quote from the *New York Times* on the back cover of Denise Levertov's *Selected Poems*: 'She is the most subtly skilful poet of her generation, the most profound, the most modest, the most moving' (are *all* those many other poets, from John Ashbery to Ed Dorn really less subtle, less skilful, less profound, less modest *and* less moving?).[4] It is easy to dismiss such comments as reviewer's hyperbole; yet they are the common currency of public discussions of poetry, and the first at least was made by a distinguished poet and Professor of Poetry at Oxford University.

There is a strong tendency in humanist criticism to associate value itself, in an ultimate or transcendent sense, with singular value. This association probably results from the Christian, monotheistic, essentialist roots of humanist values. These roots find expression in a long tradition which accords special status to the idea of poetry. In this tradition, not only is poetry held to be an art which (like other arts) embodies some form of transcendent value, but the term 'poetry' is at times used to refer to the essence of truth and knowledge, so that poetry comes to stand for transcendent value itself, in the aesthetic sphere and even beyond. This tradition emerges with the Romantic poets' linking of poetry (via the Imagination) to the spirit, as in Shelley's ringing claims that 'a poem is the very image of life expressed in its eternal truth', and that poetry is 'something divine' and 'at once the centre and circumference of knowledge'.[5] Such conceptions enter modernism in Wallace Stevens's high claims for the imagination (romantic in source, despite his wish to disassociate them from Romanticism), and persist in contemporary poetry in Seamus Heaney's description of poetry as the 'revelation of the self to the self, as restoration of the culture to itself'.[6] Unfashionable

---

[3] James Fenton, quoted on front cover of Tony Harrison, *Selected Poems* (Harmondsworth: Penguin, 1984).

[4] *New York Times* reviewer, quoted on back cover of Denise Levertov, *Selected Poems* (Newcastle upon Tyne: Bloodaxe, 1986).

[5] Percy Bysshe Shelley, *A Defence of Poetry; or, Remarks Suggested by an Essay Entitled 'The Four Ages of Poetry'*, in Duncan Wu (ed.), *Romanticism: An Anthology* (2nd edition, Oxford: Blackwell, 1998), pp. 947, 953.

[6] See Wallace Stevens, 'Imagination as Value', in *The Necessary Angel: Essays on Reality and the Imagination* (London: Faber, 1960), pp. 131–56; Seamus Heaney, 'Feeling into Words', in *Preoccupations: Selected Prose 1968–1978* (1980; London: Faber, 1984), p. 41. Stevens quotes Ernst Cassirer's observation that in Romantic thought '[i]magination is no longer that special human activity which builds up the human world of art. It now has universal metaphysical value. Poetic imagination is the only clue to reality'. Stevens, while attacking Romanticism as a belittling misuse of the imagination, in effect takes over the Romantic elevation of the poetic imagination as 'one of the great human powers' and 'the only genius' (pp. 136, 138, 139).

as it may be in the academy, humanism continues as a strong presence there and is the dominant discourse for literary discussion in much of the media. This is particularly so in relation to poetry which, for a considerable time, was found less amenable than the novel to political, post-structuralist and postmodernist theory, although that situation has now changed.[7] This humanist tradition associates multiple values with the dispersal and erosion of value itself. While giving positive recognition to richness, range, complexity and variety within certain limits (as in the New Critical ideal of ambiguity and paradox serving an ultimate unity), it postulates an essence of poetic value subsisting within various forms. Here the tendency to equate singular with absolute value, and multiple with relative value, is strong. There is a sense that, if poems can be good in many different ways and for many different purposes, then the assessment of their value becomes even more subjective and not susceptible of final decision. Logically this need not be so, given that the rating of poems on a single scale could be equally subjective. In practice, however, it is probably the case. Since the generally admitted element of subjectivity in *all* literary evaluation means that final decision is a matter of consensus rather than proof, an acknowledgement that different sorts of poetry have different value for different groups implies that consensus would be local and various. This is evidently the case in contemporary culture, not least because of its multiculturalism and transnationalism, but it is unattractive to those who wish to retain the idea of a unified common culture within national boundaries (another idea which is more often implicitly assumed than it is explicitly defended). This humanist discourse is explicitly adhered to by some critics of poetry, but is also implicitly present in the almost universal tendency to identify at least *some* poetry as 'bad' in a general or absolute sense, not merely bad in terms of a particular aesthetic or purpose. A further source of resistance to the idea of multiple value in poetry is the fear or belief that it will erode the boundaries of the poetic (even though the scholarly study of genre should, in principle, imply an acceptance of multiple forms of poetic value). The view that there is an essence of the poetic enables debates about poetic value to be phrased in the terms of inclusion or exclusion in the poetic as such. So, for example, Geoffrey Hill has commented that 'a lot of the poems one sees in magazines could very well be described as stills from home movies', adding that, 'people have every right to make home movies; all I am saying is that poems are not home movies'.[8] Here a nominalist and an

---

[7] See Anthony Easthope and John O. Thompson (eds), *Contemporary Poetry meets Modern Theory* (Hemel Hempstead: Harvester Wheatsheaf, 1991); James Acheson and Romana Huk (eds), *Contemporary British Poetry: Essays in Theory and Criticism* (Albany, NY: SUNY Press, 1996).

[8] Geoffrey Hill, interview with Hermione Lee, *Book Four*, Channel Four Television (UK), 2 October 1985.

essentialist view of poetry contend within the same sequence of thought: Hill is willing to grant the 'home movies' a certain (if clearly lesser) value, but sees this as a non-poetic value, rather than a different poetic value. Similarly, Ted Hughes has written that '[i]t's my suspicion that no poem can be a poem that is not a statement from the powers in control of our life, the ultimate suffering and decision in us'.[9] This is evidently a way of describing one sort of poetry, of which Hughes's own mythic, uncanny nature poetry would stand as a prominent example. Rather than seeing other forms of poetry (such as the satirical, humorous, political or ironic) as of differing, or even of less, poetic value, the statement sees them as simply *not poetry*; as if there can only be one essence of the poetic.

A range of influences stand opposed to this ancient but persistent impulse to singular and absolute standards of evaluation (an impulse detectable at times even in the discourse of those opposed on principle to the singular and the absolute). Various cultural, demographic, political and institutional factors in contemporary British and American society make a certain degree of plurality inescapable. At the same time, the discourses of postmodernism, postcolonialism and multiculturalism tend to associate value not with singularity but with multiplicity and relativity (at times, paradoxically, seeming to attribute absolute value to relativity and multiplicity). Each of these factors takes different though related forms on opposite sides of the Atlantic. The positive values associated by the political Left with forms of multiculturalism and by much of the political spectrum with 'democracy' and 'egalitarianism' carry over into the discourse of cultural value, and one sign of this influence in writing about British poetry is the use of unstable or ambiguous political metaphors. The introduction to *The Penguin Book of Contemporary British Poetry*, by Blake Morrison and Andrew Motion, struggles to claim some unified value for a disparate, if partial, collection of poets and ends by asserting that their common purpose is 'to extend the imaginative franchise'.[10] Whether this is a political metaphor (more poets getting the vote, or more readers?) or a commercial one (franchising opportunities for the 'new poetry' brand name) remains unclear. It perhaps derives loosely from Tony Harrison's more pointed political metaphor, 'We'll occupy / Your lousy leasehold Poetry'.[11] A comparable ambiguity to that of Morrison and Motion, though perhaps used more deliberately, is found in the title of Sean O'Brien's *The Deregulated Muse*, a survey of contemporary British and Irish poetry in which the preface, while referring to

---

[9] Ted Hughes, 'Notes on the Chronological Order of Sylvia Plath's Poems', in Charles Newman (ed.), *The Art of Sylvia Plath* (London: Faber, 1970), p. 194.

[10] Blake Morrison and Andrew Motion (eds), *The Penguin Book of Contemporary British Poetry* (London: Penguin, 1982), Introduction, p. 20.

[11] Tony Harrison, 'Them & [uz]', II, *Selected Poems*, p. 123.

Thatcherite deregulation of industry and the market, attempts to link poetry to such socio-economic and political developments in terms of a rather vague range of cultural 'anxieties'. The implication is, on the one hand, that a 'deregulated muse' encourages '*variousness* [which] seems to prevent, or at any rate dispute, the emergence of a dominant line' but, on the other, that (as in the commercial sphere) deregulation involved selling off cheap to venture capitalists what had previously been held in common, in response to ideas which 'a generation ago would have seemed ... frankly *immoral*'.[12] The confused, if suggestive, metaphor enables O'Brien to finesse the choice between a postmodernist celebration of variety and multiplicity (putatively complicit with the ideology of consumerism and the sometimes spurious 'choice' generated by a free market) and a humanist deprecation of the intrusion of commercial values into the field of the aesthetic. Such political tropes reflect in various ways the history of the class system and class struggle in Britain (the gradual extension of the franchise during the nineteenth and early twentieth centuries; language as a marker of class; Thatcherite deregulation as an attempt to destroy the power of predominantly working-class trade unions). In America, it is race and gender which are most prominent in the collective awareness of social divisions, and the importance of identity politics in the American academy and public life has meant that these divisions enter the aesthetic sphere as explicit lines of debate and contestation, rather than as metaphors. At the same time, the American avant-garde (in common with its British counterpart, but perhaps more assertively), regards all aspects of poetry, including the processes of writing, reading, publication and distribution, poetic form, and social, group and institutional configurations, as ideological and proposes a model of poetry as 'an active arena for exploring basic questions about political thought and action'.[13]

Underlying the allegiance of some to singular value is the belief that it constitutes a resistance to the fluidity and relativity of market-led consumerism, which would value poetry according to fashion and popularity rather than intrinsic literary merit. Yet, as Steven Connor points out:

> the evil of economic exchange-value is not that it melts away the fixity of use-value, but precisely that it subordinates all forms of exchange to the force of one form alone – the economic. The general

---

[12] Sean O'Brien, *The Deregulated Muse: Essays on Contemporary British and Irish Poetry* (Newcastle upon Tyne: Bloodaxe, 1998), pp. 10, 9.

[13] Charles Bernstein (ed.), *The Politics of Poetic Form: Poetry and Public Policy* (New York: Roof Books/Segue Foundation, 1990), preface, p. vii. The list of aspects of poetry held to be political derives from Roger Horrocks, as quoted by Bernstein on this page.

corruption of an era of exchange-value lies in the fact that it makes everything exchangeable according to this one standard or register.[14]

While the antithesis between exchange- and use-value is not simply homologous to that between commercial and aesthetic value, Connor's observation does suggest that objections to multiple aesthetic values, on the grounds that they corrupt or dilute the poetic, are misconceived. What erodes the specific values of the poetic is not multiple aesthetics but the cultural production of variety divorced from plurality of aesthetic values, so that the poem derives its value simply from its presence in a system of exchange and, as Connor observes, 'diversity acts in the service of uniformity'.[15] A case could certainly be made, for example (and has been made by various poets and critics influenced by or participating in forms of Language poetry), that, in the contemporary literary marketplace, 'personality' is the equivalent of money – the projected personality of the poet and the conception of poetry as the expression *of* that personality function as the universal currency according to which poetry can be accorded a notional, fluctuating value, while imposing a uniformity which displaces a whole range of other possible values, aesthetic, political and ethical.[16]

The present volume does not seek to arbitrate on such questions of value, though the contributors make clear, in various ways, their own evaluative judgements. Any attempt to survey the question of poetry and its value in contemporary culture must tread a fine line between the lure of assumed Olympian detachment and the side-step into irritable partisanship. We cannot claim to be objective – indeed, to be objective about questions of value is arguably impossible by definition – but, by the very nature of an edited collection, and by the choice of topics and contributors, we hope to have kept questions of value open rather than closed them prematurely. The book thus participates in what Connor terms 'the imperative to value', which he describes as 'not only distinct from the operation of particular values [but] opposed to it ... because the imperative dimension commands that we continue evaluating in the face of every

[14] Steven Connor, *Theory and Cultural Value* (Oxford and Cambridge, MA: Blackwell, 1992), p. 4. The whole argument of this section of the introduction is indebted to Connor's book in various ways, although I am sceptical about his vision of 'a utopia ... not of incommensurability, but of infinitely multiple commensurabilities' (p. 4), since it seems to me that this would tend to collapse back into the sort of uniformity which he describes.

[15] Connor, *Theory and Cultural Value*, p. 4. Connor discusses Terry Eagleton's attempt to unify aesthetic and use value, noting that 'Marx's implied association between the wholeness of the aesthetic and the immediacy of use-value is ... vulnerable to the objection that it sustains the very idealism which it denounces' (p. 140).

[16] On the view that the championing of the 'primacy of the individual voice' in poetry in fact serves conformity and narrow horizons of evaluation, see Charles Bernstein, *A Poetics* (Cambridge, MA and London: Harvard University Press, 1992), p. 2.

apparently stable and encompassing value in particular'.[17] The focus of the volume is on certain cultural institutions, media and literary practices through which and by which poetic value is constructed, mediated or represented. These last three processes cannot be resolved into a single term but nor can they be separated out, since, in the field of cultural value, construction, mediation and representation operate simultaneously and inextricably. When an anthology presents the 'best new poets' of a rising generation, when a radio programme interviews a poet, when poetry is selected for a university syllabus, when poets give some allegiance to a programme or group and when they perform, read or teach, existing values and acts of evaluation are represented and drawn to public attention but, in that process, are also mediated (as poets and poems are redefined by specific cultural contexts). At the same time new values may be generated: a poem on the internet, a poem filmed or recorded for radio, may acquire new forms of aesthetic value and give rise to new ways of evaluating both poetry and other cultural forms.

As an instance of the way in which a discourse on value and poetry must be itself continually subject to the challenge of the very values it examines, one might note that such interaction of poetry with other media has often been seen as itself a devaluing of poetry. When Donald Davie praised an anthology for drawing attention to the poetry not the poets, and thus 'offering poetry not as an alternative or supplement to other media but as a medium unique in what it aspires to', he participated in the modernist critique of personality which finds an echo in the poetics of the Language poets, but he also resisted the engagement of poetry with other media.[18] Against such views, Marjorie Perloff (a leading advocate of Language and other experimental poetries) has argued that 'it was [John] Cage who understood, at least as early as the fifties, that from now on poetry would have to position itself . . . in relation to the media that, like it or not, occupy an increasingly large part of our verbal, visual, and acoustic space'.[19] The well-known poetry publisher and journal editor Michael Schmidt (writing with the critic Grevel Lindop) has suggested that performance of poetry is liable to debase the 'poetic currency' and that events involving jazz and poetry are acceptable only if the jazz is treated as 'sugar' on the 'serious pill' of poetry.[20] In contrast, the programme for the 'STANZA' poetry

---

[17] Connor, *Theory and Cultural Value*, pp. 2–3.

[18] Donald Davie, review of *A Various Art* (Andrew Crozier and Tim Longville (eds) (Manchester: Carcanet, 1987)), *PN Review* 70, 16.2 (1989), 57–8, rpt. in Clive Wilmer (ed.), *With the Grain: Essays on Thomas Hardy and Modern British Poetry* (Manchester: Carcanet, 1998), p. 265.

[19] Marjorie Perloff, *Radical Artifice: Writing Poetry in the Age of Media* (Chicago and London: University of Chicago Press, 1991), p. xiii.

[20] Michael Schmidt and Grevel Lindop (eds), *British Poetry Since 1960: A Critical Survey* (South Hinksey, Oxford: Carcanet, 1972), Introduction, p. 4.

festival, at the University of St Andrews in 1999 (a festival which included events such as an open mike session with a blues band, a session with music by the performance poet Patience Agbabi and an event combining a poet, a singer and a jazz band), celebrated the interaction of poetry with other forms and practices as 'exciting and eclectic cross-overs between poetry and other art-forms', claiming that 'we will be giving poetry the status it deserves, and returning it to the domain where it is at its most powerful and enchanting: in performance'.[21]

The traditional associations of poetry with high culture, and the relative neglect of poetry within the discipline of cultural studies, have meant that limited critical attention has been paid to such institutions, media and practices, and their importance for poetry. They include publishing, reviewing, anthologizing, radio, film, television, readings, performances, academia, poetry workshops and creative writing classes and courses, poets in residence in a huge variety of locations, poetry in art installations and in the lyrics and programmes of musical performances, poetry 'slams', poetry bars and open mike sessions, poetry festivals, schools of poetry and their publicity activities, poetry 'days', poems in newspapers, poems on the underground, poems on postcards and much more.[22] The present volume cannot, of course, hope to survey all of this huge cultural field, especially given the transatlantic scope of the book. The choice of issues discussed, while influenced by the divergent interests and priorities of the contributors, has tended towards aspects of culture which, because of relative newness or distance from the traditional homes of poetry, have received less attention, but we have also aimed for variety in the forms of cultural practice addressed.[23] So there are no chapters specifically on poetry readings, nor on poetry journals (though Chapter 8 pays some attention to

[21] Stanza 99 festival programme (St Andrews, 1999), p. 1.

[22] One might note, to cite a few representative examples, the appointment of Ian McMillan as official poet to a British railway company (*The Independent*, 15 July 1999, p. 1), the poet Tracey Herd reading at a race meeting, in a lottery-funded event (*The Guardian*, 26 February 2000, p. 10), 'Wake up to Poetry: A One Day Celebration', an event held on 5 April 2000 at the University of the West of England and supported by the Poetry Development Agency; 'The United States of Poetry', a multimedia project encompassing a five-part television series on the PBS network, a book of photographs and a sound-track album, with material ranging from Joseph Brodsky to Lou Reed, and the 'Bed-Stuy Double Dutch Girls', a jump-rope team (*The New York Times*, 19 May 1996, pp. 28, 30).

[23] Notable exceptions to the tendency not to consider poetic value in relation to new media are found in the work of Marjorie Perloff, in particular *Radical Artifice*, and in Rasula, *The American Poetry Wax Museum*, which includes a telling discussion of the reasons why comparisons and links between poetry and television have been neglected (pp. 363–82). David Kennedy, in *New Relations: The Refashioning of British Poetry 1980–94* (Bridgend, Mid Glamorgan: Poetry Wales Press, 1996), considers 'poetry as media', by which he means public poetry which functions in a way analogous to, or influenced by, media such as newspapers, television and radio (pp. 214–35).

both); these continue to be of importance in defining poetry's cultural value but have received recent and well-informed critical attention.[24] There are, however, chapters considering internet poetry and poetic-photographic work, poetry on the radio and poetry on film. Anthologies, as perhaps still the central value-giving cultural site for poetry, are considered in two chapters, one for Britain and one for America, while the academy is discussed, not primarily in its role as maker of canons (a much-debated issue) but in its role as a sometimes uneasy home for poets. Other chapters widen out into major cultural and political issues – democracy, race, political violence – relating these to issues of aesthetic value.

II Media, Poets and Politics
Jonathan Allison

We read poems in traditional print media, such as books and magazines, and we may see them on posters in the London Underground and elsewhere. Increasingly, we see them on the internet. Countless poetry web sites now exist, from the single author site to the home page of The Academy of American Poets and The Poetry Society; from theme sites such as Poets of the Great War to the myriad home pages of individuals who advertise their favourite works.[25] Few understand exactly what the legal consequences are of web publishing but this seems not to hinder its proliferation. It seems unlikely, at this stage, that readers would prefer to read poetry on a computer screen than on paper but perhaps that will change with time. And with certain avant-garde works such as Kenneth Goldsmith's *Fidget*, discussed here by Marjorie Perloff, in '"Vocable Scriptsigns": Differential Poetics in Kenneth Goldsmith's *Fidget* and John Kinsella's *Kangaroo Virus*', web access is crucial in order to experience the moving imagery of the poem in non-print format. Would a decisive shift from page to screen (or from single to multiple media) alter fundamentally the ways in which we value poetry? Perloff's discussion of web poetry (and 'alternate media' works such as *Kangaroo Virus*) implies that it would. What would be produced is a 'differential poetics' involving 'an unusual degree of reader/listener/

---

[24] See R. J. Ellis, 'Mapping the United Kingdom Little Magazine Field', in Robert Hampson and Peter Barry (eds), *The New British Poetry* (Manchester: Manchester University Press; New York: St Martin's Press, 1993). On poetry readings and performances, see Charles Bernstein (ed.), *Close Listening: Poetry and the Performed Word* (New York and Oxford: Oxford University Press, 1998).

[25] Academy of American Poets: http://www.poets.org; Poetry Society: http://www.poetrysoc.com; War Poets: http://www.emory.edu/ENGLISH/LostPoets

viewer participation' and testifying both to 'a new preoccupation with material embodiment' and to 'a textual anxiety' provoked by internet culture.[26]

If readings and performances have been popular on both sides of the Atlantic since the 1960s, the broadcasting of poetry on radio, comparatively rare in America, has long been seen as a function of the BBC, with that organization's joint emphasis on entertainment and education, on representing and buttressing (British) national culture. Lilias Fraser, in '"The appreciation of real worth": Poetry, Radio and the Valued Reader', examines the history of the BBC's involvement with poetry. Apart from radio, new media for the dissemination of poetry have emerged in recent years, particularly electronic forms of publication on the worldwide web and on CD-ROM, which often allow for simultaneous electronic print publication and audio recording. Furthermore, the 1990s have witnessed, as Vicki Bertram explores, in 'Words on Film: Collaborative Work between Poets and Film-makers', growing interest among poets in collaboration with film directors to marry the spoken word with television.

We hear poetry in creative writing classes, at formal poetry readings and informal 'slams', on radio and occasionally on television.[27] The vinyl LP recordings popular in the '60s and '70s have now largely vanished, with the ascendancy of the compact disc, but recent years have witnessed the proliferation of poetry publishing on cassettes, videotapes, CDs and CD-ROMs.[28] In the US, Caedmon's vast 'Voices in Time' cassette series is popular in classrooms and, since the early 1980s, Faber & Faber have published a substantial number of their poets on tape. The Lannan Foundation have produced a videotape series entitled 'Lannan Literary Videos', profiling individual poets with excerpts from interviews and readings, while the PBS television series, *Voices and Visions*, remains a

---

[26] The claim that 'the materiality of electronic writing has changed the idea of writing itself' is explored in Loss Peqeuno Glazier's *Digital Poetics* (Tuscaloosa, AL: University of Alabama Press, 2001) (advance notice, http://www.uapress.ua.edu/authors/Glazie01.html).

[27] On the proliferation of poetry readings in the late 1960s and after, see Jonathan Raban, *The Society of the Poem* (London: Harrap, 1971), pp. 85–90, and Martin Booth, *British Poetry 1964 to 1984: Driving Through the Barricades* (London: Routledge & Kegan Paul, 1985), pp. 85–105. See also Grevel Lindop, 'Poetry, Rhetoric and the Mass Audience: The Case of the Liverpool Poets', in Schmidt and Lindop (eds), *British Poetry Since 1960*, pp. 92–106.

[28] An interactive CD-ROM accompanies the *Norton Anthology of Poetry*, fourth edition (eds Margaret Ferguson et al.) with audio recordings of poems. This is becoming increasingly common: a recording of Helen Vendler reading Shakespeare's poetry accompanies her recent book, *The Art of Shakespeare's Sonnets* (Cambridge, MA and London: Harvard University Press, 1997).

popular teaching resource in American High Schools and undergraduate classrooms.

Pedagogically speaking, audio recordings of poets reading their work have long been recognized as useful but many critics will argue that the most important encounter with poetry is reading it on the page and that, for the teaching of poetry as an academic subject, this encounter should remain primary. They would argue that listening to the poem, while valuable in many ways, does not lend itself to the sort of 'close reading' that the teaching of poetry at all levels requires. Clearly, conservative resistance to alternative modes of dissemination revolves around ideas of the contamination of art and distraction of readers from the poet's language, conventionally conceived. On the other hand, proponents of electronic media – including the sort of 'radical artifices' and avant-garde installations that interest Marjorie Perloff – welcome the construction of new means for poetic expression as liberatory and aesthetically responsible in a postmodern world.

For many readers, audio recordings of poetry remain important and pleasurable, and the broadcasting of poetry on BBC radio has long been popular and (with its 'middle-brow' associations) considered an important part of national culture. Lilias Fraser describes the changing perceptions of the poetry listener in the BBC, from the Reithian 1930s to the present, and concludes by considering the production of Simon Armitage's millennium poem, *Killing Time*, in 1999. At first, radio producers thought of the listener as a kind of reader, who would imagine the words on the page as they listened – and 'would bring a reader's method of evaluation to radio poetry'. Finally, they thought of the act of listening as 'the model, not the imitation, of how to read' – they shifted from the view that listening is a kind of reading, to the view that reading is a kind of listening. At a time when some people are predicting, in the face of web technology, the demise of print and the disappearance of the book, it is particularly interesting to read that similar gloomy forecasts were being made in the 1930s, in response to radio. Reith responded that broadcasting and publishing should be seen as mutually supportive, indeed that radio broadcasting of poetry might educate the populace to a more refined and critical taste. This is a familiar enough line of argument today, when online publishers face the criticism that their product not only 'dumbs down' but also poses an economic threat to the book trade. The radio production of *Killing Time*, with its plethora of incidental and background noises ('interjections from other voices recorded over street noise'), raises questions about the final product as a collaborative effort, overlaying authorial intentions with those of sound engineers and other production team members. But, as Jerome McGann has argued in *The Textual Condition* and elsewhere, the work of art is always a collaborative product, its meanings influenced by the publishing conditions into which the traditional solitary artist places his well-wrought urn.[29]

The situation becomes even more complex in the case of TV broadcasting, with its yoking of the voice to television imagery, not all of which can be said to be invented or controlled by the poet. Vicki Bertram focuses on seven films made since 1989 by British poets in collaboration with directors, including Jackie Kay (with Philippa Lowthorne), Fred D'Aguiar (with Mark Harrison), Simon Armitage (with Brian Hill), two by Tony Harrison (with Peter Symes) and two other ventures entitled 'Poems on the Box' and 'Poets' News'. The author raises the question, while not attempting to answer it definitively, whether making poems accessible through television endangers the traditional richness and subtlety of poetic language? It seems clear that the result of poetry-television collaboration, a 'film-poem', as it were, produces expectations and effects other than strictly poetic expectations and effects, and perhaps we have to think about new kinds of criteria with which to discuss value with hybrid media. Auden's 'Night Mail', to invoke a familiar example, is an interesting poem in itself. However, the effect of hearing it recited by Auden on the documentary film, *Night Mail*, with its skilful juxtaposition of film image to word, is different from the effect of hearing it recited on radio or, indeed, reading it on a page.[30] Readers of a poem who have heard the poem on a carefully-constructed film may feel the printed poem is a pale shadow of its visual-audio incarnation, much as a dramatic text in print can seem skeletal in comparison with a performance of a play. That is, what we value in viewing such films is not the poetry alone; we might feel the film's success can be judged by how powerful the total package is, how well the poetry is matched to pictures or how interestingly the poetry is performed. It would be possible to consider such a film-poem to be of very high quality indeed and yet to consider the poem in print, detached from its film context, to be a disappointment. Again, we must return to the question of scales of value: poems on film are being judged by different standards than poems in print.

The television collaborations explored by Vicki Bertram raise the question of multiple texts and intentionalities, whereby a printed text will vie with the TV text, in which visual imagery accompanies the poem. The poet has launched two different texts into the world, neither one

[29] Jerome McGann, *The Textual Condition* (Princeton, NJ and Oxford: Princeton University Press, 1991). McGann's web site demonstrates and illustrates in various ways the arguments propounded in his books: http://jefferson.village.virginia.edu/~jjm2f/home.html

[30] Auden supplied verse commentary for this 1936 film, made by John Grierson's Film Unit, concerning the London-Glasgow Postal Express. See John Fuller, *W. H. Auden: A Commentary* (Princeton, NJ: Princeton University Press, 1998), p. 188.

finally 'authoritative', each one bearing the hallmark of his or her 'final intentions', sacred to traditional textual scholars. This is very much in accord with Perloff's proposal for a 'differential poetics' – a concept which she links to textual scholarship, noting trends in the study of Emily Dickinson's manuscripts which grant value and validity to alternate texts and material details. Thus Perloff's argument connects the 'traditional' values of rigorous manuscript scholarship with avant-garde works based on new media, such as Kenneth Goldsmith's *Fidget*, with its multiple versions – in print, in performance and on the internet. Together the three versions might comprise a sort of variorum edition, all important, none authoritative. While clearly influenced by Samuel Beckett, Goldsmith's 'verbal/visual' *Fidget* seems to derive from a Joycean concentration on the stream of consciousness, but focussing not on the intricate play of thought and feeling but on the author's efforts to record, in painstaking detail, the movements (or fidgets) of the body. Apart from the 'plain text version' of the poem, it has also appeared as a gallery installation and has been performed at New York's Whitney Museum. It is also possible to read/ view it on the web, as a Java Applet. Each of the texts of *Fidget* involves different aesthetic expectations of the reader/viewer; as Perloff writes, the Java Applet version 'has an austere and silent beauty quite different from the printed version or from its oral enactment'. John Kinsella's *Kangaroo Virus* provides another example of a collaborative text with visual and linguistic components. A printed version is available, juxtaposing Kinsella's lyrics with Ronald Sims's photographs, but it can also be heard on CD (all sound, no photos). Perloff concludes that 'if one medium doesn't work, try another': a salutary reminder that, for certain poets, 'medium' is no longer restricted to print language, even though their status as poets is likely to continue to be judged by conservative critics primarily by linguistic criteria.

We began this introduction with the claim that poetry occupies an ambivalent space in contemporary culture as at once specialist (abstruse) and accessible (expressive and personal). If avant-garde poets such as Goldsmith can seem obscure, there can be no doubt they also have a stake in personal expression. Furthermore, there is something very audience-friendly and 'democratic', in one sense of the word, about the construction of websites or CD-ROMs, with accompanying visual imagery, which may (perhaps unintentionally) have the effect of assisting readers to come to terms with linguistic content. The same may be said of radio and television presentations of poetic voice. What about other forms of poetry that are clearly popular and intended to be democratic, but which are aesthetically disappointing? Paul Breslin, in 'The Sign of Democracy and the Terms of Poetry', argues that the most popular sorts of poetry, while effectively bridging the gap between an elite art and a popular audience, often fail aesthetically. He chooses a moralistic verse published in the syndicated Ann Landers column in the American national press and finds it complacent, conventional, unchallenging and formally lazy. He is very explicit and decisive about what he values in poetry: 'no poet I know would be caught dead with a poem like that'. Similarly, Breslin was not impressed by what he heard at an 'open mic' reading and a poetry slam in Chicago, though he himself took part in both events. Implicit here is the notion that, in making it popular, you pay the price. Evidently, he finds that the audiences for these performances do not expect such traditional poetic qualities as linguistic range, irony, and richness of diction and image, consistency of tone, philosophical depth and/or emotional complexity. He further explores two key texts in recent debates about poetry's place in society, Dana Gioia's *Can Poetry Matter?* and Charles Bernstein's *A Poetics*. For Gioia, who is taken to represent a New Formalist position, poetry needs to regain a general audience by coming out from the closed circuit of the academy and combining materials drawn from popular culture with 'the precision, compression and ambition of high art'.[31] This clearly valorizes the civic potential of poetry, while also suggesting its educative and visionary possibilities. On the other hand, Bernstein and Language poets in effect embrace unpopularity, according to Breslin, since only thus can their language remain antithetical to mainstream ideologies. Bernstein, as Breslin presents him, seems content that poets should remain prophets in the wilderness. For Breslin, poetry should be 'impure' enough to survive but 'principled' enough to challenge the reader. The implication is that a guiding ethical principle in writing and valuing poetry should allow for the interrogation of both reader and author, hence Bernstein's splendid isolation seems both purist and irresponsibly indifferent to audience.

Like Breslin, Robert Crawford is a poet who professes literature at a university. This is relatively unusual, since most poets in academia are primarily teachers of creative writing. For Crawford, the technological environment of the modern university provides the poet-academic with an unusually rich opportunity to humanize if not, indeed, spiritualize electronic media, rather than be enslaved by it. He writes:

> [p]articularly if he or she works in academia, the poet cannot simply contend that the age of information with all its computers, databases, televisions and technology did not happen but can seek to locate, in that informational world, a sense of spirituality which maintains an apprehension of the human and the spiritual among the machines that humans invented.

---

[31] Dana Gioia, *Can Poetry Matter? Essays on Poetry and American Culture* (St. Paul, MN: Graywolf Press, 1992), p. 253.

Alongside a handful of other contemporary Scottish poets, Crawford has been called an 'Informationist' poet. By 'Informationist' poetry he means work that includes catalogues, lists, and 'assemblies of unusually varied language' (Crawford) – 'spoil heaps', 'rubbish tips' and 'heaped fragments' of often 'useless information'. This embrace of 'information' represents a way of being poetically 'impure' in Breslin's terms, yet such poems cannot be said merely to reflect the detritus of popular culture. These 'spoil heaps' can trace their ancestry in epic catalogues and the floral lists of pastoral elegy, as well as in the place names of the *Dinnseanchas* (place name poems) tradition. But they absorb as much of the contemporary world as the poem can take. As such, they suggest a revolution in diction every bit as bracing as Auden's borrowings from mine engineering and contemporary psychology, and Eliot's borrowings from anaesthesiology or his invocation of the smells of steaks. For Crawford, the poet in academia is both computer-friendly ('wired' as they say) and loyal to more traditional processes of communication. Such a poet stands astride the gulf between book and computer, pen and keyboard, the national and the global and, as such, is ideally placed to take part in the building of spoil heaps.

Whereas the title 'Informationist' was one that Crawford had thrust upon him, he feels, on the whole, that it is acceptable, while recognizing that poets often do not wish to be categorized in terms of movements, groups and clubs. It is often the self-appointed task of literary historians and editors of poetry anthologies to define periods and movements. Since editors inevitably make many value judgements about the poetry they collect in a period anthology, they can get unpleasant reputations that are based on which poets they include and which they exclude. Posterity has not forgotten that Yeats excluded Wilfred Owen from his *Oxford Book of Modern Verse* and Philip Larkin's edition of *The Oxford Book of Twentieth-Century English Verse* has the dubious reputation of being anti-modernist and (worse) neo-Georgian. Andrew Michael Roberts, in 'The Rhetoric of Value in Recent British Poetry Anthologies', argues that anthology introductions frequently betray a tension between the recognition of diversity and the application of supposedly universal, neutral criteria of quality and takes this tension as indicative of contradictory ideas about the value of poetry, and about value itself, which circulate in the culture at large. Roberts also explores the 'double bind of typicality and novelty' faced by editors of anthologies which aim to represent the poetry that is typical of a period and yet also seek to propound new poetic values. Using the famous *New Lines* anthology (Conquest, 1956), *The New Poetry* (Alvarez, 1962), *The Penguin Book of Contemporary British Poetry* (Morrison, Motion, 1982) and the 1993 *The New Poetry* (Hulse et al.), Roberts explores the editorial values and assumptions underpinning these 'generational' anthologies. In this particular genealogy, he discerns a quasi-Oedipal anxiety in each anthology to outstrip its predecessor, linked to an echoing of the values of its predecessor-but-one. The effect is to obscure the real complexity of relations among poets and groups in favour of a series of artificially-limited 'new generations', and this despite the increasing dominance of 'plurality' as an avowed value. Inevitably, arguments about which poets are in some sense best or most typical of a period encourage the idea of a 'mainstream' poetic culture, which has the effect of marginalizing important work. Consequently, avant-garde poetry has been given short shrift in the anthologies under discussion, despite a thriving culture of alternative British poetries since the 1960s. Avant-garde anthologies, such as *Other* (Caddel and Quartermain, 1999), which Roberts finds in general to be more sophisticated and wary about issues of value, nevertheless encounter similar tensions to their mainstream counterparts, notably that of multiple and singular value, since they tend to homogenize mainstream poetry as an 'other', against which to define their own oppositional status. Recent anthologies which take a longer historical perspective, such as *The Penguin Book of Poetry from Britain and Ireland since 1945* (Armitage and Crawford, 1998), offer only partial solutions to the recalcitrant dilemmas of anthology-making. They escape the demand of perpetual novelty but, despite supporting plurality and the democratic voice, remain generally inhospitable to the avant-garde. At least until Keith Tuma's *Anthology of Twentieth-Century British and Irish Poetry* (2001), no anthology was in print which offered equal hospitality to mainstream and avant-garde poetry, despite the dominance of pluralism as a value.

It is precisely this phenomenon, as observed in the US context, which Alan Golding focuses on, in 'Recent American Poetry Anthologies and the Idea of the "Mainstream"'. For Golding, an American poetry establishment embodies a 'mainstream' poetic culture, while denying that such a culture exists. This establishment culture is articulated by certain influential anthologies, creative writing programs and 'workshops', lists of approved authors who are regularly invited to give campus readings, University Presses and their notions of what constitutes important and publishable work. In the words of Eliot Weinberger, the rhetoric of the mainstream anthology 'insists there is no ruling party, and thus no opposition', and hence the denial of the existence of philosophical difference prevents open debate, ensuring continued exclusion of the marginal or avant-garde and the prolongation of the conflict. As Roberts found in the case of British anthologies, avant-garde poetry is excluded from most American anthologies and avant-garde anthologies repay the compliment by excluding mainstream poetry. To judge by Roberts's and Golding's evidence, similar normative processes are at work on both sides of the pond, whereby the most influential anthologies are connected by closed circuit to a mainstream culture defined by established literary periodicals, universities, teachers and the horizon of audience expectations. Perhaps a crucial difference, however, as shown by Fraser and Bertram, is the role of the BBC in sustaining a mainstream poetic as part of national culture and the hegemony in America of the 'workshop poem' – less influential, maybe, in the United Kingdom, where writing 'workshops' and University creative writing programmes are less common.

Roberts notes that the most significant area of overlap between mainstream and avant-garde anthologies lies in the work of Scottish, black British and women poets. The problematic relationship between the avant-garde and black writing is discussed by Romana Huk in 'The Progress of the Avant-garde: Reading/Writing Race and Culture According to Universal Systems of Value'. She poses the questions: '*whose* identity is being pluralized in the quest for avant-garde unravellings of past value systems?' and 'which universalizing systems of value are (inadvertently) active in the articulation of a "postmodern" aesthetic for poetry?'. While focusing primarily on the British black poetry scene, she also explores the consequences of a different mythos of identity in the United States, mounting a critique of Charles Bernstein's project of 'post-pluralization', in which race becomes just another form of identity to be superseded. Huk's case is that the avant-garde dismantling of the subject is liable to erase particular material and historical conditions, imposing a 'universalized conception of (non)selfhood', which risks being 'a photo-negative of the bourgeois one' and, to support it, she cites the work of African American poets Nathaniel Mackey and Erica Hunt. In Britain, she detects a different risk, that black aesthetics may be found defending identity 'in a space where dominant forces are doing the same'. Huk asks whether a postmodern aesthetics allows for a critique of its own central principles, raising, like Roberts, the problem of a 'pluralism' with unacknowledged limits. She explores this question through debates among theorists and practitioners in black British cultural studies and poetry, including Gilane Tawadros's critique of the postmodern 'evacuation of history' and David Marriott's psychoanalytical indictment of an alleged disavowal of 'irreducible difference' by Language poetry. Huk finds Marriott engaged in re-examining difference and 'race-in-history' through his poems, two of which she reads in some detail for their combination of avant-garde technique with a different model of agency.

The present volume offers a variety of points of view from both sides of the Atlantic on contemporary poetry from the USA, the UK and Ireland. A guiding assumption here is that transatlantic comparisons are valid and interesting, and that the poets under discussion are prone to know about, if not read and be influenced by, transatlantic writing. While many of the essays focus on a particular national tradition, several of them point to

international traditions or media and, of course, any poetry has potentially international reception. Certainly anglophone publishing is increasingly international, although this probably applies less to poetry than
many other sorts of book; a poet can still have a substantial reputation
one side of the Atlantic and be little known on the other.[32] To what extent
does the perceived value of poetry still depend on its place in a 'national'
culture, given the rise of global media and (potentially at least) a global
cultural space? Cairns Craig, in '"Where is the Nation You Promised?":
American Voice in Modern Scottish and Irish Poetry', examines the ways
in which the voices of contemporary American poets have proved
enabling and influential to Scottish and Irish poets. For Craig, transatlantic connections have been integral to modern literary history since
Whitman but particularly since Modernists like Eliot and Pound left the
USA in search of ancient European traditions. Glaswegian poet Edwin
Morgan 're-routed' his own poetic voice 'through the voice of American
poetry', hence finding a hybridized poetic persona, rooted in Scotland but
influenced by a transatlantic identity. The result was to appropriate the
energies of American Beat poetry, among other kinds of voice, and thus
allow the industrial world of Glasgow to 'struggle towards rebirth by
reflecting, like a mirror image across the Atlantic, the styles of New
York'. Craig detects similar borrowings in the work of Tom Leonard, Liz
Lochhead, Douglas Dunn and Irish poets, Seamus Heaney and John
Montague. In the case of the Scottish poets, imitating an American poetic
and tonality was a way of escaping the tight, controlled aesthetic of the
Movement; for Irish poets, American poetry allowed an exit route from
the overwhelming influence of Yeats.

Craig's argument suggests that many contemporary poets have transatlantic allegiances which do not dissolve national identity but illustrate
how identities are always already fundamentally complex. If there is a
cosmopolitan dimension to these poetries, that is not incompatible with
fierce loyalties, and a crucial stage of his argument is the claim that
nationalism and the search for national homelands was a fundamental
force in the development of so-called cosmopolitan Modernism. What
emerged from the global fragmentation of World War One was not, in
fact, an aesthetic of internationalist, boundary-free meditation, but a
variety of modernist techniques whose practitioners (Eliot, Stevens,
Williams, Auden and Yeats) were continually conscious of nationality
and nationalism as controlling political and aesthetic factors in their
work. Hence the 'lyrical epic' was modernism's key poetic form because
its open structure reflected the crisis of historical legitimation in the

---

[32] Keith Tuma has recently argued that British poetry is effectively 'dead' in the USA. Keith
  Tuma, *Fishing by Obstinate Isles: Modern and Postmodern British Poetry and American
  Readers* (Evanston, IL: Northwestern University Press, 1998), p. 1.

nations of the West. For Craig, both the role of contemporary poetry in national identity and the fate, after modernism, of the lyrical epic, are most powerfully explored by the Irish poet, Paul Muldoon, notably via the themes of emigration and the empty search for (American) national origins in his *Madoc: A Mystery*. Craig's final gesture towards 'the poem as the resurrection of a nation' (even if subdued by his characterisation of this as an unfulfilled and unfulfillable promise) seeks to reinstall the link between poetry and nation as central to the value of each.[33]

If World War One is integral to an understanding of the development of modernism, it is also the case, as Jonathan Allison argues in 'Contemporary Poetry and the Great War', that the memory of World War One shapes contemporary understandings of personal and political identities in surprising ways, in both the UK and Ireland. Many academics and general readers alike share a fascination with World War One, and the 1960s witnessed publication of a large number of scholarly treatments of the history and literature of the war, as well as the main anthologies of war poetry which became very popular in British schools and universities. The reputation of the war poets soared in these years, which coincided with American commitment to the Vietnam War and with popular protest against nuclear weaponry in Britain and other parts of western Europe. Arguing that the memory of World War One has an important role in British nationalist discourses in Britain and Northern Ireland and that it also has powerful personal resonances for poets such as Ted Hughes and Michael Longley, whose fathers were veterans of that war, Allison explores the representation of father-son relations in elegies by Hughes and Longley, showing how war memories shape identities of both veterans and their sons, and how their sons struggle with (and write narratives in an effort to cope with) this kind of inheritance. Finally, arguing that aesthetic value is in some cases inextricably tied to 'social value', Allison considers how the social and political contexts of Longley's Northern Irish poetry provide an 'interpretative network' within which the poems have meaning and value. Drawing on Barbara Herrnstein Smith's claim that our experience of literary works *as* valuable depends in part on their 'culturally certified ... performance of certain functions', Allison proposes an affinity between poetry of the Great War and Northern Irish poetry of the 'Troubles', in that both have been judged by their performance of certain collective emotional functions. In Allison's analysis, social, aesthetic, political and emotional aspects of literary value are seen as interdependent.

---

[33] Craig's argument therefore proposes a contrary emphasis to that of Keith Tuma who, like Craig, is interested in transatlantic connections in poetry, but who admires mostly poets 'skeptical of discourses of national identity', feeling themselves part of 'a transnational republic of letters'. Tuma, *Fishing by Obstinate Isles*, p. 7.

'Vocable Scriptsigns': Differential Poetics in Kenneth Goldsmith's *Fidget* and John Kinsella's *Kangaroo Virus*

Marjorie Perloff

I

Eyelids open. Tongue runs across upper lip moving from left side of mouth to right following arc of lip. Swallow. Jaws clench. Grind. Stretch. Swallow. Head lifts. Bent right arm brushes pillow into back of head. Arm straightens. Counterclockwise twist thrusts elbow toward ceiling. Tongue leaves interior of mouth passing through teeth. Tongue slides back into mouth. Palm corkscrews. Thumb stretches.[1]

It reads at first like a section from a Beckett prose text: the late *All Strange Away*, for instance, with its graphic account of the movements made by an unspecified figure, confined in a small rotunda:

Head wedged against wall at a with blank face on left cheek and the rest the only way that arse wedged against wall at c and knees wedged against wall ab a few inches from face and feet wedged against wall bc a few inches from arse, puckered tip of left breast no real image but maintain for the moment, left hand most clear and womanly lightly clasping right shoulder ball . . . [2]

---

[1] Kenneth Goldsmith *Fidget* (Toronto: Coach House Press, 1999), with an accompanying CD by Theo Bleckmann. All further references are to this edition. *Selections from Fidget*, which covers the day's first three hours, was published in a limited edition of 100 copies, signed and numbered, on the occasion of the Whitney Museum of American Art at Philip Morris commission between Theo Bleckmann and Kenneth Goldsmith and in conjunction with exhibitions at Printed Matter, Inc. by Stadium Projects, New York, NY. See also the internet version available at http://www.chbooks.com/online/fidget/index.html. The website includes the Real Audio files from Theo Bleckmann's vocal-visual interpretation, as presented at the Whitney Museum of American Art on Bloomsday 1998, the complete text of *Fidget* in thirteen chapters from 10:00 to 22:00 and a 'Java Applet' (see below).

[2] Samuel Beckett, *All Strange Away* in *Rockaby and other Short Pieces* (New York: Grove Press, 1981), pp. 58–9.

But *Fidget*, as Kenneth Goldsmith has titled his recent verbal/visual experiment, is not literary invention but *poésie verité*, a documentary record of how it actually is when a person wakes up on a given morning. If, in one sense, it recalls Beckett, it is also written under the sign of the photographer Edward Muybridge. As Goldsmith explains:

> *Fidget's* premise was to record every move my body made on June 16, 1997 (Bloomsday). I attached a microphone to my body and spoke every movement from 10:00 AM, when I woke up, to 11:00 PM, when I went to sleep. I was alone all day in my apartment and didn't answer the phone, go on errands, etc. I just observed my body and spoke. From the outset the piece was a total work of fiction. As I sit here writing this letter, my body is making thousands of movements; I am only able to observe one at a time. It's impossible to describe every move my body made on a given day. Among the rules for *Fidget* was that I would never use the first person 'I' to describe movements. Thus every move was an observation of *a* body in space, not *my* body in a space. There was to be no editorializing, no psychology, no emotion – just a body detached from a mind.[3]

Telling the 'truth', Goldsmith quickly discovers, may be the biggest 'fiction' of all, it being humanly impossible to track all of one's bodily movements. At this very moment, I am moving my fingers over the computer keyboard as I type, flexing my left foot, wiggling my left toes and running my tongue over my upper lip from right to left. As I note those movements, I am making others that go unrecorded. Indeed, as Goldsmith admits, after five hours of the experiment in which he monitors his body as it gets out of bed and interacts with objects like coffee cups, he 'began to go crazy'. The exercise becomes harder and harder, the verbal equivalents to physical motion more and more abbreviated. By 6:00 PM, 'as a defense my body put itself to sleep'. When Goldsmith awakes and realizes he has another five or six hours to go, he panics:

> I went out and bought a fifth of Jack Daniels, walked over to an abandoned loading dock by the West Side highway and drank the entire bottle, all the while continuing my exercise. Needless to say, I got trashed. I found my home and fell asleep by 11:00 PM, never once having stopped my narrative.

---

[3] Goldsmith, letter to the author, 9 October 1998.

Later, when he plays the tapes, Goldsmith finds that, in the drunk sequence, his words have become completely slurred and, in the last chapter (22:00), quite incomprehensible. So, in a Beckettian move, 'I ran the first chapter backwards, mirrored it, then reversed every letter' (Fig. 1.1). For example, 'Tongue runs across lower lip, moving from right side of mouth to the left following arc of lip', becomes

.pil fo cra gniwollof tfel ot htuom fo edis thgir morf gnivom pil rewol ssorca snur eugnoT.

The sentences from this last chapter were then put into reverse order, with the last actions coming first and the first coming last.[4] The only exception is the very last line of the book, 'Eyelids close', which is printed in standard order, 'creating a full circle of closure for the day'. Furthermore, the tapes were then rigorously edited: all unnecessary words such as 'the' were removed as were all possible literary and art references. The aim was to make the text 'very dry and very descriptive' and 'to divorce the action from the surroundings, narrative, and attendant morality'.

These statements must be taken with a grain of salt. For one thing, the 'closure' provided by the final sentence of the thirteenth chapter, 'Eyelids close', is called into question by the various versions in which *Fidget* exists. The piece, which exists as a plain text version,[5] was given a gallery installation at Printed Matter,[6] a performance at the Whitney Museum of

---

[4] This seems to be a direct allusion to Beckett's *Watt*, Chapter III, in which Watt, unable to cope with 'reality', begins to invert, first the words in a given sentence and then 'the letters in the word together with that of words in the sentence together with that of the sentences in the period', as in (spelled phonetically) '*Dis yb dis, nem owt. Yad la, tin fo trap*' ('part of night, all day. Two men, side by side'). See Beckett, *Watt* (New York: Grove Press, 1959), p. 168. I discuss Beckett's reversals here in *Wittgenstein's Ladder: Poetic Language and the Strangeness of the Ordinary* (Chicago: University of Chicago Press, 1996), pp. 139–40.

[5] The Whitney edition was published in April 2000 by Coach House Press (Toronto, Canada), whose online site is www.chbooks.com.

[6] The gallery installation, according to Goldsmith (letter to the author, 9 October 1998) consisted of 'twelve paper suits (one for each hour of the day). Each suit had the entire hour of the day printed on it. Following the trajectory of the day, the earlier suits were printed with very light text and the suits later in the day were printed in reverse, with white letters on black paper. Also, following the emotional/psychological trajectory of the day, as my mental state grew shakier, so the text on the suits grew less legible and more smeary (this was achieved with a Xerox machine).'

22:00 .etarapes regniferof dna bmuht thgiR .flac thgir sehctarcs dnah thgiR. .ydob dhiheb
tsiF .regnif elddim thgir fo pit yb del ,swercskroc dnah thgiR. .sllup wolbE .rsir skcottuB
.nethgiarts seenK .thgir petsediS .tnorf ni sevom mrA .snepo dnah tfeL .tnorf sehcniP .petS
.drawkcab teeF .tfel snruT .ydob morf sevom dnaH .esolc sregniF .ydob ot sevom dnah tfeL
.petS .petS .petS .petS .petS .spets toof thgiR .taorht fo kcab morf dehsup sucuM .sdnetxe
toof thgiR .nethgiarts seenK .llab yb deL .sesir leeH .drawkcab petS .dnuorg stih toof thgiR
.tfel stfihs thgieW .sllaf toof tfeL .leeh no thgieW .stih llab thgiR .petS .petS .llab ta sdnE
.leeh ta snigeB .spets toof tfeL .swollof toof tfeL .tfel sgniws toof thgiR .tfel snrut ydoB
.dniheb seyE .stfil toof tfeL .dneb seenK .deb stih gel tfeL .thgiew ydob stroppus toof thgiR
.dnuorg ffo stfil leeh thgiR .revo sdneB .osrot morf sdneB .ydob sdneb dnah tfeL .sdneb
kcaB .ydob sleporp gel tfeL .sesiar toof fo llaB .dtawkcab seenK .tfil eot eiknip ,eot htruof
,eot driht ,eot dnoceS .spord eot gib fo piT .roolf morf stfiL .stcartnoc toof thgiR .deb fo
egde morf sevom eenk thgiR .snettalF .snethgiartS .tfel spilF .elpmet ta stratS .egacbir reppu
ta sdne hctertS .tcartnoc seenK .nwaY .elkna separcs gel tfeL .sesir ylleB .sllaf ylleB .sesir
ylleB .levan morf sllaf ylleB .sesir ylleB .sllaf ylleB .sesir ylleB .tcartnoc sgnuL .seitpme ylleB
.slliF .gel ni doolB .hgiht tfel ni ssenllitS .deb ffo stfil gel tfeL .taorht morf dehsup sucuM
.dnuorg ffo stfil eenk fo edis thgiR .gel tfel fo sriah sehsurb leeh thgiR .eenk thgir fo edisrednu
morf evom seot tfeL .snethgiarts gel tfeL .srhcra kcaB .senthgiarts gel thgiR .wollip otni
sknis deaH .tfel ot thgir pil reppu skcil eugnoT .avilas sdiovA .ecaf morf sevom dnah tfeL
.staerter sivleP .sesneT .stcartnoc gel tfeL .sneffits osroT .nwaY .nwod seyE .thgir seyE .eson
eliforp seyE .pu seyE .tfel seyE .xaler selcsum daehrof .pord sworbeyE .esolC .tfel ot eson
eliforp seyE .snepO .wodahs yb decnahne noisiV .thgir ot eliforp eson sweiV .snepO .elgnis
esoN .nepo seyE .eson seyE .wollaws fo o dnuor smrofed htuoM .spil seyE .wollawS .sdneB
.snethgiartS .llits gel tfeL .srhcrA .deb morf sevom eenk thgiR .snthgiartS .trapa seenK
.stcatnoc mra tfeL .haed fo tnorf ni evom sdnaH .snethgiarts gel tfeL .selgnaD .spord gel
thgiR .nwaY .elahnI .stacrtnoc hcamotS .stcartnoC .stsurht sivleP .snettalf kcaB .daeh tnorf
ni kcolnu smrA .sepiW .lirtson ot sucum dekac sdda regniF .lirtson tfel fo epahs ot mrofnoc
ton seod regnif fo epahS .regnif fo epahs ot mrofnoc ton seod lirtson tfel fo epahS .lirtson
edisni segdir sdiova regnif fo piT .sevaeL .lirtson morf sevom regniferoF .stfil dnaH .snethgiarts
wolbE .nwaY .stcartnoc mrA .skcottub otni dna xyccoc htaeneb sedilg regniF .pitregnif yb
deilppa erusserp thgilS .suna dna skcottub fo kcarc morf sedecer regnif xednI .llits slianregniF
.skcottub morf stfiL .kcab morf sevoM .spord dnaH .snesool elpmet tfeL .reppu morf
etarapes hteet mottoB .stsurht sivleP .snepo waJ .xaler hteeT .nettalf seoT .nethgiarts seenK
.hctertS .nwaY .edis no ydoB .hctertS .sgel neewteb sdnaH .stsurhT .eye tfel yawa sevom
regnif elddiM .worbeye tfel segassam regnif xednI .eye sbur eikniP .ecaf morf sevom dnah
thgiR .sucum sretslob avilas yretaW .wollawS .hteet morf yawa eugnot sehsup riA .elahxE
.nessol selcsum kceN .wollawS .lrucnU .avilas kciht secudorp eugnoT .swollawS .htuom fo
tnorf ot hsuP .hteet fo wor pot sesnaelc eugnoT .keehc thgir fo hcuop morg slepsiD .htuom
fo tnorf sdooolF .taorht morf eson ot dehsup sucuM .snethgiarts wolbE .rae thgir morf straped
dnah tfeL .tfel spilf ydob sa nethgiarts seenK .seenk morf sevom mra thgiR .noitisop letaf
morf sdnapxe ydoB .enilriah ot worbeye morf sevom regniF .semit ruof sehctI .darherof ot
enilriah morf sevom regnif xedni thgiR .warD .elahnI .lirtson srevocnu bmuht thgiR .eson
morf sevom dnah thgiR .wollawS .sucum dna avilas slespsid eugnoT .eson otni taorht fo
kcab morf dehsuP .tcartnoc skcottub tfel dna hgiht thgir ni selcsuM .deb morf stfil eenk
thgiR .stcartnoc pih thgiR .drawkcab skcottub sleper toof thgiR .stsiwt dnah thgiR .ehtaerB
.bmuht fo roiretni sesserac regniferoF .esolc sregniF .stcartnoc wolbE .elahnI .lirtson thgir
morf sevom regnif xednI .sepiW .sesripsid sucuM .daerps regniferof dna bmuhT .pil no
sucum sdragersiD .sgnul ot nward eson morf riA .esolc sregniF .daerpS .eson morf sevom
wolbE .snepo dnah thgiR .stcartnoc gel tfeL .deb morf sesir eenk thgiR .deb morf sesir eenk
tfeL .tfel stsurht sivleP .seenk ta nethgiarts sgeL .ni smrA .stcartnoc redluohS .lruf sregniF
.stcartnoc smrA .siart sbmuhT .spit sessim riaH .darh fo edis diova sregnif fo spiT .srae
revocnU .swaj morf evom sdnaH .gnirps sbmuhT .kcen esarler sregniF .spord wolbE .waj
morf yawa hsup sdnah fo sleeH .kcen morf evom sdnah fo kcaB .lruf sdnaH .kcen fo edis
morf evom selkcunK .stsurht woble thgiR .redluohs thgir morf sevom tsiF .selkcunk sbur
bmuhT .snepo dnah thgiR .drawnwod snrut wolbE .kcen sdiova tsiF .specib morf sevom
bmuhT. .redluohs morf sevom bmuhT .snethgiarts wolbE .nepO .esarler sregniferoF .sexaler
bmuhT .swercskroc mlaP .htuom fo tou sedils eugnoT .hteet hguorht gnissap ,htuom fo
roiertni sretne eugnoT .gniliec morf yawa woble stsurht tsiwt esiwkcolcretnuoC .sbned mrA
.daeh fo kcab morf yawa wollip sehsurb mra thgir thgiartS .spord daeH .wollawS .tcartnoC
.dnirG .xaler swaJ .wollawS .pil fo cra gniwollof tfel ot htuom fo edis thgir morf gnivom
pil reppu ssorca snur eugnoT Eyelids close.

Figure 1.1 Kenneth Goldsmith, *Fidget* (Toronto: Coach House Press, 1999),
Chapter 22.00

American Art at Philip Morris (16 June 1998) (Fig. 1.2),[7] and a 'fidgetty' 'Java Applet' electronic site, made in collaboration with programmer Clem Paulsen.[8] But more importantly, the ostensibly 'dry' and 'descriptive' report of successive body motions quickly takes on an air of surreality as the artist poses the question of what it would mean to be aware of every physical motion one makes. The more empirical and

Figure 1.2   Kenneth Goldsmith and Theo Beckmann, *Fidget* 1998. Performed at Whitney Museum of American Art at Philip Morris, New York City. Photo credit: Paula Court. Courtesy of the Whitney Museum of American Art.

---

[7] In performance at the Whitney Museum of American Art (June 16, 1998), Theo Bleckmann, the lead singer for Meredith Monk, 'stood high on a balcony in the museum and dropped sheets of paper printed with each word as he sang them. These sheets of paper were picked up by a pair of twin children and brought to a team of seamstresses, who sewed them into a suit during the course of the hour-long performance. When Bleckmann had finished singing, the then-finished suit was hoisted up to his balcony, where he donned the language/actions that he had just spoken/sung. Hence, a full circle was created' (letter to the author, 9 Oct. 1998). In an article for *Poliester* (Fall 1998), Bill Arning, who attended the performance, reports: 'To hear the expulsion of morning mucus from the nostrils ethereally sung by Bleckmann was as startlingly incongruous as to read such an unsensational act described by Goldsmith as if it were a recipe for a difficult but exquisite souffle.'

For further discussion of the Bleckmann performance ('a cross between a Gregorian chant and a medieval Book of Hours'), see Nancy Princenthal, 'Artist's Book Beat', in *Art on Paper* (November/December 1998), 70–1.

[8] The site may be accessed on http://www.chbooks.com/online/fidget/index.html.

detailed the verbal transcript, the more absurd the attempt to 'translate' body motion begins to seem. Faced with a welter of ceaseless and simultaneous movements, the mind filters out about ninety-nine per cent of these movements and subjects the rest to increasing interpretation. The 'factual' account thus becomes more and more idiosyncratic, and what *Fidget* celebrates with perverse charm is the victory of mind over matter and the inability to convey what we call body language except through language. The text is thus a devastating send-up of the now all-pervasive Foucault-inspired discourse on bodily primacy, a discourse that, in the wake of Elaine Scarry's famed *The Body in Pain*, generates such book titles as *Apocalyptic Bodies*, *The Body in Parts*, *Leaky Bodies and Boundaries*, and *Performing the Body*.[9] Consider, for example, the narrator's account in chapter 2 (11:00) of going to the bathroom and urinating:

> Walks. Left foot. Head raises. Walk. Forward. Forward. Forward. Bend at knees. Forward. Right foot. Left foot. Right foot. Stop. Left hand tucks at pubic area. Extracts testicles and penis using thumb and forefinger. Left hand grasps penis. Pelvis pushes on bladder, releasing urine. Stream emerges from within buttocks. Stomach and buttocks push outward. Stream of urine increases. Buttocks push. Sphincter tightens. Buttocks tighten. Thumb and forefinger shake penis. Thumb pulls. Left hand reaches. Tip of forefinger and index finger extend to grasp as body sways to left. Feet pigeon-toed. Move to left. Hand raises to hairline and pushes hair. Arm raises above head. Four fingers comb hair away from hairline toward back of head. Eyes see face. Mouth moves. Small bits of saliva cling to inside of lips. Swallow. Lips form words.[10]

Why is this description of the most ordinary and trivial of human acts so unsettling? Whereas a satirist like Swift, in 'A Voyage to Brobdingnag', reveals the inherent hideousness of the human body by means of gigantism ('[The Nurse's Breast] stood prominent six Foot and could not be less than sixteen in Circumference. The Nipple was about half the Bigness of my Head, and the Hue both of that and the Dug so varified with Spots, Pimples and Freckles, that nothing could appear more nauseous'),[11]

---

[9] I take these titles at random from a recent Routledge book catalogue (1998/99): Tina Pippin, *Apocalyptic Bodies: the Biblical End of the World in Text and Image*; David Hillman and Carla Mazzio (eds), *The Body in Parts: Fantasies of Corporeality in Early Modern Europe*; Margrit Shildrick, *Leaky Bodies and Boundaries: Feminism, Postmodernism and (Bio)ethics*; and Amelia Jones and Andrew Stephenson (eds), *Performing the body: Performing the Text*.

[10] *Fidget*, pp. 7–8.

[11] Jonathan Swift, *Gulliver's Travels*, in *The Writings of Jonathan Swift* (New York: W. W. Norton, Norton Critical Edition, 1973), p. 71.

Goldsmith is determined to keep his eye, so to speak, on the ball, to record noncommittally and non-judgementally the way the body actually works. And yet that very 'objectivity' has the Swiftian effect of demonstrating the stark disconnection between the physical and the mental, between the rote performance of the bodily function and the human ability to 'form words'. As the 'eyes see face' in the mirror, the implicit question seems to be Hamlet's: 'Is man no more than this?'

In breaking down bodily functions into their smallest components, Goldsmith defamiliarizes the everyday in ways that recall such Wittgensteinian questions as 'Why can't the right hand give the left hand money?' In ordinary discourse we take a verb like 'walk' for granted, without dwelling on the fact that 'Walk' means to alternate the forward motion of right foot and left foot. When we refer to a man urinating, we don't usually note that the steam of urine 'emerges from within buttocks'. And when we say someone 'speaks', we don't bother to add that 'Mouth moves' or that 'Lips form words'. 'Four fingers comb hair away from hairline toward back of head': it couldn't be a more common gesture but the standard reference would be 'to push the hair out of one's face'. The near-rhyming locution 'four fingers comb hair . . . from' takes a moment to recognize for what it is. And when, in chapter 3 (12:00), Goldsmith has his morning cup of coffee, the ritual becomes more elaborate than a ballet routine or an athletic contest:

> Back on back of chair. Legs touch legs. Arms parallel arms of chair. Hands grasp end of arms. Legs push back. Feet flat on ground. Elbow on arm. Arms out. Cup to mouth. Swallow. Cup put down. Teeth outside mouth. Legs lift. Legs stretch on legs ninety degrees. Grasp paper towels. Slide to front. Left hand grasps right. Pull away from left. Left hand stretches. Fold.[12]

The relation of human arms and legs to the metaphoric arms and legs of a chair, the place of the teeth as one opens one's mouth wide enough to drink, the movement one makes when folding a paper towel – all these take on an aura of gravity as if something of great importance is taking place, something in need of urgent commentary.

But, of course, such self-consciousness or, more properly, body consciousness cannot be sustained and so the entries get shorter and shorter and, by the time we get to chapter 9 (18:00), we read the following:

> Reach. Grasp. Reach Grab. Hold. Saw. Pull. Hold. Grab. Push. Itch. Push. Push. Turn. Walk. Two. Three. Four. Five. Six. Seven. Eight. Turn. Chew. Massage. Gather. Heavy. Slower. Reach. Open.

[12] *Fidget*, p. 14.

> Swallow. Exhale. Stand. Burp. Grab. Turn. Pick. Grab. Grab. Grab. Open.[13]

The chapter consists of permutations of mostly monosyllabic verbs without subjects or objects, often distinguished by a single letter as in 'Grasp'/ 'Grab', and ends with the rhyme 'Raise. Gaze'. In the next chapter ('19:00'), drinking has begun and all hell breaks loose. The objective reporter now gives way to the inventor of language play:

> Refinger. Sneeze cross. Length of fore wipes free. Hand sad. Runs at bottom of thigh, no eye. Calflex. Peripheral movements spoken. Breath cools down right side. Jaws find teeth clenched. Outer part of lower fang, most pronounced grinding backward and forward.[14]

And two pages further down:

> Spinger thumb. Now is lift. Thumb to flip. Now thumb. Indents forefinger. Crease unnaturally lumpy. Right and right is face down on ground. Riched lightly. Arching four and blade middle and not touching ground. Still harrow. Body is sit. Licks wet.[15]

The more the language of description breaks down into non-sense and neologism, the greater, ironically enough, the need to make value judgements. The hand is now unaccountably 'sad', the 'eye' missing, the 'crease' (of the forefingers?) 'unnaturally lumpy'. One cannot, it seems, remain detached from one's body, from one's *own* reactions. 'Slight pleasure gained from dig into finger and then pleasured by sharpness', remarks the narrator, now wanting to put *his* stamp on events as they occur.[16] The language becomes *his* language and the next chapter ('20:00') opens with the sentence 'Whitehead and watch after left hand', where the first word in initial (and hence capitalized) position, refers not only to a whitehead or mole found on the left hand but to the philosopher, Alfred North Whitehead, whose famous Fallacy of Misplaced Concreteness (for example, if a tree falls in the forest when no one is there to hear it fall, does it make a sound?) is apropos to Goldsmith's narrative. The poet further puns on 'watch', which looks ahead to the phrase 'In the pocket worthwhile' in the next sentence. And the creation of a new language field leads to the finale with its reversal of words (see Fig. 1.1), giving us new

---

[13] Ibid., p. 55.
[14] Ibid., p. 57.
[15] Ibid., p. 58.
[16] Ibid., p. 59.

entities like '.petS .drawkcab teeF' ('Feet backward. Step'). The reversed linear flow makes a key word of 'morf' ('from'), a word highly applicable in the context along with 'woble' ('elbow'), 'pil' ('lip') and the mysterious 'evom' ('move'), which looks like a number or symbol in a cabbalistic game. The morphing landscape is full of 'sredluohs' ('shoulders'), 'eugnot' ('tongue') and there is much 'dna' ('and') about. It seems, finally, that the language game has occluded the multiform activities of the moving body. And so 'Eyelids close'.

Here, then, in Beckett's words about *Finnegans Wake*, 'form *is* content, content *is* form ... [The] writing is not *about* something; *it is that something itself*.[17] But the paradox – and this is a new development in poetics at the turn of the twenty-first century – the written text is only one of *Fidget*'s realizations. Earlier, I mentioned the Whitney installation, the musical performance score and the Java Applet. Let me now say a further word about this latter electronic version, which reconfigures the text of *Fidget* by substituting the computer for the human body. As Goldsmith explains:

> The Java Applet contains the text reduced further into its constituent elements, a word or a phrase. The relationships between these elements is structured by a dynamic mapping system that is organized visually and spatially instead of grammatically. In addition, the Java Applet invokes duration and presence. Each time the Applet is downloaded it begins at the same time as set in the user's computer and every mouse click or drag that the user initiates is reflected in the visual mapping system. The different hours are represented in differing font sizes, background colors and degree of 'fidgetness', however, these parameters may be altered by the user. The sense of time is reinforced by the diminishing contrast and eventual fading away of each phrase as each second passes.[18]

Time is speeded up in the Applet so that each hour period takes approximately five to seven minutes to complete. The viewing of the Java Applet from any specific site would take about eighty minutes, and then the cycle begins all over again. No one, of course, is likely to sit at the screen for the full cycle, but even a few minutes of access reveal

[17] Samuel Beckett, 'Dante . . . Bruno . Vico . . Joyce', *Our Exagmination Round his Factification for Incamination of Work in Progress* (Paris: Shakespeare and Company, 1929); rpt. in Beckett, *Disjecta: Miscellaneous Writings and a Dramatic Fragment*, ed. Ruby Cohn (New York: Grove Press, 1984), p. 27.
[18] See http://www.chbooks.com/online/fidget/index.html.

some interesting facets of *Fidget*. When the text's linear momentum is replaced by spatial organization, words interact in new ways. Thus, in the case of the opening sequence ('Eyelids open. Tongue runs cross upper lip ... Grind. Stretch. Swallow), in the electronic version 'swallow' appears centre stage and rests on top of 'Tongue runs across upper lip'; it is then replaced by 'grind' and 'stretch', the words grinding against one another and causing a kind of traffic jam as the screen fills up with what looks like a spider web of action verbs connected by lines that appear straight, then bend and stretch. But, in the visual mapping system, verbs like 'bend', 'clench' and 'swallow', detached from their subject and object nouns, and given relatively equal weight, become less referential, less narrative and – oddly – less male-oriented. In its book version, *Fidget* is quite obviously a man's narrative, especially in the masturbation passage in the fourth chapter ('13:00'). But in the Applet, words appear as *words* rather than as *signifiers* of X or Y, morphology and physical appearance taking precedence over denotations. In the '15:00' chapter, for example, the sentences 'Right hand saws' and 'Arm and elbow move toward body' (Fig. 1.3, lines 2–3) are transformed into overprint, intersecting and coming apart on the yellow 15:00 background (Fig. 1.4), marking their symbiosis. As one watches, phrases appear, replace one another and disappear in what looks like a balletic structure. As a visual and kinetic space, *Fidget* has an austere and silent beauty quite different from the printed version or from its oral enactment, for, as seen on the screen, this language has neither memory nor agency. Indeed, the elegance of the clean, undifferentiated visual space suggests that, as the poet Tan Lin put it, 'the mind is only vestigially connected to the body "it speaks" through'.[19]

And yet – and here is a further irony – the training ground for producing this electronic text, I would argue, may be found in Goldsmith's earlier, and by no means 'elegant', written work, *No. 111 2.7.93–10.20.96* – his encyclopedic poem based on words ending in the sound *ah* (*schwa* according to phoneticians), a collection of words drawn from conversations, books, phone calls, radio shows, newspapers, television and, especially, the internet, that was arranged alphabetically and by syllable count (from single-syllable words beginning with A – 'A, a, aar, aas, aer, agh, ah air' – to D. H. Lawrence's complete 'The Rocking Horse Winner') so as to create a gargantuan poetic reference book

[19] Tan Lin, 'Information Archives, the De-Materialization of Language' and Kenneth Goldsmith's *Fidget* and *No. 111 2.7.93–10.20.96*', *Art Byte*, Feb–March 1999, as posted on Goldsmith's web page, http://wings.buffalo.edu/epc/authors/goldsmith/lin.html, p. 1.

15:00

Left hand grasps. Right hand grasps. Left hand pulls. Releases. Left hand grabs. Right arm sweeps to right. Left hand reverses. Elbow out. Turns around. Right hand saws. Arm and elbow move toward body. Arm and elbow move away from body. Toward body. Away from body. Fingertips hold. In and out. In and out. Right hand releases and grabs. Left hand drops. Right hand brushes left fingertips. Left hand moves, turning entire body. Right arm extends. Right hand grasps. Right hand opens. Left hand closes. Body spins three hundred sixty degrees. Right hand grabs. Body bends. Left hand drops. Opens. Left hand reaches. Twists counterclockwise. Right finger slides across bottom of nose. Mucus coats upper surface of right finger. Left hand on left buttocks. Right hand reaches. Twists clockwise. Body turns. Left arm extends. Left hand grasps. Right hand sweeps with blade. Body turns. Right hand grasps. Left hand grasps. Right hand grasps. Left hand grasps. Right hand grasps. Moves back and forth repeatedly. Left hand grasps. Slides. Elbow out. Elbow back. Elbow back. Body spins one hundred eighty degrees. Right hand sweeps. Right hand plunges. Right hand plunges. Right hand jingles. Shakes. Back and forth. Back and forth. Left hand grasps. Body spins. Left hand grasps. Moves to right. Body weight rocks back and forth. Shifts left to right. Quick motion. Left hand pushes. Thrusts. Right hand crunches. Right hand moves on top of left. Fingers open. Left palm up. Left hand closes. Fingers clench. Right hand turns. Thumb and forefinger push away from body. Push away from body. Push away from body. Twist. Hand twists. Hand back. Tension in muscle. Hand moves. Muscles in hand tense. Left hand eliminates. Body turns one hundred eighty degrees. Pushes on top. Thumbs press. Fingers push. Press. Body shakes. Back and forth. Body shakes. Back and forth. Body shakes. Thumb pushes. Mouth opens. Lips lick. Hands lift. Plunge. Emerge. Immerse. Elbow out. Hands open. Grasp. Pull out. Emerge. Scoop. Shift. Scoop. Shift. Scoop. Scoop. Scoop. Left hand grabs. Both hands lift. Raise. Shake. Twist. Turn. Pull counterclockwise. Upend. Drop. Turn. Spin. Right arm spins clockwise. Elbow twists. Stops. Reverses. Meat of thumb quickly twists counterclockwise. Meat spins. Repeats. Spins faster. Hips sway counterclockwise. Stop. Tips of fingers grasp. Clockwise spins. Whole body shakes back and forth. Back and forth. Pelvis thrusts right. Releases. Arms outstretch. Raise. Arm tips parallel. Grasp. Pull. Right hand tears. Pats. Left hand smoothes. Left hand grasps. Right hand dumps. Body spins. Grasp. Right hand dumps. Right hand pinches. Turns. Right hand twists. Elbow moves toward body. Twists. Right hand twists. Elbow draws in. Right hand twists. Left hand grasps. Right hand twists. Right hand twists. Twists. Releases. Right hand trims. Left hand reaches. Wrist drops. Left hand grabs. Steps right. Lifts. Lifts. Thumbnails dig. Water releases. Twists. Peels. Pokes. Releases. Pushes. Right hand crashes. Right arm raises. Repeats several times. Left hand twists. Pulls. Steps. Stops. Body spins to left. Walks right. Bends down. Scoops. Dumps. Digs. Drops. Walks. Right arm extends. Twists counterclockwise. Left. Right. Drops. Arm extends. Hands grasp and move across body. Hands immerse. Drops one. Drops two. Drops three. Drops four. Grasps. Middle, fore, and ring finger rub against each other. In and out. Tongue smacks against palate. Grabs and wipes. Walks. Left. Right. Bends. Picks. Turns counterclockwise. Grasps. Rips. Left. Right. Two. Lifts. Turns. Elbows outstretch. Right. Drops. Up. Turns. Twists. Drops. Grasps. Slices in and out. One. Picks up. Back and forth. Two. Back and forth. Three. Drop. Turns right. Left. Grasps. Drops. Right hand shakes two three four five six. Twists counterclockwise. Dumps. Drops. Twists. Walks softly. Right. Moves in. Drops. Sit. Drops. Chews repeatedly. Shuttles left to right. Presses. Elbow drops. Deep inhalation. Chews right. Swallows. Stops. Clears throat. Breathes. Deep exhalation. Burps. Breathes in through nose. Stomach protrudes. Belly pushes out. Chest cavity collapses. Chest expands with breath. Out through nose. Shoulders raise. Sits. Legs spread. Hands in front, elbows on thighs. Teeth grasp thumbnail. Push. Push from center of stomach. Push. Urine dribbles from tip of penis. Breathe steadily. Urine flows from tip of penis. Bowels open. Push from abdomen. Sphincter opens. Bowels fall. Push. Push. Urine trickles. Lips form words. Hands intertwine. Sphincter closes. Urine spews. Left hand reaches. Palms up. Both hands grasp. Pull toward body. One hand wraps over another. Stops. Pulls. Moves forward. Left hand moves between legs and rubs crack of buttocks. Sphincter loosens. Middle finger glides over anus. Pressure on coccyx. Arm reaches and grasps. Hand flattens. Twists back and forth. Hand moves between legs. Pressure on anus. Pulls. Drops. Hunches. Pulls. Lifts. Stands up. Drops. Turns. Hand reaches and pushes. Left hand grasps. Moves to right. Right hand twists counterclockwise. Right hand shakes. Left hand squeezes. Right hand surges. Lips purse. Quick strokes. Quick strokes. Lips purse. Expel saliva. Quick strokes. Expel. Drops. Wipes. Moves left. Steps. Grasps. Both hands pull. Left leg lifts. Left leg drops. Right leg lifts. Right leg drops. Crouches down. Grasp two fingers. Flips. Stretches. Right leg passes. Left leg lifts. Body bends over. Snaps. Pull out. Grasps. Elbows out. Right leg opens. Up. Step through. Left leg lifts. Step through. Grasp. Pull out. Shoulders expand. Suck in. Stomach lifts. Pull. Grasp. Fidget. Fidget. Fidget. Pulls. Twist. Turn. Finger pulls. Tightens. Loops. Leg drops. Leg moves forward. Drops. Pull. Tightens. Loops. Hands move to knees. Step forward. Bend down. Grasp. Grasp. Reach. Pulls down. Slide through. Shoulders hunch. Crimp. Pull out. Drop. Plug. Hear. Press. Right ear turns out. Grasps. Bends down. Pulls straight. Pulls tight. Grasp. Pulls. Step. Step. Stops. Inserts. Turns to right. Step. Step. Three. Four. Five. Step. Six. Seven. Eight. Nine. Step. Step. Eyes scan. Left hand pulls. Stop. Waits. Breathes. Again. Grasp. Step. Bend. Breathe in through nose. Steps. Vision shifts. Head nods. Rubs genitals. Pace quickens. Drop down over shoulder. Stop. Sit. Right leg crosses left. Dangles. Ankle moves up and back. Breathe from stomach. Left hand falls over. Tongue protrudes from mouth. Caresses upper lip moving from upper left to right. Tongue probes back of front teeth. Tongue chafes against sharpness of front tooth. Tongue moves to gums. Runs over crevice between two front teeth. Relaxes into slumped tongue. Probes bump on front tooth. Reaches up and grasps.

Figure 1.3 Kenneth Goldsmith, *Fidget*, Chapter 15:00.

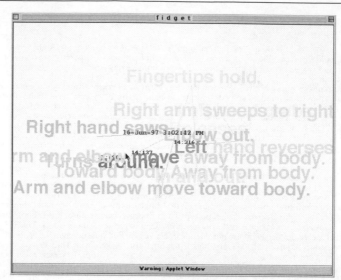

Figure 1.4   Kenneth Goldsmith and Clem Paulsen (screen-shot). Java Applet, Stadium Projects, *http://www.chbooks.com/online/fidget/index.html*, 1998, Chapter 15:00.

archive on the *argot* of our times (see Fig. 1.5).[20] The sensitivity to language displayed in *No. 111,* a text still subject to conscious arrangement rather than the empiricist recording of chance movement as in *Fidget*, clears the ground for the on-screen paragrammatic possibilities we now witness in Goldsmith's work.

[20] In a letter to the author of 14 March 1997, Goldsmith explains his technique in *No. 111* as follows:

> I was inspired by the explanation given to me regarding the sacred significance of the Sanskrit word *aum*. It seems that when one speaks this word, all parts of the mouth are engaged. . . . My function for the next 3 years was that of a collector of language . . . I would carry around a portable dictaphone and a notepad and whenever I would encounter one of these [*ah*] sounds, I would 'capture' it. At first, my idea was to take all sounds regardless of their content . . . perhaps, I thought, with this system I could subvert the normal function of language (communication) and invoke a less conventional idea (although not without precedent) of language as pure music. And language is a great medium to do this with because no matter how much one collects for sound alone, there is *always* meaning.

Goldsmith's arbitrary limits (600 pages of material gathered between 2 July 1993 and 20 October 1996) and arrangement via the alphabet and syllable count give us such bravura passages as the following sequence of three-syllable units beginning with *wa* (see *No. 111 2.7.93–10.20.96* (Great Barrington, MA: The Figures, 1997), p. 27:

> Wadada, waheena, wahoodler, waiting for, wallflower, wallpaper, walls have ears, WankStoppers, Ward Cleaver, warm moisture, warmaster, warrior, Warszawa, wassailer, wasted years, watch out for, watch the wear, wave-lover, wayfarer, Wayfarers.

I

A, a, aar, aas, aer, agh, ah, air, är, are, arh, arre, arrgh, ars, aude, aw,
awe, Ayr, Ba, ba, baa, baaaahh, baar, bah, bar, bard, bare, barge, barre,
Bayer, beer, bere, beurre, bier, bla, blah, Blair, blare, blear, bleh, blur,
boar, board, Boer, boor, bore, bored, Boz, bra, bras, Brer, brrrr, bur,
burr, C.O.R.E., ca, cah, car, card, care, caw, cha, chaar, chair, char, chard,
chaw, cheer, cheere, Cheers, Cher, chiere, choir, chord, chore, Claire,
claw, clear, cleere, coeur, Coors, cord, core, corps, course, craw, crore,
cur, curr, curs, czar, d'or, da, där, dare, daw, dawed, dear, deer, derre,
dire, diur, door, dor, dore, dour, draw, drawe, drear, droor, duh, dure,
dyere, e'er, ear, eere, eh, Eh?, eir, 'er, Er, er, ere, err, eyr, fa, få, fair, faire,
far, fas, faugh, fawe, fayre, fear, fer, fere, ferre, fier, fiord, fir, flair, flaw,
fleer, floor, flour, floure, foiah, for, för, force, Ford, ford, fore, fors, four,
IV, foure, fra, frere, frore, fur, fyr, ga, ga', gah, gair, gar, gaw, gear, geere,
giour, gnar, gnaw, goore, gore, gourd, grah, grarh, gras, graw, grrrr,
Grrrrr!!, guard, gyre, ha, haah, hah, Hair, hair, här, hard, hare, harr,
harre, haw, hawe, hear, heer, heere, heir, her, here, herr, hir, hire, hoar,
hoard, horde, hors, hour, houre, huh, Huh?, hurr, hwor, ia, ier, ire, ja,
jaar, Jah, jar, jaw, Jaws, jeer, ka, kar, ker, kir, kna, knar, knarre, knur,
Kurd, la, La!, lair, lard, lare, laud, law, lawe, lawed, Lear, leer, leh, lere,
lier, Loire, loore, lor, Lord, lord, lore, lough, lourde, Ma, ma, mar, mare,
Mars, Maude, maw, mawe, mere, mha, mire, mirre, moi, Moor, moor,
moore, more, mors, moure, mwa, myre, myrrh, na, nah, nahhh, Nair,
nar, nard, naw, ne'er, near, nerd, nha, noir, nor, nur, nya, nyeh, o'er, oar,
oor, oore, or, ore, our, oure, Pa, pa, paar, paas, pah, pair, paire, par,
pard, pare, paw, pear, peer, per, perr, perre, pers, pier, poire, por, pore,
pour, poure, prayer, preyere, pshaw, pur, purr, qua, quaa, quaer, Quah,
quaire, quar, queer, quire, R, r, Ra, raa, rare, raw, rawe, rear, rer, rere,
rh, roar, ruhr, sa, saar, sard, sarge, saugh, saw, sawe, scar, scare, schmeer,
schwa, score, scour, sear, Sears, seer, sere, serr, Shah, shard, share, Shaw,
shawe, shear, sheer, shere, shire, shmeer, shore, shour, shoure, shur, Sir,
sir, sire, slaw, slur, smear, smeer, smore, snare, sneer, snore, soar, soor,
soore, sore, sour, spa, spar, spare, sparre, spear, spere, sphere, spoir, spore,
spur, square, squaw, stair, star, stare, steer, steere, stir, stoor, store, straw,
sur, sure, svår, swa, sward, swear, swere, swoore, sword, swore, t'a, ta,
taa, tar, tare, Tarr, Taur, taw, tawe, tear, tear, teere, ter, tha, thair, thaire,
thar, thaw, their, ther, there, they're, Thor, tor, tore, tour, toure, trois,
Tsar, 'twere, tweer, Tzar, ugh, uh, Ur, ur, urr, urre, vair, var, veer, Vuh,
wah, War, war, ward, ware, wear, weer, Weir, weir, wer, were, werre,
wher, where, Where?, whir, whirr, whore, whurr, wir, Wire, wire, word,
wore, worre, wors, worse, ya, yaar, yard, yare, yaw, yeah, year, yeer, yer,
yere, yheere, yoore, yore, you're, your, youre, yr, yre, Za, zha, Zsa;

Figure 1.5   Kenneth Goldsmith, *No. 111 2.7.93–10.20.96* (Great Barrington,
MA: The Figures, 1997), p. 1.

II

'If literature is defined as the exploration and exercise of tolerable linguistic deviance', write Jed Rasula and Steve McCaffery in the introduction to their new anthology *Imagining Language*, 'the institutional custodianship of literature serves mainly to protect the literary work from language, shielding it from the disruptive force of linguistic slippage'.[21] In the age of digital reproduction, such slippage has increasingly taken the form of what James Joyce called 'vocable scriptsigns', a writing that is 'verbovisivocal'.[22] A second intriguing example of such *differential* poetics – differential in that the text in question is neither single nor autonomous but a set of variants – is a recent collaboration between two Australians, the poet John Kinsella and the sound artist/photographer Ron Sims, called *Kangaroo Virus*.[23] Like *Fidget*, *Kangaroo Virus* exists in electronic form, like *Fidget*, it has a performance score – this time on a CD that accompanies the book – and, like *Fidget*, it is a documentary, informational poem that relies heavily on empirical observation. But, unlike *Fidget*'s reliance on the tape recorder, *Kangaroo Virus* is made up of short free-verse lyrics by Kinsella, each of which has an accompanying photograph by Sims, lyrics whose spoken version deviates, both rhythmically and semantically, from the printed text.

Kangaroo Virus has introductions by both Kinsella and Sims, and these are seemingly straightforward, like Goldsmith's account of *Fidget*. Here is the opening of Kinsella's introduction:

> I'd not long been back from Cambridge, England, when my partner and I decided to spend a day with my brother in Dryandra Forest near his home in Williams [in Southern Australia]. We visited Congelin Dam not far off the York-Williams road. My brother had been there a week earlier and found a number of dead kangaroos through the bush. On arriving, we immediately found a corpse floating in the dam like the rotting hulk of a whale. The dam was built to service the railway that used to cut its way through the forest late last century. Gnarled and petrified corpses in grotesque fetal-like positions were to be found through the bush. My brother recounted how in recent months kangaroos, not only in this district but throughout the wheatbelt, had been struck down by a mysterious 'virus' that left them blind. He'd seen them hopping into fences and ploughing into tractors, dead in their dozens along the roads.

---

[21] Jed Rasula and Steve McCaffery, *Imagining Language: An Anthology* (Cambridge and London: MIT Press, 1998), p. x.

[22] James Joyce, *Finnegans Wake* (New York: Viking Penguin, 1976), p. 118.

[23] John Kinsella and Ron Sims, *Kangaroo Virus* (South Freemantle: Folio/Fremantle Arts Centre Press, 1998); cf. http://www.johnkinsella.org.

Farmers had been shooting them in the fields, rangers had been shooting them in the bush. We talked about the release of the calici rabbit virus, how it had 'escaped' before 'release' from Kangaroo Island off South Australia.[24]

'Greatly disturbed', Kinsella starts writing his Kangaroo Virus Poem and enlists the sound-artist/photographer, Ron Sims, to work on the project. He reports:

> Without scientific methods at hand, we decided to approach it through art – words, sound, and images. Science and art have much in common. As a poet, I explore the data of language for codes and truths. I develop hypotheses and search for answers. Of course, much never progresses beyond the state of exploration but it is the search that counts.[25]

This is a sentiment Goldsmith could well endorse even though his own heavily inflected New York irony could hardly be less like Kinsella's romantic ecology. This poet's highly interpretative, subjective responses to the landscape are, in any case, curiously qualified by the dispassionate realism of the photographs. In his own introduction, Sims writes:

> Poetry abstracts and fractures the 'real' world, and then reassembles our understandings into a new 'reality' – that of the poet ... The photographic image has quite a different strength. Unlike any other visual art form, the photograph portrays 'truth' – we believe the image! No matter how distorted, whether in colour or mono-chrome, essentially the photograph is a split second of actuality, captured.
>
> For *Kangaroo Virus* my very happy dilemma has been to find a tenable bond between the 'expressionistic' poetry and the 'representational' quality of the photograph. It seemed pointless that the one should merely mirror the other at the narrative or subjective level. So I began to consider the intrinsic value of the photograph image: the line, texture, density, form. I felt that if there should be a bond with the poetry then it was here, in the common 'musicality', not the 'meaning' of the two art forms.[26]

The two artists worked separately so that 'illustration', if it occurred at all, became what Sims calls an 'organic accident, not an artistic

---

[24] *Kangaroo Virus*, p. 9.
[25] Ibid., p. 9.
[26] Ibid., p. 10.

contrivance'.[27] Kinsella's poems, after two longer lyrics, 'Death of a Roo Dog' and 'The Visitation', are free-verse quatrains like the following:

> They might call it 'rail country'
> as the tell-tale signs are there
> immediately – the skin deeply
> scraped, the bones grey and strewn about.[28]

Read against Sims's photograph on the facing page (Fig. 1.6), with its dead grey tree trunks, some still standing, bone-like, silhouetted against the sky, the 'tell-tale signs' are very much 'there'. Or consider the following:

> The eye is black too and from
> the core like an exotic ache
> . that'd be noticed only by tourists:
> the vacuum elemental, or cabbalistic.[29]

The 'eye' (Fig. 1.7) is indeed frightening, but perhaps not as frightening as the well-meaning tourists themselves, who are unwittingly the source of the terrible virus.

Kinsella is much more traditionally 'poetic' than Goldsmith. Metaphor, for example, is a pervasive device, as in

> The twisted eye of wire
> works as a lyre in the small
> shifts of air scratching
> close to the surface,

accompanied by a photograph in which the wire loop on the tree trunk creates a stark, abstract design, or as in

> The crypt of the forest
> cracked like sodden rag
> dry-boned and calqued
> cavities replete, idling,

which accompanies a photograph of a kangaroo skull covered by debris – a picture so horrible, the eye turns away in pain.[30] Kinsella's figurative images culminate in the quatrain:

---

[27] Ibid., p. 11.
[28] Ibid., p. 20.
[29] Ibid., p. 26.
[30] Ibid., pp. 34, 58.

Figure 1.6   Ron Sims, photograph, *Kangaroo Virus*, p. 21.

Figure 1.7   Ron Sims, photograph, *Kangaroo Virus*, p. 27.

> Imprint: like they've seen it before,
> these old-timers, cast in plaster,
> referencing the direction of a roo,
> even so, the forest thinner, shrinking.[31]

And here again the photograph of footprints in the slag (Kinsella's or Sims's, not a kangaroo's) has none of the comfort provided by talking about 'old-timers'; it is merely – and horrifically – desolate and bleak (Fig. 1.8).

To conclude the book, Sims provides a series of observations on the process of photographing this terrible landscape ('Steam trains once ran through here. The rail mounds, sidings, bridge are left-overs of that time and I am quite comfortable filming the evidence. It is integral to the condition of this area and to our story'), and Kinsella has a long poem called 'Narrative' that recapitulates the horror of

> new viroids
> sprouting from the paddock's surface,
> memory prompted by shifting fences,

and blames the eco-tourists who invade the former wilderness for their contribution to its destruction.[32] The concluding note is a shade

---

[31] Ibid., p. 62.
[32] Ibid., pp. 67, 70.

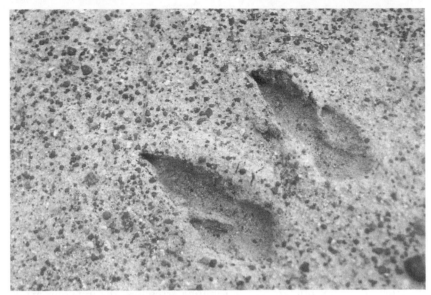

Figure 1.8   Ron Sims, photograph, *Kangaroo Virus*, p. 63.

moralistic, but Kinsella's didacticism is offset by both visual images and the soundtext, which is nothing short of extraordinary.

The thirty-minute CD is by no means a straightforward reading of the poems; indeed, their sequence is markedly altered and lines and stanzas are often repeated. Kinsella and Sims read antiphonally, circling round and round the same words and phrases beginning with the word 'static'. For the first few minutes we hear violent noises: a train hooting through the countryside, dogs barking, machinery crashing, the galloping of kangaroos.[33] Throughout the sequence, there is wailing and gnashing, a fence opening with a squeak, sheep bleating, and an occasional bird cry. The choral phrase throughout is the opening of 'The Visitation':

> Old timers reckon they've seen it before
> but others have their doubts . . .

Simms will chant these lines from a distance and then Kinsella, in the foreground, repeats them. Then after more frightening and violent noise, Kinsella recites, very matter-of-factly, the opening of 'Death of a Roo Dog': 'One of the dogs chased a boomer / right down from the forest's edge'. The words from the first two poems cycle in and out, interspersed with sounds of water dripping, dogs lapping water, a buzz saw and

---

[33] I must add a disclaimer here since I have no idea what that movement would really sound like. But it seems to be a very imaginative simulation.

occasional metapoetic conversation between Kinsella and Simms, figuring out where to place the camera and what to say next.

In the course of the sound piece, Kinsella reads almost all the quatrains, some of them twice, as in the case of 'The living, cased in lichen / holds up the movement'.[34] Then after the sound of a herd in the distance, Kinsella repeats lines from 'Death of a Roo Dog', especially

> Before I could grab the mad dog's collar
> it launched itself straight in after
> a roo that I'd swear stood higher
> than me by a head.[35]

We hear sheep, the perennial train shooting into the night, then silence punctuated by a faint sound of bees buzzing and bird sound. Silence.

What I find so interesting in this sound poem is that, as in the case of Goldsmith's Java Applet, it is not simply a repeat of the linear text but an artwork in its own right. The choral speaking, chanting, litany-like structure, the total human silence for long stretches, the amazing array of forest, animal and weather sounds frightening in their clamour: all these have the effect of putting the listener squarely into the scene. As someone who (dare I confess it?) is not fond of animals, has no pets, pays little attention to problems of animal preservation and even less to the eco-problems of the Australian Southwest, I nevertheless find *Kangaroo Virus* wholly captivating. Reading the poems, studying the photographs, listening to the soundtrack and surfing the internet site, I find myself keenly interested in the fate of the kangaroo.

Perhaps this is just another way of saying that such 'differential' poetry – a poetry in which no single version necessarily has priority – can be as instructive as it is compelling. Like Goldsmith's *Fidget*, which alternates verbal, visual, aural and kinaesthetic images of motor activity and the reaction of mind to body, *Kangaroo Virus* gives us alternate ways of tackling a given problem. The works in question are not so much intermedia (for example, word + image or word set to music or recited on film) as *alternate* media, their differential production implying that *knowledge* is now available through different channels and by different means. Such work allows for an unusual degree of reader/listener/viewer participation: it is the reader, after all, who must decide whether to access the 20:00 chapter of *Fidget*, in which case she or he cannot 'read' the other twelve chapters, or whether to 'read' linearly by moving from page to page of the written text. In either case, the 'reader's' experience frustrates a conventional experience of reading the book.

[34] *Kangaroo Virus*, p. 40.
[35] Ibid., p. 12.

The same holds true for *Kangaroo Virus*: the reader can choose whether to begin with the lyric sequence or to match poem or photograph to sound track version. In his epilogue 'Process', Ron Sims remarks: 'Steam trains once ran through here. The rail mounds, sidings, bridge are left-overs of that time, and I am quite comfortable filming the evidence. It is integral to the condition of this area and to our story'. But then he adds, 'The sounds, of course, are gone with the trains but I will keep them in mind for the audio production'.[36] As Jasper Johns might say, 'Do something to it. Do something else to it'.[37] Or again, if one medium doesn't work, try another. 'Quiddity', as we read near the end of Kinsella's final poem in the series, 'is the word'.

Yet it is also important to note that such 'quiddity' has always been with us, although we have not known quite what to make of what I am calling 'differential' poetics. Take the case of Emily Dickinson, whose poetry, almost all of it published posthumously was, for years, read as a series of neat rhyming hymn stanzas, normally punctuated.[38] Even after Thomas Johnson published his definitive edition of the poems in 1955, reinstating Dickinson's original dashes (rather than commas) and recording the variant words and phrases Dickinson had listed in the margins, the stanza form and 'look' of Dickinson's lyric remained uncontested. It was only when the manuscripts themselves came under close scrutiny in the past two decades that the situation changed. In her brilliant studies *My Emily Dickinson* (1985) and *The Birthmark* (1993), both of them part poetry, part documentary history, part literary criticism, the poet Susan Howe argued that any valid reading of Dickinson must honour the actual form of Dickinson's manuscripts – the so-called 'fascicles',[39] which

[36] Ibid., p. 67.

[37] Jasper Johns, 'Sketchbook Notes, 1963–64,' in *Writings, Sketchbook Notes, Interviews* (New York: Museum of Modern Art, 1996), p. 54. Johns's famous entry reads:

> Take an object
> Do something to it
> Do something else to it

[38] For a concise treatment of the publication history of the poems, beginning with Millicent Todd Bingham's edition of *Poems by Emily Dickinson* (1891), see Martha Nell Smith, 'Dickinson's Manuscripts,' in Gudrun Grabher, Roland Hagenbüchle and Cristanne Miller (eds), *The Emily Dickinson Handbook* (Amherst: University of Massachusetts Press, 1998), pp. 113–37.

[39] In his Introduction to *The Poems of Emily Dickinson Variorum Edition*, 3 vols (Cambridge and London: Harvard University Press, 1998), R. W. Franklin explains:

> Dickinson copied poem after poem onto sheets of letter paper, already folded by the manufacturer to form a bifolium. She kept the sheets separate – not inserted inside one another to form a larger signature – and thus copied them individually ... To bind, Dickinson stacked the assembled sheets, with the overflow leaves (if any) in place, and punched two holes through the group, threading it with string, tied on the front. She did not put her name on the fascicles, give them titles or title pages, or label, number, or otherwise distinguish them. (vol. I, p. 7)

exhibited, especially in Dickinson's later years, a kind of free verse, the lines almost always running over so as to break the seemingly boxlike stanza patterns. As for the variant words listed at the bottom of a given page, Howe read these as an integral part of the respective poem.[40] This line of reasoning has been developed in such scholarly books as Sharon Cameron's *Choosing not Choosing: Dickinson's Fascicles*, Martha Nell Smith's *Rowing in Eden: Rereading Emily Dickinson*, and Marta L. Werner's *Emily Dickinson's Open Folios*.[41] Werner's study, which focuses on a group of forty late drafts and fragments hitherto known as the 'Lord letters' (the reference is to Dickinson's friend Judge Otis P. Lord), goes so far as to envision every stray letter, ink mark, blank space, crossed-out word or variant as part of the poetic fabric of a given text; indeed, for Werner, there is no distinction between Dickinson's poems and her letters or verbal fragments. As for the poems themselves, these critics argue that there is not one definitive version of any given poem and that, moreover, the fascicles provide essential contexts for each text so that only a variorum can give a particular poem its identity. And not only a printed variorum, but a reproduction of the manuscript itself, in all its materiality.

Is such attention to manuscript versions merely fetishistic as some Dickinson scholars have argued?[42] The question may well be falsely posed. For the interesting issue, so far as the New Poetics is concerned, is not whether it is *necessary* to read Dickinson's poems in their variant manuscript versions, but that poets and critics should now *want* so to read them. The current thrust of Dickinson scholarship, in other words, testifies to a new preoccupation with material embodiment rather than with a hypothetical urtext that will remain the same no matter what the medium, the publication conditions and so on. Indeed, read in the context of recent Dickinson studies (and similar materialist study is now being given to other 'classic' authors), Goldsmith's *Fidget*, Kinsella's *Kangaroo Virus* and related contemporary 'poems' take on a new resonance. Internet culture, these books suggest, has produced a textual anxiety beyond anything one might have imagined a few short decades ago.

---

[40] Susan Howe, *My Emily Dickinson* (Berkeley: North Atlantic Books, 1985), *passim*; *The Birthmark: Unsettling the Wilderness in American Literary History* (Hanover and London: Wesleyan University Press, 1993), pp. 131–53.

[41] Sharon Cameron, *Choosing Not Choosing: Dickinson's Fascicles* (Chicago: University of Chicago Press, 1992); Martha Nell Smith, *Rowing in Eden: Rereading Emily Dickinson* (Austin: University of Texas Press, 1992); Marta L. Werner, *Emily Dickinson's Open Folios: Scenes of Reading, Surfaces of Writing* (Ann Arbor: University of Michigan Press, 1998).

[42] See, for example, Heinz Ickstadt, 'The American Emily Dickinson', keynote address to 'Emily Dickinson at Home', biennial conference of Emily Dickinson International Society, Mt. Holyoke, MA, August 1999.

In his classic essay 'The Work of Art in the Age of Mechanical Reproduction' (1935), Walter Benjamin observed that, given the increased possibilities for readers to become writers, 'to publish somewhere or other comments on [one's] work, grievances, documentary reports' or 'letters to the editor', 'the distinction between author and public is about to lose its basic character'.[43] How prophetic these words have turned out to be! Half a century later and especially in the Internet chat groups and on LISTSERVs, authorship as such has indeed become ubiquitous. The response of poets has been to control the *material* conditions of the work as assiduously as they once controlled their poems' choice of words, verse form and lineation. At the same time, material conditions now offer many more choices. The page, the screen, the Java Applet, the CD, the videotape, the illustrative photograph: all these can become part of the poetic text. Poets, in Dickinson's words, thus 'dwell in possibility' – a possibility as challenging as it is dangerous.

[43] Walter Benjamin, 'The Work of Art in the Age of Mechanical Reproduction,' in *Illuminations*, ed. Hannah Arendt, trans. Harry Zohn (New York: Schocken, 1969), p. 232.

2

Words on Film: Collaborative Work between Poets and Film-Makers

Vicki Bertram

'Poets are the guardians of the language', MP Alan Howarth declared on BBC Radio Four, in his eloquent protest at Oxford University Press's notorious decision to scrap its contemporary poetry list.[1] Yet how can such guardianship operate, when only a tiny minority of people ever read the poets' work? Poetry, like other art-forms, is currently engaging with debates about elitism, 'dumbing down' and accessibility. In such discussions, accessibility usually relates to perceived difficulties in comprehension.[2] However, it is perhaps more productive to consider the varying accessibility of particular media. Television is by far the most accessible medium in the west (probably also worldwide) in terms of its potential audience, and a few contemporary poets based in Britain – working in close collaboration with dedicated directors and film crews – have created some striking and innovative programmes over the last two decades. In this article I shall consider generic and technical developments in these ventures, concentrating on a selection in order to do justice to the range of work: Tony Harrison's *Blasphemers' Banquet* (1989) and *Black Daisies for the Bride* (1992); *Poets' News* (1993) and *Poems on the Box* (1993), both directed by Peter Symes (working with various poets); Jackie Kay's *Twice Through the Heart* (1992); Fred D'Aguiar's *Sweet Thames* (1992); and Simon Armitage's *Drinking*

---

[1] The decision was announced late in 1998.

[2] The more 'accessible' poetry is, the less complex and – by implication – valuable it is. This is a typical example of the argument, from a review in the *TLS*:

> On the plus side, all this activity has introduced more people to contemporary verse ... old prejudices are breaking down and the audience is being extended. Yet the urge to be accessible can work against complexity and nuance. It encourages such gifted poets as Carol Ann Duffy and Simon Armitage to maximize their appeal by giving the age what it demands.

John Kerrigan, 'England of the Mind', *TLS*, 14 November 1997, pp. 16–17 (p. 16).

for England (1998).[3] I am interested in both the creation and the reception of poetry on film. What do these films offer that is different – in terms both of the poetry itself and of the style and technique of the film? How does the poets' involvement affect their writing, as well as the general perception of poets? Does the speed of the medium require simpler poetry and does simpler equal less good? Can these collaborations produce something more than simply poetry on film: can they stretch the capabilities of both poetry and film in original ways? If so, perhaps critics need to move away from our traditional concentration on page-based poetry and pick up the challenge presented by poetry's new relationships with film.

For a long time I have been bewildered by the gap between ordinary people's perceptions of poetry – in which emotional expression and subjective response play a big part – and academic criticism where both these aspects are largely absent. Those contemporary poets who come closest to being 'household names' (Roger McGough, John Hegley, Benjamin Zephaniah, Jean Binta Breeze) are either ignored by academics or treated with a mixture of disdain and embarrassment. I suspect this is because their style of poetry does not *need* elucidation of the sort academics are best equipped to offer. The poets favoured by academics are read by a minute section of the population and attract small, if erudite, audiences to their readings, while poetry slams draw hundreds of punters. Does 'popular' poetry's neglect by academics mean that they don't consider it important? Or is it an implicit admission that they don't have the tools that would enable them to say much of value about it? In these postmodern days, in which distinctions between high and low culture have supposedly been dissolved and the influence of cultural studies has encouraged scholars' interest in genre fiction and other popular forms of prose fiction, why are poetry critics still only interested in such a narrow band of work? Is it possible to be accessible (and, perhaps, popular) *and* to produce important, valuable, original, quality poetry? Is it accessibility or popularity that disqualifies this work from serious critical attention?

The relationship between poetry and film has a long history. Viktor Shklovsky recognized both poetry and prose genres within film and argued that, in practice, the boundary between the two was often blurred. He differentiated 'semantic constants', associated with the contingencies and impetus of plot, from what he labelled 'formal constants' – parallelism, use of symbol, image and montage. These latter, when prioritized over and above the plot, were the hallmark of poetic cinema. He argued that the two genres were:

---

[3] While I have cited the poet's name, the director obviously plays a crucial role in the production. For a full list of directors, see Appendix 1.

distinguished one from another not by rhythm, or not by rhythm alone, but by the prevalence in poetic cinema of technical and formal over semantic features, where formal features displace semantic and resolve the composition. Plotless cinema is verse cinema.[4]

In contemporary texts about literary analysis, parallels are often drawn between film and text, since film-making employs similar techniques to narrative.[5] Usually the emphasis is on adaptation or on the analogous methods of critique appropriate to the two media. As Shklovsky's distinction implies, a film with a strong plot is less conducive to poetic strategies, since it is driven by the narrative. It is the documentary – associated with factual materials – rather than, say, drama, that has proved so welcoming to poets. Documentary is a very open form and can, therefore, accommodate a high degree of experimentation.[6] Free from the impetus of plot, documentary can incorporate diversions or vary the pace; Shklovsky's 'technical and formal' features take pre-eminence over the semantic. As viewers, we probably don't realize the technical opportunities offered by this openness, but it is this greater scope that excites the film-makers, because it gives them space to maximize the artistic potential of the genre.

The earliest collaborations between film-makers and poets involved documentary-style films: Symes cites W. H. Auden and Benjamin Britten's *Night Mail* and John Betjeman's *Metroland*.[7] More recent attempts to transfer poetry to the screen have often fallen victim to clumsy literalism: an actor's voiceover accompanied by photography replicating the poem's imagery. The effect of these techniques is overkill; the two media cancel one another out, distracting the viewer. Film poetry projects offer the possibility of a genuine collaboration, in which both media and creators are changed by the process, resulting in a film that

---

[4] Viktor Shklovsky, 'Poetry and Prose in Cinema', in R. Taylor and I. Christie (eds), *The Film Factory: Russian and Soviet Cinema in Documents* (London: Routledge, 1994), quoted in John Hill and Pamela Church Gibson (eds), *The Oxford Guide to Film Studies* (Oxford: Oxford University Press, 1998), p. 66.

[5] In a chapter entitled 'Narration in Film and Prose Fiction', Montgomery et al. identify many of the fundamental differences between the two media: the capital-intensive teamwork of film versus the individualism – of production and reception – of prose fiction. They also cite C. S. Peirce's distinction between signs (where the relationship between signifier and signified is arbitrary) and icons (where the relationship is based on resemblance). Film's reliance on icons makes it closer to mimesis: 'the film image resembles the portions of reality which it signifies'. Martin Montgomery, Alan Durant, Sara Mills, Nigel Fabb and Tom Furniss, *Ways of Reading: Advanced Reading Skills for Students of English Literature* (London: Routledge, 1992), p. 193.

[6] I am grateful to director Philippa Lowthorpe for this insight.

[7] Peter Symes, 'Verse on Film: Notes from the Last Ten Years' (unpublished paper, 1996).

challenges viewers' expectations and makes new demands on them. Peter Symes, a film director based at BBC Bristol, has pioneered such projects by directing seven films with Tony Harrison (an eighth is underway), as well as serving as executive producer on three other poetry series (see Appendix 1 for full details).[8] Symes has also written valuable accounts of the working methods that he and Harrison have evolved.[9] Here, I focus on *The Blasphemers' Banquet*, inspired by Harrison's anger at widespread indifference to Ayatollah Khomeni's fatwa against Salman Rushdie.

Tony Harrison and Peter Symes: *The Blasphemers' Banquet*

Symes had first worked with Harrison on a four-part series on death and commemoration, *Loving Memory*. It was during this project that the pair discovered the potential of their collaboration. Prior to this, Harrison's film experience had been limited to writing poetry commentary to accompany a pre-shot film.[10] For the first time, he became fully involved in the whole process, requesting shots of specific lengths and objects, and making use of the research team to ferret out arcane information on whatever subjects captured his imagination. He realized the similarities between his own work, as poet, and that undertaken by the film editor: both preoccupied with image and rhythm, and the relationship between the two. Symes was excited by the emotional depth poetry could add to a documentary's narrative; he writes of 'its ability to draw people in, and then tell them uncomfortable things without having them turn away; its ability to be subjective; its ability to transform and illuminate'.[11] He recognized the greater versatility poetry could offer: the narrator can move around, one moment assuming the persona of a widow, the next stepping back into the role of observer and guide, interpreting events to the viewers. *The Blasphemers' Banquet* gave them the opportunity to explore these insights on a subject close to Harrison's heart: the censorship of writers.

Reading Symes's accounts of the process and watching the film, his claim that the poet is 'the engine of the production' is incontestable. Harrison's charisma and drive are evident throughout. What is underway

[8]   *V.*, probably Harrison's most famous television film, was directed by Richard Eyre and first broadcast on Channel 4 on 4 November 1987.

[9]   Peter Symes, 'Blasphemy and Death: On Film Making with Tony Harrison', in Neil Astley (ed.), *Tony Harrison: Bloodaxe Critical Anthologies: 1* (Newcastle-upon-Tyne: Bloodaxe, 1991); Introduction to *The Shadow of Hiroshima and Other Film/Poems* (London: Faber, 1995), pp. 384–94; 'Verse on Film'.

[10]   The film was called *Arctic Passage* and was directed by Andree Molyneux; see her article, 'Cutting His Teeth: Working with Tony Harrison on *Arctic Paradise* and *The Big H*', in Astley (ed.), *Tony Harrison*, pp. 367–76.

[11]   Symes, 'Blasphemy and Death', p. 387.

is the creation of an epic poem that feeds off, and resonates into, its accompanying visual and aural components; while the soundtrack and film footage are physically created by others, their inspiration is 'driven by the poetic imagination' that lies at the centre.[12] Harrison steeps himself in the mass of material collected by researchers; out of this, a few themes emerge, which guide his input into the film shoot. The bulk of the actual writing is done very late in the proceedings and it is not until then that the skeleton of a structure emerges. Symes describes an intensely collaborative scene: Harrison, composer Dominic Muldowney, himself and the film's editor working in separate rooms along the same corridor, meeting up to test their latest version, trying cuts against quatrains, altering speed and soundtrack, all the time sparking ideas off one another. In the finished programme, the different media function wholly inter-dependently: 'images, words, music and sounds all contribute to the whole on their own terms, and not as some weaker accompaniment, so while the verse remains the lynchpin of the whole operation the other elements are never downgraded.'[13] *The Blasphemers' Banquet* was cre-ated under great time pressure: three months from the start to transmis-sion in July 1989.[14] It offers a mature example of the potential of a fully collaborative venture between film and poetry. Traditional poetic themes, like transience, are politicized, as Harrison draws on his own personal experience of vilification by religious authorities and carves out one of his favoured dichotomies: art on the side of freedom, disobedience and revolution; repression, authority, religion as the enemies. It is a piece written with both heart and brain fully engaged, motivated by deep anger. The poetry is sinewy with ideas and thought, as well as being gripping and ideally suited to its polemical end; alliteration is used to good rhetorical effect and the poet avoids the obvious rhymes that mar some of his film work. The editing has tremendous energy and includes some dramatic footage of the Ayatollah's funeral. The sound track, which uses an Islamic scale and makes ingenious use of background noises, also indicates the great artistic originality that went into the film. Special effects are used thoughtfully, with fades from colour to black and white; text appears on screen (something Symes is especially keen to do) to great effect when a quotation from Khomeni appears:

> There is no humour
> There is no laughter
> There is no fun

---

[12] Ibid., p. 384.

[13] Ibid., p. 393.

[14] It achieved viewing figures of 3.9 million, as part of the *Byline* series screened on BBC1. Symes points out that it was only because of an unexpected gap in the series that the project was given the go-ahead at all.

A few seconds later, 'in Islam' is displayed on the screen to the right of these lines; after a few more seconds, the lines are attributed to Khomeni. Symes singles out a memorable sequence composed entirely of visual and sound effects to prove his claim that 'the structure [is] always carried by the verse, but [there are also] sequences where image alone or sound alone or a powerful combination of the two are interwoven with the rest'.[15]

The film's underlying unity is ingenious. Bradford, where much of the film is set, was the town where a copy of *The Satanic Verses* was burnt. But it is also a town with an enormous number of churches, now mostly redundant and used as warehouses, restaurants and auction rooms. These contemporary commercial premises form settings for many of the sequences, all of which are tied in to the theme of impermanence and the inevitability of change. But this coherence is not clear at the start. For the viewer, the initial experience is bewildering. The first few minutes include several brief snippets of film that are repeated later, in their full version; our curiosity may be engaged, but so much is going on that little sense can be made of it initially. Such disorientation is offset by thematic and imagistic coherence. The letter/shape 'O' forms a recurring motif, featured in close-ups of the 'Omar Khayam' restaurant, at which the banquet is to take place, and echoed in shots of wedding rings for sale at auction. Fittingly, Harrison chooses the quatrain, used by the English translator of Omar Khayam's work, as his stanza form. Only towards the end are we told that Khayam despised the paradise offered by the Koran to virtuous Muslim men and deliberately flouted religious instruction by drinking wine. One of the final shots in the film is of the letter 'O' being removed from the restaurant front; the last shot is of its new frontage and name, now the 'Bombay Brasserie'. The voice of soprano Teresa Stratas singing the refrain 'O I love this fleeting life' is repeated several times to great contrastive effect, its semantic and melodic inference juxtaposed with the passionate fury of anti-Rushdie demonstrations. Footage of mourners after Khomeni's death, and of enraged Muslims protesting at Rushdie's book, is shown in colour then black and white, to imply parallels with other scenes of impassioned demonstrations, with the threat of violence lurking.

Several commentators have expressed misgivings about the film, on the grounds that it uses anti-Islamic stereotypes. The way the marches are edited does, in my view, invite comparison with fascist demonstrations and the whole structure of the film groups 'extremist' movements together without acknowledging the tensions facing a minority ethnic/religious community in an overwhelmingly white, secular country. But it is not fair to claim the film is anti-Islamic; the attack is against

---

[15] Symes, 'Blasphemy and Death', p. 393.

fundamentalist religions and shots of Ian Paisley, amongst others, make this clear. *The Blasphemers' Banquet* is polemical and was made for a series that featured hard-hitting, provocative viewpoints. It raises the difficult issues of freedom of speech versus respect for different religious traditions: precisely the issues that triggered the fatwa and the film's production in the first place.[16]

Words on Film: Philippa Lowthorpe and Jackie Kay: *Twice through the Heart*

Because of the success of *The Blasphemers' Banquet*, Symes was given the green light for his next proposal: six documentary films, each made by a director working with his or her choice of poet (see Appendix 1 for full list). The programmes were made during 1991–2 and screened shortly after. As executive producer, he organized seminars at which those involved could share experiences and ideas. While his own work with Harrison provided the blueprint and clearly shaped his expectations, what is striking about the series is the variety of work produced, partly in terms of the individual style of each poet, but also the way in which the combination of film and poetry is used. I have chosen to focus on two films that illustrate this variety. In its entirety, the series proves the versatility of both method and end result.

According to Symes, it was difficult to find poets willing to participate and several backed out when they realized what was involved: 'in effect we were asking them to write an epic poem'.[17] Director Philippa Lowthorpe worked with Jackie Kay on a film about the judicial system's treatment of women who murder their abusive partners. Choosing to focus on the real case of a woman in her sixties, Amelia Rossiter, they were denied access to her – a disadvantage which stretched the ingenuity of both. Unlike Harrison, Kay took little part in the actual filming although, like him, she did the bulk of her writing at the cutting-room stage. Her poetry concentrates on the imaginative recreation of Rossiter's thoughts and emotions, exploring the subjective potential of the form. Kay herself appears in the film as narrator/investigator, asking ostensibly simple questions rendered fiercely subversive by interrogative repetitions and the clever juxtapositioning of image and text. For example, as the footage shows women absorbed in the intricate job of making judges' wigs, Kay asks:

---

[16] It seems to be these very oppositions that excite Harrison most. Writing of *V.*, John Lucas has suggested that, 'whatever hope for reconciliation the poem may gesture towards, its real energies are in the versuses'. John Lucas, 'Speaking for England?', in Astley (ed.), *Tony Harrison*, 351–61 (p. 354).

[17] Peter Symes, unpublished interview, conducted 30 March 1999, at BBC Bristol.

> Who made the wig? Who puts it on?
> Who decides between right and wrong?

The court room's theatricality is emphasized throughout: Kay opens up her battered suitcase and a paper fold-out court scene is revealed; the jury are represented as clothes hung on coathangers and the accused herself appears as a neat blue suit poignantly arranged on a dressmaker's dummy. In this way the metaphor is extended not only throughout the poetry but also into the visual properties of the film.

Lowthorpe's account of the experience suggests that working alongside a poet she admired liberated her own poetic instincts and enabled her to develop ways of expressing them in her own chosen medium. Certainly the wig-making sequence and the use of props like the coat hangers carry poetic resonance. The camerawork in the opening scenes is particularly evocative, using wide lenses to create angular shots suggestive of someone being pursued in a threatening manner while, to a silent soundtrack punctuated only by a dripping kitchen tap, close-ups on ordinary objects like a teapot and cup render the domestic sinister. This was the first time Lowthorpe worked with film editor Fred Hart; they have since collaborated on several projects, developing a mutual interest in the rhythmic and poetic qualities of film-making, but both remember *Twice* as a landmark in their experience. They wanted to exploit the power of poetic images to suggest and imply, rather than risk sensationalizing their material. They discovered that, by combining image, text and music, it was possible to achieve a resonance far more powerful cumulatively than in its individual parts. In their later documentaries, they concentrate on the rhythms of people's speech, creating sequences, rather like musical themes or motifs, that are repeated several times throughout the film.[18] 'Ordinary people are very poetic in the way they talk,' Lowthorpe suggests, 'and my films are more like a long poem than a documentary.'[19]

Words on Film: Mark Harrison and Fred D'Aguiar: *Sweet Thames*

Fred D'Aguiar, working with director Mark Harrison, also made substantial use of repetition and juxtaposing. *Sweet Thames*, their film about the racism of the British immigration system, is more technically ambitious, making use of mask, multiple locations and archive footage. D'Aguiar's poetry, like Harrison's, carries a great deal of information but the film's most memorable aspect is its skilful deployment of metaphor.

---

[18] See, for example, 'Three Salons at the Seaside', broadcast 1994, BBC Bristol.
[19] Philippa Lowthorpe (1999), unpublished interview conducted with Lowthorpe and Fred Hart, 30 March, BBC Bristol.

The river Thames's flood barrier serves as an image for the immigration system's exclusionary practices. Words like flood, influx, swamp and tide, used by D'Aguiar about the river, appear on the screen and recur in extracts from speeches by Enoch Powell, Margaret Thatcher and others, alluding with disdain to 'flotsam and jetsam'. The metaphor resonates on several levels: it was the river Thames that brought the early, forced immigrants (as slaves) to London, as well as the booty from their home-lands. The river is an icon of the former Empire's greatness, as well as a dumping ground for today's inhabitants' rubbish. The slave trade and the vital role played by sugar from the West Indies form a recurring theme in the film, which includes an interview with the manager of a sugar refinery near the river as he talks matter-of-factly about 'impurity removing operations'. Without the strong metre and the powerful oratorical delivery of Harrison's poetry, D'Aguiar's poetry makes less impact; it does not form the pulse of the film in quite the same way. Kay's poetry, also lacking an insistent metre, derives its power from her compelling repetitions and also from the force of her delivery. Voice – its tone, and the poet's style of reading – seems to play a vital role in these films' effectiveness.

Symes was most impressed by those films in which the poetry really uses and draws on the visuals, and vice versa: where both media are fully integrated, rather than where one serves as accompaniment to the other. But his real regret – echoed by Lowthorpe and Hart – is that he has been unable to get a further series commissioned. *Words on Film* was an ideal opportunity for new directors and poets to experiment in the genre.

Poems on the Box

Poems on the Box was a different kind of project, again spearheaded by Symes. The series was a collaboration between two departments: Music and Arts and Bristol Features. Its aim was to find a novel way of transmitting already-existing poems on television. The title itself, with its friendly colloquialism, signals the programme's accessibility and its playfulness, immediately – albeit subtly – reminding viewers of the plasticity and tricksiness of language. (When is a box not a box but a television? Why is a television called a box?) Director Richard Kwietnowski and his colleagues chose the minimalist background of a plain wall that filled the screen, with a small television set in the left-hand background, serving the dual function of creating three-dimensional depth for the wall and providing the series with an icon in keeping with its interest in words as iconic. This set remained identical for each poem in the series. Instead of mimetic visual potential, the designers focused on graphics. Starting from the assumption that words are the heart, meat and bones of poetry and motivated by fashionable interest in language as an arbitrary system of signs, they played with words and the letters that formed them. Graphics, typography and layout were their tools, and they exploited them to the full (as Concrete and Language poets have also done) to draw attention to the processes of textual communication. The resulting films strip bare the poems' structures by orchestrating the appearance and disappearance of individual words (or letters) at various places on the screen; they never attempt literal duplication of the poems' content. Instead of actors, recordings of the poets themselves are used, presumably on the grounds that there is no one better placed to reveal the intended rhythms and inflections than the poet him/herself.

During Stevie Smith's 'Tenuous and Precarious', the poet's playful repetition of Latinate suffixes and their transformation from words into people is translated to the screen by the clever use of typography and timing. Accompanying a 1966 recording of the poet's reading is a scroll of repeated 'ous' in a vertical line down the right hand side of the screen. As the poem progresses, each character is evoked and dismissed (by use of the past tense); as this happens, one suffix in turn is erased. During the last verse, which begins:

> My name is Finis,
> Finis, Finis,
> I am Finis,

the Roman font 'I' appears at the close, the word 'Finis' then appears on the small television set, signalling both closure and the ambiguous quality of the narrator's status: evidently a survivor, but whether triumphant or suffering (tenuous and precarious) is unclear.

Such techniques complement, rather than replicate, the poetry. The intense concentration on letters and words as signifiers and the removal of the signifieds leave the viewer's imagination uncluttered by competing images. During John Betjeman's 'Meditation on the A30', the grim tale of a reckless driver's death, the wall becomes a car windscreen with the viewer positioned as driver or passenger. This is communicated through the appearance and disappearance of words by invisible windscreen wipers whose action erases the text as they swing from left to right. Again, it is the simplicity of the idea and its enactment that is so effective. At the close, an emergency siren is heard; such minimal but powerfully evocative use of sound is again characteristic of the series. These strategies represent an important shift from a focus on content to rhythm and structure. The original poem isn't altered by its transmission but its reception *is*, I think, affected: the structure is foregrounded and use of the poet's voice, undisturbed by dynamic visuals, maximizes the viewer's experience of an intense, unusually intimate televisual communication.

This focus on structure has been taken much further by John Cage, an American composer well known for his experiments in multi-media. Marjorie Perloff's analysis of his *Roaratorio* provides some useful insight into the similarities between *Poems on the Box* and his work. Inspired by James Joyce's *Finnegans Wake*, Cage created sixteen multi-track tape recordings superimposed over a recital of the text, creating a symphonic installation piece. Some were soundtracks of natural noises that happened to be going on in specific places named in the text; others were recordings of familiar Irish folk songs. He also mined the text for inspiration, finding words within words and using upper case to reveal them (tOwn); adding letters to yoke opposites together, just as Joyce does in the *Wake* (Perloff cites the example of adding one letter to 'laughter' to make 'laughtear'). He dispenses with linearity, logic and causality, and his intricate systems are quite randomly – if rigorously – pursued. Perloff believes his intention is 'to produce simultaneous layers of sound and meaning that correspond to the complexity of the parent text'.[20] Cage, unlike *Poems on the Box*, is *not* trying to enhance the meaning of the verbal via the visual and aural, but to present several different signifying systems working in parallel, their separateness preserved. Nevertheless, his experiments may suggest the potential that could be exploited by a new generation of poets and film-makers working collaboratively.

Poets' News

Poets' News marked a further radical step, this time challenging perceptions about the poet's role in contemporary society in a way that has since been taken up and developed in initiatives like the Poetry Places scheme.[21] Back in 1993, this was a bold and radical idea. Poets, associated in the popular imagination with secluded garrets and Lakeland landscapes, were commissioned to make a news item and were given one day in which to do it. The commission's timescale was certainly realistic: there was an editorial meeting in the morning, at which the topic was decided; the remainder of the day was spent filming, researching and writing, before the final edit and transmission. About five such items were broadcast together in several fifteen-minute programmes. The process demanded quite different skills from poets accustomed to the slow process of drafts and edits. News is, by definition, ephemeral; poetry is

[20] Marjorie Perloff, 'Music for Words Perhaps: Reading/Hearing/Seeing John Cage's *Roaratorio*', in *Postmodern Genres* (Norman: University of Oklahoma Press, 1988), pp. 193–228 (p. 216).

[21] The scheme, run by the Poetry Society, aims to put poets on writing residencies in unusual places. Examples include a rubbish-recycling depot in Norfolk, a City legal practice and the department store, Marks & Spencer. The project received National Lottery funds of £450,000.

– traditionally anyway – intended to last (although the example of poets from predominantly oral cultures provides a different model, in which poets play vital roles as social and political commentators on topical events). 'Literature is news that STAYS news' as Pound put it succinctly.[22] I have not heard from any of the poets involved but I suspect this was one of the hardest commissions they had ever tackled. The finished results betray the haste of their composition and the few that had longer than a day reveal an enviable polish. One of these was Roger McGough's item on National Backpain Week. Like several of the most effective, this piece parodies the genre's format, imitating the weather report that follows the national news. With a map of the British Isles on the screen behind him (also functioning metonymically as a representation of the human body) McGough appears as the friendly weatherman, delivering warning of an impending cold snap ('keep well wrapped up, won't you?'). The piece is based around common metaphoric connotations of types of weather:

> Well, tonight depression centred on the brain will lift.
> Dark clouds move away, and pain will be widespread but light.

The usual symbols for mist, wind and high pressure flash up, wittily transformed ('a belt of high pressure, if worn too tight, may cause discomfort'). Only in the concluding couplet is the topic revealed:

> So the outlook for the week is pretty black:
> it's one long pain in the back.

The *Poets' News* project raises interesting issues about poets' place in society. National Backpain Week is not exactly hard news. Other topics included the publication of the Wolfe Report, the official enquiry into the Manchester Strangeways prison riot, famine in Africa, coal pit closures, the Maastricht Treaty and the latest unemployment figures. Of course, the particular event may be ephemeral but its implications and effects are not. Poets had to think about the medium as much as the message. Tony Harrison's determination that poetry can and should secure a public platform and resist relegation to the cosy arts media is clearly shared by Symes. Harrison spoke recently of his struggle for a public poetry, not 'poetry on the page where people overhear you talking to yourself'[23] and, in his commissions for *The Guardian,* he has insisted that his poetry appear in the news section, rather than the arts or tabloid. However,

[22] Ezra Pound, *The ABC of Reading* (1951; London: Faber, 1961), p. 29.
[23] Reading and discussion, followed by screening of his new film, *Prometheus*, held at Magdalen College, Oxford in April 1999.

the choice of poets involved in this enterprise is surprising and a bit disappointing: Simon Rae, Alan Jenkins, John Whitworth, Fleur Adcock are not the poets I would expect to perform well with such a commission. Lemn Sissay, Ben Zephaniah, Carol Ann Duffy and McGough – poets with a sense of theatre – seem, unsurprisingly, much more at home in the medium. Their use of slick satire and wit works more effectively than the earnest solemnity of others' approaches. Their work for *Poets' News* proves that poetry can be pithy, political and topical. It may not be poetry that repays repeated study, but poets with the appropriate skills and style for the commission showed what is possible and, at the same time, drew attention to the narrowness of expectations surrounding poetry.

Tony Harrison and Peter Symes: *Black Daisies for the Bride*

Black Daisies was filmed in 1992 and broadcast the following year. It won the Prix Italia and was chosen, along with *Poems on the Box* and *Poets' News*, to be shown at the international showcase festival, *Input*. *Black Daisies* is a bold venture by a poet not often associated with such an intimate subject as the frailty of Alzheimer's sufferers. Focusing on four women, it is filmed on the ward in a Yorkshire hospital and, to Harrison's great pleasure, is a truly hybrid film: funded jointly by the drama and documentary departments at Bristol and using actors alongside real hospital staff and patients. Harrison himself does not appear and very little of the poetry is delivered by him. Most of it is sung, following the metre and tunes of two well-known songs that would have been familiar from the women's youth: the Christmas carol, 'In the Bleak Midwinter' and 'Daisy, Daisy'. Harrison was intrigued to discover that the last thing to leave human memory is melody and the film includes footage of a music therapist and a local banjo player's visit to the ward, where one of the women sings along with him, the words forgotten. Appropriately, then, most of the poetry is sung by actors playing the women on their wedding days and contains information about their lives and their husbands, in an attempt to reinstate their three-dimensionality before the disease took hold.

When I interviewed him, Symes told me that, in his view, the fundamental challenge for documentary-makers was 'how not to make someone a victim'. Clearly these imagined recreations of the women's lives are an attempt to avoid that, in a film that risks censure by using individuals who cannot give their consent to appearing in it. Symes is particularly enthusiastic about poetry's ability to get inside individuals, to explore their subjective reality, but *Black Daisies* presents individuals with a striking theatricality. Where Kay's evocation of Rossiter's shame seems utterly convincing, we get little insight into the personality or feelings of the brides in this film. It is unlikely this is due to a lack of information; Symes speaks of the diligence of the researcher, Harriet Bakewell, and the brides' songs are packed with factual detail about motorbike rides and vegetable growing. It is the personalities that remain somehow opaque. These characterizations entirely lack the empathy evident in *Twice through the Heart*, although the stylized operatic presentation and the leap back in time that these bridal scenes enact may imply that this kind of emotional empathy was not what Harrison sought.

Black Daisies is a powerfully visual and aural film. The accompanying poetry seems much less significant; it is as though the poetic devices and working method devised by Harrison and Symes have been fully absorbed and integrated within the process, so that the finished product is a profoundly poetic film, even without the poetry.[24] Above all, it is the use of imagery that characterizes this film: the hospital ward door, requiring a combination number to open, forms a poignant image of entrapment and isolation, while a cloud of confetti turns into a blizzard in a dramatic visual manifestation of the onset of oblivion. The black daisies of the title form part of the pattern of the mosaic floor in the hospital foyer; they also, of course, symbolize loss, the reversal of normal expectations (like memory), as well as death. As Symes describes it, the process of making the film followed a similar pattern to their earlier collaborations, with the structure only emerging finger-bitingly close to completion. However, unfired by Harrison's personality, the verse is – in my view – thin and too generalized to carry much power. The music demands more of the viewer's attention and the use of the song and hymn as framework for much of the poetry inevitably restricts the complexity of what can be said. Furthermore, the subject matter is hardly conducive to the kinds of rhetoric more usually associated with Harrison's writing. As an innovative film, *Black Daisies* has won great admiration; as poetry, it is less interesting.

Brian Hill and Simon Armitage: *Drinking for England* and *Saturday Night*

Drinking for England, which won the Royal Television Society award for Best Documentary, is a film about people's attitudes to alcohol. As such, it has to confront Symes's challenge of avoiding making victims out of its subjects. Hill had been impressed by Simon Armitage's first film-work, *Xanadu*, which was part of the *Words on Film* series. He had already commissioned Armitage to write a commentary for his earlier

---

[24] Lowthorpe and Hart praised the film for its 'fusion of cinematic visual and poetic visual', unpublished interviews, 1999.

documentary, *Saturday Night*, but *Drinking for England* experimented with a totally new technique. In the usual way, Hill advertised for people in whose lives alcohol played an important part. He interviewed them, then gave transcripts of the interviews to Armitage, along with some information about their personalities and lifestyles. Armitage then drafted poems for each of them. Apparently, none of the individuals concerned were perturbed by the news that they would be expected to perform a poem, as well as speak to camera. They were shown the verse Armitage had written for them. In one or two cases, changes were made where they felt the verse didn't get it right; in others, they were shocked at just how effectively and accurately the words conveyed their experiences. What is extraordinary is how naturally and unselfconsciously they all perform in the finished film – even Jane and Duncan, who sing rather than recite their poems.[25]

Drinking may have won an RTS award but the newspapers were lukewarm. The liberal press were most hostile, with several critics expressing unease at the way in which the film put words into people's mouths. Hill's response is challenging: he claims that on this film the subjects knew in advance what they would be saying to camera, unlike in most documentaries, where individuals are filmed and may say things they later regret, or their words may be edited in ways that misrepresent them. Other criticisms concerned the artificiality of subjects speaking verse, suggesting that this destroys authenticity. Hill response is to ask, 'what is real in documentary making?' – a pertinent question at a time when several reputable documentary series have been accused of constructing ostensibly 'real' situations and of using shoddy research methods.[26] According to him, the reaction of those who took part in the film has been 'pretty favourable'. For Jane, who is filmed at a detox clinic, the film has played an important part in her fight to stay off alcohol; she still doesn't drink. 'Television can change things,' Hill noted wryly.[27]

But the critics were, indeed, hostile. Desmond Christy wrote in *The Guardian* that '[o]ne of the troubles with alcoholics is that they are

---

[25] Hill told me that Duncan's song shoot took only two hours, including rehearsal (Hill, 1999).

[26] The increasingly blurred boundary between fact and fiction has been widely noted and is frequently associated with postmodernism. A recent news item on Radio 4 discussed new research revealing that a very high proportion of the population get their medical knowledge from television programmes like *Casualty* and considered the implications of this fact. Perloff argues that poetry is affected by this kind of development: 'Poetry, that is, now functions in an arena where the simulacrum exerts increasing influence over the way business is actually done in the "real" world.' Marjorie Perloff, *Radical Artifice: Writing Poetry in the Age of Media* (Chicago: University of Chicago Press, 1991), p. 198.

[27] Brian Hill, unpublished telephone conversation, March 1999.

boring ... The verses were ... well, the kind of thing you might compose if you were drunk'.[28] This is clearly intended as a criticism, yet if the remit is to produce poetry appropriate to a particular individual who is regularly drunk, perhaps it could also be seen as evidence of Armitage's success. It also suggests a reluctance to entertain the possibility that poetry can be something other than genteel, elegiac or highly wrought. The implication is that poetry is not for ordinary folk. The protectionism that surrounds poetry is unique amongst the arts: in prose, there is room for the blockbuster, the sitcom and Henry James but, in poetry, writing that is accessibly political, topical, ephemeral, 'light' or funny causes unease.

What the criticisms also reveal is reviewers' resistance to any departure from the conventions of the documentary. Christy expresses disorientation when Jane starts singing: 'Jane was so good I wondered if she was miming'. And Karl French in *The Financial Times* comments: 'The programme maybe just about gets away with the poetry, but the singing was a terrible idea ... this takes the documentary form off on a bizarre and unnecessary tangent'.[29] It is certainly shocking when Jane and Duncan start to sing, precisely because it takes the programme way outside its expected terrain, but the effect is powerful: each reveals so much of their personality, as well as their attitude to alcohol, in the way they sing. Duncan comes across as an intelligent man who can produce a convincing line on the joys of constant drinking. Armitage has scripted lyrics that are well-suited to his clever flippancy; they pun on the substitution of 'think' for 'drink'. As he sings, Duncan moves easily, performing like a natural:

> I walk to the bar and I think like a fish.
> Thinking's a beautiful thing for a man,
> Thinks from a bottle and thinks from a can.

Shots of him singing are cleverly superimposed on to footage of the busy pub, so that he sits down, singing away, next to three older men with their pints, and they just continue with their conversation. This is effective as a way of naturalizing the artificiality of a solo song; the viewer can relax like the old men, accepting that the song isn't about performance, so much as self-expression. Jane's song is shot very differently: she is pictured walking along the corridors of the detox clinic, sitting on her bed or staring out of the window. The elegiac refrain

---

[28] Desmond Christy, review of *Drinking for England*, *The Guardian*, November 1998, G2, p. 11.

[29] Karl French, review of *Drinking for England*, *The Financial Times*, 10 November 1998, p. 21.

'Sherry and me we go back a long time' forms the core of a melancholic, introspective piece. She is very self-conscious and carries herself with a precarious pride marvellously expressive of her tentative grasp on a brand new self-respect. It is almost embarrassing to watch her perform-ance, not because it is bad (she sings very well, as Christy notes) but because so much is at stake: her new-found confidence and determina-tion are on show for the first time and in such a public manner.

Armitage is an ideal choice for this kind of work; his poetry has stretched the form since his debut collection, *Zoom*, in which he showed that the anecdotal and demotic could be incorporated naturalistically within traditional poetic forms.[30] He drew subject matter from his experience as a probation officer and the stuff of ordinary life. As his film-work reveals, he can write poetry that has the colloquial feel of prose, yet with the heightened intensity of poetry. In *Drinking for England* he has worked, in effect, like a dramatist: catching the person-ality of each person, condensing it and then handing it back in a poem. When the subject reads, she or he imbues the text with his or her own emotions, claiming it as their own, in just the same way that an actor comes to inhabit a part.

In *Xanadu*, *Saturday Night* and *Drinking for England*, Armitage has developed a very different working method from Harrison.[31] On neither of Hill's films has he participated in the filming process. He operates rather like a caricaturist, catching the essence of a person and, in doing so, he shows impressive versatility. Donna's traumatic past is given plain expression; her refrain – 'don't you know, tell you why; mother drinks, so do I' – forms a stark contrast to the elegant wordplay between 'gills' and 'gills' in the lines 'two or three gills to moisten the gills' for G&T tippler Dennis. His poem brilliantly conveys the lifestyle and temperament of this prosperous Toad-like chap 'in the west of his days', while Kerry and Amy, in their late teens, get 'shit-faced' and 'don't give a Fosters'. At the same time, it builds in its own obsolescence, using contemporary slang and brand names to convey these young women's experience authentically. Armitage's work in *Drinking for England* produces impressive character studies. These aren't, as Christy knows, poems anyone is likely to want to re-read – they are written for a specific context. Like the work in *Poets' News*, what they really call into question is the assumption that poetry,

---

[30] Simon Armitage, *Zoom* (Newcastle-upon-Tyne: Bloodaxe Books, 1989).

[31] In an interview about his work, Armitage was explicit about his determination to carve out his own way of working on film: 'I think I said to Peter [Symes] that every time I felt Tony Harrison breathing down my neck I kind of rolled up my collar a bit because I'd got my own way of working.' Peter J Atkinson, *Verse Commentary on TV Documentary: The Work of Peter Symes* (unpublished BA Dissertation, University of Leeds, Ripon and York St. John, 1994), Appendix 2.

by definition, has to be striving towards immortality in order to qualify as real poetry.

Hill's work is an original blend of naturalism and stylized effects. He is not afraid to experiment, making use of grainy shots, fast cuts, slow motion and even blurring the focus to imitate the drunk's double vision. He also makes full use of music, giving each individual their own sound-track: computer-generated club sounds for Kerry and Amy, pub back-ground noise for Shaun and a languid, playful saxophone for Dennis. The influence of Dennis Potter is detectable. Music plays an even more important part in *Saturday Night*. In this earlier film, Armitage's pum-melling repetitions form an effective backdrop to the dramatic sound-track, which works by counterpoint, contrast and surprising juxtapositionings. Club scenes and a junkie shooting up are accompanied by a classical music soundtrack and fast cuts. Despite the fact that Armitage played no part in the filming, he captures the tangible excite-ment and its transformative effects. His voiceover speaks of another city, a 'Leeds of the mind', brilliantly conveying the tab of fantasy we slip into our big nights out. Young boys playing with a dog amidst the back-to-backs are, through the poet's eyes, training for the Chinese State Circus; a cat nosing around a yard is a Bengal tiger; three lads walking down a street are walking on the moon.[32]

Conclusions

Where Harrison insists on the whole script being in poetry, Kay, D'Aguiar and Armitage work by incorporating poetry amidst prose. His purism contrasts to the hybrid quality of their work, which shows in the style of their poetry: less tightly bound within traditional forms, more influenced by contemporary music and ordinary speech.[33] But, despite such distinc-tions, what all these projects share is the inseparability of text from film: it is this that is the hallmark of this kind of collaborative undertaking.

Symes, Lowthorpe and Hill all share a refreshing belief in poetry's emotional power: that is what they have wanted to harness for their films. As Lowthorpe put it, 'poetry appeals to down here, mostly ... if you start looking at it too closely you analyse yourself into a nothing ... our films are not cerebral'. [34] Symes is most excited by the intensity that poetry can

---

[32] The fact that the text is written during the editing process also enables the team to compensate for earlier technical failures. Hill told me that Armitage's extended riff on the theme 'what drugs is' was devised to accompany footage shot in the toilets at a club, after the crew realized that they had shot the sequence without sound. Hill, unpublished phone conversation, 1999.

[33] Atkinson comments, in addition, on the influence of pop music videos over this younger generation of poets. Atkinson, *Verse Commentary*, Introduction.

[34] Lowthorpe, unpublished interview.

deliver. Confessing that he didn't read much and wondering aloud who did, he nevertheless claimed that 'in all of us there's something that appeals about rhythm and about rhyme'.[35] He advises poets to use a strong metre and rhyme when writing for television. Once again, Harrison differs from the others in the degree to which this is true of his film-work.

In these projects, poets work in ways that clash with traditional ideas about what poets are like and what they do. In the expectations of many academics, poets are wordsmiths writing for the page, they work alone, they seem to stand back from ordinary life and the lyric, with its intimate address, is their preferred genre. In reality, most poets spend a large proportion of their time working with others, in workshops and residencies. Mixed media projects are increasingly popular with funding bodies, so they may also collaborate regularly. Writing for television films could hardly be further from the intimacies of the lyric poem. Symes's expectation that poets, like journalists, should be able to respond fast, work collaboratively, and use their talents flexibly, is marvellously at odds with the reverential attitude that often hovers around the academy's chosen few.

Marjorie Perloff has criticized the heads-in-sand attitude that dominates poetry critique in the United States, describing a tendency to approach a poem as an 'object detachable from its context, as if a "poem" could exist in the US today that has not been shaped by the electronic culture that has produced it'.[36] She has been in the forefront of attempts to move critical methods on from page-based traditions. In her introduction to *Postmodern Genres,* she claims that it is the minor artists, imitators of a worn-out tradition, who continue to write for the page; 'real' poetry is happening in installation and performance work, innovative practice that redefines the very nature of the genre.[37] I believe in the continuing significance of page-based work but it does seem as though the potential for poetry offered by television has, so far, received little attention.

But what of the effects of these collaborative films? It is hard to gauge how such a commission might affect a poet's future writing style and I have no feedback from poets themselves on this issue. In terms of film-work, there are clear effects. From my conversations with directors Lowthorpe and Symes, and editor Fred Hart, what was most striking was their appreciation of the formal and technical challenges opened up by the use of poetry. These include the greater subjective scope offered by a poetry commentary, the setting of text against images and the rhythmic

---

[35] Symes, unpublished interview.
[36] Perloff, 'Music for Words Perhaps', p. xiii.
[37] Perloff, *Radical Artifice*, p. 7.

potential of poetry, to be complemented by the film editor's cuts. The combination produces highly-crafted films; only a fraction of the combined artistry can be absorbed at a single viewing. Even if the text is available, it is so dependent on the film that the poetry alone conveys only a very partial impression of the whole. [38]

The other significant difference about such films lies in the work they demand from their audience. Relationships between image, text and sound are not mimetic; for the most part they work by counterpoint and juxtaposing, and viewers have to decide for themselves on the relevance of such organizational decisions. Viewers also have to follow metaphorical trails and make their own connections. For example, there is a stark contrast in *Black Daisies* between the unselfconscious, mundane atmosphere on the ward, with people lost in their own mysterious inner worlds, and the high theatricality of the brides' appearances, performing direct to camera. What are viewers to make of this? It is too deliberate to be an accident but it is left up to us to decipher its intention and effect. These are subtle and demanding activities, expectations far from the role of viewers of most broadcasts. In such ways, these films do seem quantifiably distinct from most other forms of television. Furthermore, these hybrid forms take off in unexpected directions. Whereas familiarity with the rules and conventions of a genre usually guide the viewer, in films like *Drinking for England* the feeling of disorientation is palpable. Television is still such a young medium; perhaps we are less used to witnessing the evolution of its genres. If the techniques piloted in *Drinking for England* successfully avoid the pitfalls of turning documentaries' subjects into victims, it may well pave the way for more of this kind of experimentation.

Most crucially, such collaborations produce a different kind of poetry. However skilfully handled, it seems to me incontrovertible that the presence of a dynamic visual dimension takes attention away from the accompanying poetry. *Poems on the Box* is a fine illustration of how television can actually intensify viewers' experience of poetry, but this is done by *minimizing* visual distraction and yoking what does appear very carefully to the poem itself. The series seems to work by the principle of less is more: the vast potential of the screen harnessed to produce such minute visuals has the effect of concentrating attention. The other films are different because the poetry in them has been produced for the film. In these cases the text is less highly wrought, less dense or complex than page-based poetry. It is not written for publication, not designed to stand alone. Here there are similarities with the work of poets who write

---

[38] Harrison has reluctantly agreed to publication of some of his television work and prints brief film directions alongside the poetry. The BBC Education department published the text for the *Words on Film* series but sales were poor.

predominantly for performance. They create a different kind of poetry. But why should there not be room for poetry for different purposes?

If the academic world's poetry critics were to accept this broadening of the genre, they/we would need new skills: familiarity with several media and the dynamics of performance, as well as the confidence to explore work that is not fixed by a printed text. Critics have been slow to respond to the growth in poetry in performance for similar reasons.[39] These developments require a wholly different set of analytic and evaluative tools; maybe it is easier to side-step the challenge by assuming that, because it has to be reasonably accessible on a single hearing, such poetry is too simple to warrant academic critique. But does the absence of nuance and complexity make William Blake's *Songs of Innocence and Experience* or Stevie Smith's lyrics less good poetry? To criticize Armitage's writing in *Drinking for England* on the grounds that it is not poetry that will endure, or that it can't stand alone, is simply to use inappropriate assessment criteria. Is 'simpler' equivalent to 'less good'? The work that has been completed to date proves the exciting potential latent in multi-media collaborations and the impact that they can have over the perception and role of poets in contemporary society. It remains up to us to take on the challenge.[40]

[39] Commenting on this critical neglect, Ruth Harrison cites Peter Forbes's suggestion that it is the lack of ability to copyright performance (and therefore market it) that militates against the full acknowledgement of such work. Vicki Bertram (ed.), 'A Round-Table Discussion on Poetry in Performance: Jean Binta Breeze, Patience Agbabi, Jillian Tipene, Ruth Harrison and Vicki Bertram', in *Feminist Review* 62 (Summer 1999), 24–54.

[40] Video copies of all the films discussed are available at the Poetry Library, South Bank, London. Tel. 020 7921 0943/0664; e-mail info@poetrylibrary.org.uk.

Appendix 1: Recent Film and Poetry Collaborations, with date of first transmission

Loving Memory: BBC 2

Letters in the Rock (Dir: Peter Symes) 16 July 1987
Mimmo Perella (Dir: Peter Symes) 23 July 1987
Muffled Bells (Dir: Peter Symes) 30 July 1987
Cheating the Void (Dir: Peter Symes) 6 August 1987

The Blasphemers' Banquet: BBC1

(Dir: Peter Symes) 31 July 1989

Words on Film: BBC 2

Devices of Detachment (Dir: Hugh Thomson) 5 June 1992
Xanadu (Dir: Kim Flitcroft) 12 June 1992
Twice Through the Heart (Dir: Philippa Lowthorpe) 19 June 1992
Pieces of Peace (Dir: Kate Broome) 26 June 1992
Sweet Thames (Dir: Mark Harrison) 3 July 1992
Dressed to Kill (Dir: Peter Symes) 10 July 1992

The Gaze of the Gorgon: BBC 2

(Dir: Peter Symes) 31 October 1992

Poems on the Box: BBC 2

1993 (Executive Producers: Peter Symes & Roland Keating; Directors: Richard Kwietnowski, Teresa Griffiths, Paul Tilsey)

Poets' News: BBC 2

(Executive Producer: Peter Symes; Producer: Michael Davies) 1993

Black Daisies for the Bride: BBC 2

(Dir: Peter Symes) 30 June 1993

Saturday Night: BBC 2

(Dir: Brian Hill) 3 April 1996

Drinking for England: BBC 2

(Dir: Brian Hill) 10 November 1998

Prometheus: General cinema release, funded by FilmFour

(Dir: Tony Harrison) 1999

Acknowledgements

Many thanks to Peter Symes, Philippa Lowthorpe, Fred Hart and Brian Hill for sparing their time for my questions and for their invaluable contributions to this article.

3

'The Appreciation of Real Worth': Poetry, Radio and the Valued Reader

Lilias Fraser

I

'The broadcasting of poetry probably arouses the critical, indeed the combative, instinct in listeners more acutely than any other part of the programme,' announced the *B.B.C. Yearbook* for 1931. 'This fact seems to be an additional proof – if additional proof were needed – that poetry has very deep and therefore very individual roots in the English character. People usually get angry about things in proportion as they care for them'.[1] Has radio's idea of the poetry listener changed since? 'Were you intelligent, were you the ideal listener, you would appreciate this difficulty,' Harold Nicolson wrote of complaints about BBC scheduling and scolded in reproachful italics, '*A University is at your command. Attend it*'.[2] Clearly, something has changed. Certainly broadcasters got angry about things in proportion as they cared for them and perhaps still do; Nicolson and others cared deeply about the development of the ideal listener, one who could learn to criticize poetry on radio with discrimination and sympathetic judgement. Yet the one problem then seemed to lie in how to educate ordinary listeners to match an ideal, one which was being constructed as the programmes were made. Those convictions about poetry on radio, which were revealed by that process of construction, are the foundation of current ideas of the listener and, in part, pre-empt ideas of the contemporary reader.

The gradual evolution of the idea of the perfect listener, with whom programme makers gradually fell a little in love, falls into three stages. At first, the listener was constructed as an imitation of the reader. Then, moving into the second stage, the identity of the listener was subject to debates over how poetry could develop on radio, responding to the forays into new techniques and the sometimes reactionary returns to a more

---

[1] 'The Broadcasting of Poetry', *B.B.C. Year Book* 1931, p. 222.
[2] Harold Nicolson, 'A Word to Listeners', *Broadcast Talks*, No. 449 (September to December 1930), pp. 3–6 (p. 6).

familiar broadcasting discipline. The final stage appears in an acceptance that the ideal listener had either undergone enough formation or that a policy of formation was not the right approach; in this construction, the listener was, and is, held to be capable of exploring a certain degree of risk. Although the concept of the ideal listener originated in an examination of the poetry reader and reading practices, its eventual maturity is signalled by its arrival in critical theory as the model, not the imitation, of how to read.

The first stage was influenced by the cautious reception of radio as a new medium and the intermediate, adolescent stage ran in parallel with the increased credibility of radio poetry as a form in its own right: these stages, and suggestions towards allowing the ultimate maturity of the listener, were recurring topics in the *B.B.C. Quarterly* during the 1940s and early 1950s. Although the phrasing of these articles may have the anachronistic ring of a received pronunciation, the stages they describe still form the basis of discussion about listening; two of these stages of development can appear concurrently within the same article, just as a cross-section of current radio programming presents poetry in ways which are individually sympathetic to each stage's interpretation of the continuing passion over radio poetry. Barbara Herrnstein Smith wrote about her readerly love affair with the Shakespeare sonnets that she understood evaluation not as an appreciation of the constant ideal, but as an involved, responsive process of judgement; like the judgement of a lover, it is 'always compromised, impure, contingent'.[3] The evaluation involved in listening to radio poetry, both of the poetry and of the listener, is constantly compromised by allegiances with other methods of evaluation borrowed from other media; yet, without these formative influences, the impurity and contingency of the relationship between radio poetry and its listeners could not thrive.

Listening's most significant other was, and it seems still is, reading. Along with the argument that radio can compete with visual media like cinema and prove superior, one of the most long-running arguments for radio is that it is wedded to print publishing. This radio review, written in 1999, is not guilty of any apparent anachronism, yet its opening comments are essentially familiar with, if not obedient to, the rhetoric of early broadcasters:

> I've had it with clichés about radio (and God knows I've perpetu-
> ated a few myself). If I hear the one about the scenery being better
> on the wireless once more, it'll be pistols before dawn. *Yet there's no*

---

[3] Barbara Herrnstein Smith, *Contingencies of Value: Alternative Perspectives for Critical Theory* (Cambridge MA: Harvard University Press, 1988), p. 1.

denying that when it comes to ideas, radio is second only to the printed page as a conduit.[4] [my italics]

Broadcasters initially worked on the assumption that listeners were simply readers who needed guidance in tailoring their listening to their reading needs and assumed too that listeners would bring a reader's method of evaluation to radio poetry. The earlier writing on broadcasting, particularly, shows the influence of a popular contemporary training of the reader. In 1929 I. A. Richards published *Practical Criticism*, his analysis of readers and reading behaviour. The basis of the technique was a concerted effort on the part of the reader to attempt repeated and cumulative readings over a period of time. If a session of reading was unsuccessful, it 'left the reader with nothing but the bare words before him on the paper' but, when readers successfully articulated their opinion, Richards maintained they could contribute extra dimensions both to their individual practice of the method and to a communal understanding of other readers' judgement. He described these communicated opinions as lending both community and individual a solid superstructure:

[it] is as though we were strolling through and about a building that hitherto we were only able to see from one or two distant standpoints. We gain a much more intimate understanding both of the poem and of the opinions it provokes.[5]

Despite the stress on the visualization of permanence and on the importance of the students' repeated contemplation of a tangible text over a period of time, this approach provided broadcasters with a blueprint for the construction of the ideal listener as an individual engaging in a communal discipline. The foundation of comprehension of a poem was the sight, and perhaps touch, of bare words on paper. The threat to the structure of understanding was the excess of 'heterogeneous' information which breached the reading communities. Richards likened it to the heir of a small business attempting to maintain an untroubled parochial routine in the face of global economic problems; by implication, learning to read in a discriminating fashion was the only way to retain the inherited value of the reading business. The recommended reading practice was directly paralleled with equipping oneself with a survivalist knowledge in defiance

---

[4] Anne Karpf, 'Strong Shades of Gray', *The Guardian*, Saturday 27 February 1999. The review went on to praise two programmes, one of which was an interview with Derek Walcott by David Dabydeen. Retrieved 17 October 2000, from the World Wide Web: http://www.guardianunlimited.co.uk/Archive/Article/0,4273,3828310,00.html.
[5] I. A. Richards, *Practical Criticism: A Study of Literary Judgment* (1929; London: Routledge and Kegan Paul, 1987), p. 9.

of an onslaught of information and the insidious new media which provided it: the only alternative, he maintained, was the hurried defence of 'stereotyping and standardising' in the ordinary reader's critical expression, '[a]nd this threat, it must be insisted, can only grow greater as world communications, through the wireless and otherwise, improve'.[6] *Practical Criticism* did hint obliquely at some of the pleasures of reading poetry by warning of 'the difficulties of *sensuous apprehension*', since '[w]ords in sequence have a form to the mind's ear and the mind's tongue and larynx, even when silently read'[7] but pleasure was overshadowed by a schooling in crisis economies of reading and critical sanctions.

Radio's apologists were already aware of how much the marketplace might affect the value of radio literature. In a way that is particularly familiar to a contemporary audience, there was a certain amount of gloomy prediction that radio and cinema, jointly and separately, would cause the death of the book. John Reith, with his fervent agenda of education and discrimination for the BBC's programming, mounted his defence with an attack on those who might be more worried about book sales than the development of the skilled and discriminating listener:

> One cannot deny, however, that there is some ground for the fears which are occasionally expressed. It is pertinent to ascertain whether they emanate from those who are simply concerned with the commercial benefits or losses which accrue to them, according as the market for their products rises or falls, or whether it be the expression of an anxious concern on the part of those who, with no financial interests involved, are apprehensive of any new operation which may be to the detriment of the advance of the general intelligence.[8]

Despite this slight assumption of the moral high ground, he did unbend a little to reassure 'those who write or publish books ... [and] those who desire that the reading and study of good literature be encouraged' that the alliance between broadcaster and publisher could be beneficial. By introducing the listening public to 'what is commonly called good literature', in preference to 'the exploitation of sensationalism, vulgarity, crime', broadcasting would even develop discrimination in the book-buying habits of the public: 'the market for certain kinds of music and printed matter will become more limited as appreciation of real worth is fostered.'[9] There was an uneasy truce. Solid pages of publishers' advertisements appeared in

---

[6] Ibid., p. 340.
[7] Ibid., p.14.
[8] John Reith, *Broadcast Over Britain* (London: Hodder & Stoughton, 1924), p. 131.
[9] Ibid., p. 133.

BBC publications, which were further enforced with the encouragement of the study groups formed by listeners in local libraries. *The Listener* printed selected poems beside transcripts of broadcast talks, including the BBC's first National Lecture, by Robert Bridges, on the subject of poetry. It also gave details of recommended editions and occasionally reviewed published poetry collections. The emphasis on returning the listener to their readerly activities is unmistakable; the index of the real worth of broadcast poetry was initially the level of its popularity in print.

In the first stage, then, the listener is perceived primarily as a disadvantaged reader, lacking the structural props of even the bare words. In consequence, this listener must not be in any way distracted from the form that appears to their mind's ear, since the task is not only to concentrate on the words to the exclusion of everything else but to conjure up and maintain a mental substitute for the missing print form. The ideal listener was expected to make an instantaneous conversion from an aural to a visual medium, in order to compare the value of what was heard with the value it might be given as a piece of text. Listeners, like readers, are initially trained to develop a disregard for anything surrounding the words of a poem, for the literally marginal white noise which has its equivalent in any medium; the size and thickness of the paper on which a poem is printed, or the impress of theatrical training on a reader's voice, are to do with the economies of the medium. As the ideal listener began to take shape, its creators assumed that even these marginal economies would compete with the illusion of the listener's intimacy with the poem; the distractions of 'sensuous apprehension' for the concentrating listener were deceptively expensive.

'Not all poetry lovers like hearing poetry read aloud; but most have their own views as to how this should be done,' *The Listener*'s editorial remarked dryly in 1929.

> Those who have had most experience of broadcasting poetry, however, are inclined to stress the importance of simplicity and absence of all exaggeration of effect. Poetry read aloud *must* be unobtrusive, so that it fits harmoniously with the mood of the listener.[10]

Anything might create discord and distraction in the listener's mood, from the hated over-exaggeration of some radio voices, to the listener's own surroundings. The writer, in the *B.B.C. Year Book* for 1931, who observed how much listeners cared about radio poetry, urged that:

> [the reader] must understand the nature and structure of poetry, so that he can strike the right balance between bringing out the words,

[10] Editorial, *The Listener*, 13 March 1929, p. 316.

and the meaning of the content, neither unduly obtruding his own personality nor repressing it by any trick ... poetry broadcasts must aim at something which will give the illusion of a reader at one's own fireside, i.e. a reading, not a performance.

But he also amplified the listener's responsibility to engineer their own sound environment and their degree of concentration:

Broadcasting ... may seem on the face of it a wholly unsuitable medium. It has of necessity a more or less universal appeal; how can it be brought to serve a peculiarly individual art like poetry? The loud-speaker sends out what it receives in whatever company it may find itself – a noisy street, a busy kitchen, a living-room containing half a dozen people of different ages engaged in different occupations. How can an English lyric, however lovely, find the right reception in such circumstances? The answer, of course, is that it cannot; poetry, possibly more than any other kind of programme, demands some degree of co-operation on the part of the listener.[11]

Richards had promised that the reader who made the effort to concentrate on different communal structurings of a poem would, paradoxically, be rewarded with the privacy of a more intimate understanding: the *Year Book* writer exhorted the listener to make equal effort and be rewarded with an intimate space away from the distractions of communal noise. Intimacy, in this first stage of moving from reading to listening, is both a requirement and a reward for taking the necessary care with a poem. The broadcast poem's capacity for intimacy is derived from the reader's capacity for concentration; it is not necessarily a quality inherent in the broadcast poem itself.

The specific idea of *intimacy*, often with that connotation described by Herrnstein Smith of the contingency of an involved judgement, is still used throughout discussions of broadcast poetry. Susan Roberts, a producer of poetry programmes on radio, said recently:

we tend to listen to the radio on our own. It is a direct medium – the voice in your ear ... Like the experience of reading a poem, it is intimate and allows you to concentrate on the voice alone with no distractions.[12]

---

[11] 'The Broadcasting of Poetry', p. 222.
[12] Susan Roberts, 'Exploring Connections between Poetry and Radio', conference entitled *Unnatural Selection: Media and Value in Contemporary Poetry*, University of St Andrews, 9 October 1999.

A slight shift in the definition of radio's intimacy was symptomatic of a move to the next stage of listening. The listener at his fireside, in thrall to the intimate, even whispered, voice of a poetry reading, was an enduringly popular image. However, when Herbert Read, in 1949, made what sounds like a moderately whimsical case for the adaptation of genre to environment, he was voicing a critical shift in this image of the appropriate responsibilities of the listener. Although the tone of his piece was lightly speculative, it was voicing an accepted mood of radio's adolescent rebellion from the limitations of a reading mentality. 'A new art generally inherits an old aesthetic,' he began and added that '[b]roadcasting was at first treated as merely the diffusion of what already existed'. He proposed that '[i]nstead of Home, Light and Third Programmes, we would have Theatre, Hall and Room Programmes ... [t]he aesthetic principle underlying this new style might be indicated by the word Intimacy'.[13] In suggesting that the new art of broadcasting should adapt its inherited aesthetic, in order to explore the particular possibilities of the listener's situation, Read was implying that the criteria of broadcast poetry selection would change as well.

Inevitably, when the discipline of listening began to change from an imitation of reading to a skill in its own right, there was a revaluation of what sort of poetry might best exploit radio's new understanding of intimacy. Rather than protect listeners' reading skills or rearrange their sitting rooms, Bonamy Dobrée asked if it might be 'one of the functions of the B.B.C. to inaugurate the process of hooking in the consciousness of the ordinary listener', protesting that 'difficult poetry is almost impossible to seize through the medium of the disembodied voice'.

> [A]n opportunity should be seized in the recent return of poets to clearly defined forms – canzones, sestinas, villanelles. Not that the listener's ear need be trained to expect the repetition of a phrase, as we learn to look for in classical music, but that when the return comes it not only brings the delight of recognition, and a little relaxation, but also binds the fleeting sounds and ideas together ... The question is: What do you and I, sitting by our hearths, alone, or with one or two others, want to hear? We want, as far as possible, to hear the voice of the poet such as we imagine it to ourselves when we read him.[14]

There is still an element of the readerly panic in the seizure of 'fleeting sounds and ideas', but this is an example of transition towards a new

[13] Herbert Read, 'Sotto Voce – a Plea for Intimacy', *B.B.C. Quarterly*, IV (1) (April 1949), 1–6 (pp. 1–2).

[14] Bonamy Dobrée, 'Poetry on the Air', *B.B.C. Quarterly*, VIII (3) (Autumn 1953), 153–7 (p. 155).

confidence in managing the medium, in pursuing rather than educating the listener. Instead of insisting on the listener's capacity to visualize text, broadcasters were exploring the wider possibilities of visual imagination; new horizons were still the reward of careful listening but they were horizons in which the influence of textual reading was explained as more hindrance than virtue. Herbert Grierson praised the BBC for 'teaching us to hear' and 'reminding us that poetry is written ... to be heard in imagination even if we have to read in silence', and he reproved the backwardness of 'try[ing] to *see* the word as well as *hear* it'.[15]

At the same time, an increasing freedom from a print-based, readerly construction of judgement was accompanied by a concern over evaluation and ephemerality. Although writing for radio might flourish, what was the point if the constructed listener was still unsure of what the new achievements were worth? '[A] chance to experiment ... is probably radio's greatest gift to the modern poet,' D. G. Bridson wrote, arguing that the epic had every chance to flourish in the broadcast medium, where the pressures of publication space had restricted poetry. He continued '[h]ere is a medium in which he can blaze new trails for himself and his times' and issued the challenge that 'for the modern poet to ignore that immense radio audience is tantamount to his admitting that he has either nothing to say worth people's hearing – or that he lacks the technique for making them understand and appreciate it'.[16] As writers like Louis MacNeice and Dylan Thomas began to explore the possibilities of radio, it became imperative that new criteria were developed to deal with work which was not only broadcast on radio but written specially for it. If the ideal listener were to be allowed more independence from readerly behaviour, then broadcasters acknowledged that they needed a way of judgement that would allow both the medium of radio and the perceived radio listener to come of age.

If they were to do so, producing the kind of understanding listener that Nicolson had hoped for, then a way had to be found to discuss, if not settle, the value and evaluation of radio poetry. There was the literal value of work, paid per line – and, in case this encouraged very long poems with very short lines, there was even during the late 1940s a graded scale of fees which meant that writing anything above twenty-four lines specially for radio broadcast would be scarcely worth the effort.[17] In fact, poets wanting to accept Bridson's challenge to explore radio's possibilities

---

[15] Herbert Grierson, 'The Spoken Word', *B.B.C. Quarterly*, IV (3) (October 1949), 148–53 (pp. 150, 153, 148).

[16] D. G. Bridson, 'Radio's Approach to Poetry', *B.B.C. Quarterly*, V (3) (Autumn 1950), 167–72 (p. 171).

[17] Based on BBC fees outlined in c. 1948. See Kate Whitehead, *The Third Programme: a Literary History* (Oxford: Clarendon, 1989), p. 161.

faced a compound problem of which fees were a large part. Since experimental radio poetry was unlikely to be suitable for publication, the already low fees for its broadcast would be unsupplemented by print sales. In addition, poetry which would only be heard once or twice, and would remain unpublished, was unlikely to be valued critically as part of the poet's work.

Henry Reed, despite suggesting that the future of radio work lay in drama, felt that no established poet or dramatist could afford – in either sense – to write for radio: 'It could only be done as a handsome, recklessly self-denying *beau geste*.' He argued that a return to the support of print by publishing radio plays would lessen the risk to writers' identities, although he implied that this would encourage 'bookish' rather than particularly experimental radio work. But his main solution was an increasingly popular one amongst broadcasters. It was not enough to argue for a particular style or approach to writing for radio; the split between radio's requirements and 'bookish' writing should be acknowledged and young writers should be encouraged to take the step of devoting themselves to radio careers. (Quite how this could practicably be achieved, given his concern over the low fees, he does not explain.) But if writers were to make such a commitment to the medium of radio, he argues, the listener would be able to follow suit.

> It is bound to remain an art for the young writers; a mature and established one could not possibly afford to devote the necessary time to it. I think this brings us back to the uncertainty of our expectations of radio literature ... If radio is to mature it must compel writers to involve their whole selves in its art when they write for it. It too must become for them, if only for a time, a means of examining and criticising life. Only when an author's radio-drama is to be observed as being a part of his seriously developing *œuvre* will radio show signs of being reliable: *then* indeed shall we know what to expect, how much to 'give' to it as we listen.[18]

He adds that radio-writers could also allow themselves more freedom in subjectivity, so that 'the results might be a bit more healthy and a bit more grown-up all round'. Rather than posing as maturely untroubled by subjects, audience or medium, these younger writers should acknowledge the concerns and inconsistencies of artistic and personal growing-up and, in doing so, allow the audience the element of risk that would help them develop artistically:

[18] Henry Reed, 'What the Wireless Can Do for Literature', *B.B.C Quarterly*, III (4) (January 1949), 217–22 (p. 219).

> it is the parts of an artist's self most familiar to himself as puzzles and obsessions and regular preoccupations that really produce anything worth offering to a serious listener or reader ... [i]t is, and has long been, a fatal fact in radio that the writer has tended, when confronted with anything difficult to express, not to master it but to omit it.[19]

The listener was first allowed a sense of intimacy as a reward for concentration, then was granted intimacy as a passport to a private sound territory: perhaps the third stage of the listener's development is being considered secure enough in their listening abilities, and solid enough as a construction, to accept, explore and survive a certain degree of risk.

Risk might be a matter of facing possible boredom or the incomprehension of something difficult to express. It is also, according to Reed, a matter of knowing how much critical concentration to invest in the art of listening. Why should a listener learn how to listen and why should they keep listening? Can they simply pronounce a radio poem to be 'good' or would it be more satisfying to know what it is good as? When they are listening to radio poetry, what are they listening *for*? C. Day Lewis proposed a shift which would involve a risk for the writer, paralleling that of the reader and involving not just changes in reading voice, subject or form, but a radical vision of what poetry's function on radio should be.

> The great majority of listeners, let us accept it, are indifferent to poetry, or positively hostile. It is futile to go on telling them that poetry is good for them and really tastes very nice too if only they'd try it. The way to break down, or rather to by-pass, their resistance is to use poetry, persistently and as a matter of course, in contexts which are already of popular interest. We complain today, for instance, that the masses are apathetic about Britain's economic crisis. We agree that this is because it has not been brought home to their imagination as individuals. Yet we continue to coax them with pre-digested statistics and prosy pep-talks, while the one instrument which can go straight to the heart, can awake the sleeping imagination, is left unused. I suggest that, ideally, every documentary feature programme on a subject of topical interest, whether it be the Mines, the Pools, Atomic Energy or a Royal Occasion, should modulate here and there into poetry, should use the heightened form of language we call poetry to make its imaginative points.[20]

---

[19] Ibid., p. 220.
[20] C. Day Lewis, 'Broadcasting and Poetry', *B.B.C. Quarterly*, V (1) (Spring 1950), 1–7 (p. 5).

The radiogenic poem, in making itself both uniquely appropriate for the medium and keeping the listener involved in the contingency of an intimate affair, risks its status as a broadcast poem by becoming an element of a radio programme, just another feature of the aural syntax. In making a poem which is irrevocably radiogenic – practically indistinguishable from other elements of radio, like news bulletins or the other parts of its documentary context – the reward might be that listeners can recognize and accord value and, in turn, invest radio poetry with serious critical listening. Radio poetry gains new vocabularies and the documentary gains, amongst other things, a 'hooking' device to catch the listener and force a re-evaluation of its subjects.

Lewis's slightly wry suggestion that poetry might 'go straight to the heart', where other media coverage resulted in apathy, is borne out by one reviewer of the radio production of Simon Armitage's poem *Killing Time*, who wrote that he 'felt tears pricking'.[21] *Killing Time* was commissioned as a 1,000-line poem on the last year before the official millennium celebration;[22] it is a public poem in the sense that, as Lewis recommended, it reviews the last year of the century in verse as a way of making its imaginative points about the news format. The Faber blurb on the published version of the poem continues to evoke a traditionally readerly distrust of broadcast media when it explains the poem's context as 'a world picked clean by microphone and camera, a world where nothing is sacred, secret or even true'.[23] *Killing Time* is split into lengthy narrative sections, read by Armitage, and laconically sound-bitten quatrains, which interject the looser single rhyme scheme, and are frequently read by voices of passers-by, recorded over street noise. At the outset, Armitage describes the grotesque of communication turned into a feeding frenzy; a monkey has evolved which thrives on a merciless intake of news, yet still craves an existence outside its own ephemerality. Later in the poem, the narrative voice takes up the protest, retrieving it as a complaint which can compromise each human consumer of broadcast media. The news items of 1999 are delivered in a suspension of what might happen if ephemerality and urgent time-driven regulations were not a threat; for example, the shots in the Colorado high school slow down until they form a choreographed presentation of a flower to each victim. Richard Branson's attempt to travel round the world by balloon leads to a fantasy of living in one:

---

[21] Phil Daoust, 'Killing Time', *The Guardian*, Monday 20 December 1999. Retrieved 17 October 2000, from the World Wide Web: http://www.guardianunlimited.co.uk/Archive/Article/0,4273,3943510,00.html.

[22] *Killing Time* was broadcast on Radio 3 on 18 December 1999, in a production by Kate Rowland. A film version of the poem, with Christopher Eccleston and Hermione Norris, was directed by Brian Hill and shown on Channel 4 on 1 January 2000.

[23] Simon Armitage, *Killing Time* (London: Faber, 1999), back cover.

> We could do worse,
>   couldn't we, than balloon? Could do worse than peel
>   the skin from the soul
>   and dither and drift in the miles of airspace between heaven
>   and Earth,

a fantasy which depends on the instruction, 'Be quiet and listen'.[24]

Rhyme is not solely in the structure of the poem: it is present in the assonant sound effects and music. When Bonamy Dobrée encouraged the formal properties of poems which would bring 'delight of recognition, and a little relaxation' for the listener, he had written only about the recurrent or rhyming words. Although *Killing Time* provides that sort of recognition of formal features, the recognition provided by its broadcast medium is equally in the two main sorts of sounds outside the poet's voice. There is the collage of 'media' in action; the sound of newsreaders' voices, stalling sometimes on repeated phrases from news headlines and wrapped in radio static. There is also the musical soundtrack of eclectic styles linked by repeated notes which echo a range of urgency, from an alien sonar to the insistent ticking and chiming of Big Ben and the smaller timepieces that regulate the poem's subjects. Piano blues, ubiquitously familiar electronica (by, appropriately enough, the French band Air) and a minimalist *Dies Irae* build around repeated cadences and single notes in a kind of structural sonar, detecting new developments on the poem's preoccupations – the compromise between the unfeeling detachment encoded in reports of aerial bombardments and a longing for the freedom of apolitical, unnewsworthy, flight:

> Impossible of course,
>   but couldn't we just, couldn't we just?

For example, an echoing, repeated sonar-like noise is first heard during the first narrative section, directly after a description of Christmas shoppers and round the words:

> But tonight the bright star over the Middle East is the burn
>   of a cruise missile homing in.

It continues with a soothing string accompaniment, through the visual morse of

> tracer-bullets [rising] like Amaretti papers aflame
>   before the connection goes dead,

---

[24] Ibid., pp. 18–19.

and beneath the introduction of a newsreader's voice repeating 'no-fly zone'. The sonar reappears in a later narrative section, which introduces round-the-world balloon flight, so that narrative and sound effect can get close to heaven but never quite touch it:

> all the mental energy
> and tax dollars pumped into that Stealth bomber thing
> ...
> when all along we could have sided with the angels.

Rising above the problem is only a temporary respite for the listener, since, as Armitage was quoted as saying in an interview, 'with this length of poem, you can keep coming back ... you can let the scab heal over and then pick it off again'.[25]

Opening up old wounds is scarcely the kind of comforting recognition that Dobrée had urged, but he would surely approve that Simon Armitage reads most of the poem himself with interjections from other voices recorded over street noise, some of which sound slightly bemused. Repeatedly, his voice cuts in apparently closer to the microphone than it was before, sometimes in the whisper of a nature programme commentary. But this is not focused towards the security of intimate, fireside listening: reminders that broadcast news is made, not organically developed, come in the flashes of white noise, the undercurrents of familiar newsreaders' voices describing the events. As one of the street readers fades in, the end of a conversation – 'if you like, start again'– is a prompt that this is another attempt at making a recording rather than the pronouncement of a disembodied and infallible voice.

Working through the news monkey's meals of human violence and vanity, the poem fights to slow down the frantically ephemeral progress of news media. In that respect, its criticism is reflexive: the function of documentary, which lent radio poetry credibility in the ears of the ideal listener, is now what the poem most criticizes. Harman Grisewood, discussing criticism as the modern listener's form of pietas, even insisted that learning to listen could redeem the critic's humanity:

> [a] man owes it to himself, to his own fulfilment according to his capacities, to evaluate what he observes and what he hears ... to distinguish the torrents of sound that pour upon one each day merely by what makes a pleasant or an unpleasant sensation can hardly be said to earn the description of a human response.[26]

[25] Robert Potts, 'Mean Time', *The Guardian*, Wednesday 15 December 1999. Retrieved 17 October 2000, from the World Wide Web: http://www.guardianunlimited.co.uk/Archive/Article/0,4273,3941854,00.html

[26] Harman Grisewood, 'Response and Responsibility', *B.B.C. Quarterly*, IV (3) (October 1949), 165–9 (pp. 168–9).

If the poem itself can now criticize its medium's more inhuman devices, then, by this reasoning, it has grown up along with the listener and become a public-spirited art. Yet an alternative definition of listening offered in these pieces is that, like reading, it is a compromised, impure process; a developing relationship as contingent on pleasant or unpleasant sensations, as Richards warily acknowledged over 'the difficulties of *sensuous apprehension*', as on a more premeditated set of criteria. In the act of questioning the values by which it is judged, the radio poem and its listeners have, perhaps, grown up; their particular love affair proves itself to be more than a matter of devising an idealized criteria and constructing a petrified art form to match.

The three stages of listening are, of course, compromised by an allegiance to reading but, equally, reading has been presented as revelling in the impure seductions afforded by listening. Allowing writing to become more challenging and, therefore, listening to become more concentrated and difficult need not mean a reversion to text and a panic over how much time an act of comprehension can afford. After being shaped by the modernist tools of reading, listeners can now choose to deploy the authority of postmodernist reading which explores, as its model, contingent listening.

> Listening is, of course, shaped by a labyrinth, the labyrinth of the ear itself. Modernist demystification – the tendency to disillusion or 'disenchantment', an attempt to escape magic which characterises the modernist project – produced one dominant understanding of flight: as exile. But exile itself implies a stable territorialised home. Postmodernism is able to sustain the possibility of enchantment – known conventionally as the 'postmodern sublime' – and will take the risk of enchantment in listening, the risk of self-amazement; as a result, the flights which it has privileged are those which have no root and no landing: a state of exile without territory.[27]

We could do worse, couldn't we, than balloon? The disorientating enchantment of listening is not, in this case, a very long flight from the exclusive intimacy of readerly concentration. Learning to listen like this, with every intention of getting lost, does allow a freedom from the values imposed by a textual cartography; it also implies release from the civic obligation to return criticism on what is heard.

The most interesting route to follow in evaluating contemporary poetry on radio might be this appreciation of loss and being lost. Perversely enough, it might allow yet another justification of the sort of intimacy to which early broadcast poetry aspired:

[27] Thomas Docherty, *After Theory* (Edinburgh: Edinburgh University Press, 1996), p. 176.

What do you and I, sitting by our hearths, alone, or with one or two others, want to hear? We want, as far as possible, to hear the voice of the poet such as we imagine it to ourselves when we read him.[28]

Bonamy Dobrée advised the security of recognition that would come from a strictly formalized poetry – a familiar aural territory. But John Burnside, interested in exploring different sorts of absences in his poems, describes a different sort of travel itinerary for a listener trying to understand a poem through its sounds. His suggestion for the realization of radio's potential is to combine the creative disorientation of the listener with the physical and aural geography in which a poem is developed.

People like to hear the poet's voice, but the voice I use in a reading is nothing like my voice – it's as competent a voice as I can assume to read a poem to an audience. Starting a poem involves an inner voice – my real voice – speaking the poem as it develops. It belongs in a different space. The only way to deliver that inner voice to an audience would be to take a tape recorder to the place [the poem] was made, or spoken, and then play that recording, which would be more real than reading to an audience in a room ... If you're absorbed in listening, you get lost at the end – you reorientate yourself ... It moves you to another space.

The experience of writing is unrepeatable. When you write a poem you don't want or expect the next person who comes along and reads it to have exactly the same experience. If recording [in situ] like that is the closest you can get to the experience of making a poem, then it's like creating a room and then leaving it and someone else will come into it and have a different experience.[29]

This doesn't mean a helpless abandonment of all evaluation, although it does upset any idea of a universal set of criteria – 'someone else will come into it and have a different experience'. Reading which is modelled on listening, rather than listening modelled on reading, describes the intimacy of understanding which Richards included in his architecture of interpretation; it even helps to free the ideal reader from a cycle of investment and return. When C. Day Lewis suggested that merging poetry and news documentary was the way to develop radio poetry, he made his proposal of the radiogenic poem as an alternative to a marriage of convenience: 'Theoretically, it should have been love at first sight and an ideal marriage between poetry and radio ... Yet the courtship has been

---

[28] Bonamy Dobrée, 'Poetry on the Air', p. 156.
[29] Interview with John Burnside, 8 February 2000.

a suspicious one, the marriage on the whole perfunctory'.[30] Perhaps the
marriage is happier when the radio poem and the listener are valued with
the contingency of a love affair. The readerly listeners were offered the
possibility of orienting themselves in communal sound and communal
judgement, never quite escaping from even the most fantastical aural
landscape created for them. The postmodern love affair with listening
also offers the reward of intimacy but its sound effect is contingent upon
disorientation.

[30] C. Day Lewis, 'Broadcasting and Poetry', p. 1.

4

Contemporary Poetry and Academia: The Instance of Informationism

Robert Crawford

> Where is the wisdom we have lost in knowledge?
> Where is the knowledge we have lost in information?[1]

When I asked him in a university context if he thought there was a clear distinction between knowledge and information at the close of the twentieth century, Richard Rorty shrewdly quoted these lines from T. S. Eliot's *The Rock*. He made the point that, for Eliot, there was a clearly hierarchical distinction between knowledge and information. Rorty's opinion was that the word 'information' was linked to once fashionable cybernetic ideas developed around MIT and Harvard by Norbert Wiener. In the late twentieth century, phrases like 'the knowledge industry' demonstrated that knowledge and information had coalesced.[2]

While agreeing with this view, I would argue that it marks a more significant shift than Rorty was inclined to allow. The very existence of a term such as 'the knowledge industry' shows how much knowledge in late capitalist society has come to be regarded not in terms of academic worth but almost entirely for its economic value as information. It is hard to think of Matthew Arnold viewing his dreaming spires as part of 'the knowledge industry', but it is easy to see the 1998 decision of Oxford University Press to axe its poetry list as taken in a climate where poetry was valued less as the Wordsworthian 'finer spirit of all knowledge' than as a commodity whose financial returns appeared low in a world of information-trading.[3] Though Sir Keith Thomas, Chairman of OUP's Finance Committee, wrote a lengthy article in the *Times Literary Supplement* arguing that this decision might 'receive the gratitude of

---

[1] T. S. Eliot, *The Complete Poems and Plays* (London: Faber and Faber, 1969), p. 147 ('The Rock, I').

[2] Richard Rorty, discussion with the present writer, St Andrews, 1 May 1997.

[3] William Wordsworth and S. T. Coleridge, *Lyrical Ballads, 1805*, Second Edition, ed. Derek Roper (London: MacDonald and Evans, 1976), p. 35 (Wordsworth's Preface).

posterity', the Press was eventually shamed into a face-saving agreement with Carcanet after a good number of OUP poets had already left the list.[4] It may be to the Press's credit that it could be shamed but, before that happened, the matter had been raised in the House of Lords and, with pointedly Arnoldian ululation, James Fenton, Arnold's modern successor as Oxford's Professor of Poetry, lamented, 'The Philistines are upon thee, Oxford.'[5] Meanwhile a brigade of poets and professors of English (some of them Oxford dons) including Gillian Beer, John Carey, Tony Harrison, Seamus Heaney, Tom Paulin and Craig Raine denounced the 'disgraceful decision' of the University Press.[6] This may be the most striking recent manifestation in Britain of a complex and sometimes bruising encounter between poetry and competing notions of value in contemporary culture. It is part of the same Thatcherite and post-Thatcher climate which has resulted in the energetic promotion of selected 'New Generation Poets' by an advertising agency and in the increasing employment of poets by ambitious, competitive universities.

For some people, poetry can have nothing to do with market economics, national politics or the politics of academia. On one level they are right. Yet, after the death of Ted Hughes, the spectacle of several highly distinguished English, Irish and Scottish poets lining up to say 'no' to the job of British Poet Laureate reminds us that poetry can intersect with political as well as economic values. When Tony Harrison, reacting to his reported 'shortlisting' for the Laureateship, reserved his right to be

> free to say up yours to Tony Blair,
> to write an ode on Charles I's beheading

he made a significant public statement about the freedom of the poetic imagination in the politics of late twentieth-century Britain.[7] In late 1998 and early 1999, the widely-reported debates over the Laureateship and over the OUP beheadings came as strong reminders that poetry, as well as being a matter of aesthetic finesse, intersects with issues of political, economic and academic value in contemporary culture.

If we remember that the university subject of English Literature began some distance from the dreaming spires of Oxford and that one of its founders was the Scotsman Adam Smith, then we are recalling that the relationship between the academic teaching of poetry in English and the writing of verse has been shaped from its outset by commercial and

---

[4] Keith Thomas, 'The Purpose and the Cost', *TLS*, 5 February 1999, pp. 14–15; '"Oxford Poets" Saved', unsigned piece, *Observer*, 7 March 1999, p. 4.

[5] James Fenton, 'Beware the Philistines of Publishing', *The Times*, 25 November 1998, p. 22.

[6] Hermione Lee et al., 'Oxford's Poetry List' (letter), *TLS*, 4 December 1998, p. 17.

[7] Tony Harrison, 'Laureate's Block', *The Guardian*, 9 February 1999, p. 15.

national as well as aesthetic forces. Since the eighteenth century, English Literature has been a university subject involving close, sometimes politically sensitive collaborations and flytings between writers and academics. The symbiotic relationship between Hugh Blair and James 'Ossian' Macpherson is the most striking early instance of this. Not only is the university subject of English Literature in important senses an eighteenth-century Scottish invention, it is also one that, from its beginnings, included instruction in what we would now call creative writing.[8] Throughout the nineteenth century, it was not unusual to find poet-academics bound up with English Literature's exploitation and development. Whether in the Edinburgh of William Edmondstoune Aytoun, the Glasgow of John Nichol, the Harvard of Henry Wadsworth Longfellow or the Oxford of Matthew Arnold, poets of varying temperaments and abilities were involved in the proliferation of academic literary studies. To think of links between poetry and the academia of literature departments purely as a contemporary English or even as a mid-twentieth-century American phenomenon is wrongheaded.[9] Complex networks of economic and cultural considerations which have a bearing on poets and on academics have brought both together in the business of teaching literature throughout the English-speaking world for well over two centuries.

While the pressures of institutional commerce may sometimes harm them, it is often money which lures poets into academia. The attraction of a salary cheque can be strong and it may be a good thing to have at least an element of structure to one's creative life. For universities in Britain, poets on campus still add a smidgen of high-cultural allure. Creative Writing courses are a marked growth area at undergraduate and post-graduate level, so poets can enhance an institution's teaching portfolio. They are also a bankable asset in terms of research, on which funding in part depends. The regular UK national 'Research Assessment Exercise' defines 'research' not just in terms of 'the needs of commerce and industry' but also as 'the invention and generation of ideas, images, performances and artefacts including design, where these lead to new or substantially improved insights'.[10] Legitimately, this covers poetry.

---

[8] See Robert Crawford (ed.), *The Scottish Invention of English Literature* (Cambridge: Cambridge University Press, 1998) and Robert Crawford (ed.), *Launch-site for English Studies: Three Centuries of Literary Studies at the University of St Andrews* (St Andrews: Verse, 1997), especially the chapters by Robert Crawford, Douglas Dunn and Neil Rhodes.

[9] Crawford (ed.), *The Scottish Invention of English Literature*; see also D. G. Myers, *The Elephants Teach: Creative writing since 1880* (Englewood Cliffs, NJ: Prentice Hall, 1996) and Robert Crawford, *The Modern Poet* (Oxford: Oxford University Press, 2001).

[10] Anon., *Research Assessment Exercise 2001: Key Decisions and Issues for Further Consultation* (Bristol: Higher Education Funding Council, 1998), p. 40.

Pragmatic considerations may be to the fore as far as the entry of poets into academia is concerned but there are also more altruistic reasons. Not all poets go to university as students, but many do. Higher education can offer the time to write as well as to read, alongside opportunities to encounter kinds of knowledge which nourish the production of verse. Academia may shape poetry in questionable ways, producing anthologies which surround even new poems with walls of commentary. So the special experience of poetry gets blocked in and blocked off. For a number of student readers, poems come indissolubly bonded to explicatory, contextualizing or, at least, biographical prose. Classrooms can not just condition but also contaminate poetry. Despite that danger, there remain people who are interested in taking into poetry kinds of knowledge most readily accessible through the channels of the modern university. To give two examples from my own student days, there will be poet-academics such as Norman MacCaig at Stirling University who drew his salary from an academic institution but liked to present himself in his verse and his person as anti-academic; on the other hand, there will also be poet-academics like Edwin Morgan at Glasgow University who made unashamed use of the world of knowledge and information in which his professional life was led.

The professional lives of poets in academia involve some of the most valuable human resources: imagination and literary expression. It is important that courses in creative writing are not seen as a soft option or a convalescence. It is equally vital to recognize that they frequently summon highly motivated students whose energy is channelled productively into the shaping and refining of verse. The poet in higher education may share technical advice and solutions. He or she may become tired out by students' demands for more and more close attention. Yet, at root, the poet's presence on campus involves (as in an art college or a music conservatory) the principled and rigorous transmission of a treasured art. The poet works often with students who share a deep love of verse. In the writing classroom, however theoretically informed, such aesthetic essentials as enjambment, word-choice and rhythm can move centre-stage, while in seminar rooms along the corridor they may seem lightly regarded in comparison with other criteria for judging cultural value. The poets' workshop may be a focus for sustaining idealism as well as developing technical skill.

However, the poet in academia is also part of an institutional mechanism. He or she is surrounded by a policed culture of publishing and perishing where the pressured accumulation of printed and electronic texts seems often at odds with writerly ideals or risks. In the wider world of information (a cyber-zone increasingly structured round that internet which depends on a convergence of academic, military and other systems), the poet unites the imaginative skills and gifts of the seer with those of the participant in a sometimes banal virtual-reality environment. Today's poet in academia negotiates between these extremes of vision and screen-bleariness. She or he is familiar with traditional notions, developed by Romanticism, of a poetry alert to the physical and trans-cendental glories of the world. Yet the poet is also shaped, either directly or indirectly, by intellectual phenomena such as poststructuralism and information technology which have moved language into a virtual-reality world severed from the tangible referents assumed by earlier ages. Where structuralism may be seen as belonging to the older, cybernetic order of pre-chip computers, cheques and paper money, poststructuralism is a philosophy in harmony with the deincarnation of knowledge and the proliferation of the virtual-reality domain of information. In this, finances, texts, images and identities are alike produced through 'dematerialized' digital transfer. Even the previously separate areas of human genes and electronic encoding are in convergence. The poet in academia, working in an atmosphere where there remain strains between the older, hierarchical world of 'knowledge' and the newer world of traded 'information', is well placed to register and respond imaginatively to shifts in what we value.

In this essay I write as a poet and critic active in a School of English. I have made poetry out of the environment described above, most recently in *Spirit Machines*.[11] Rather than attempting a wide-scale survey of poetry and academia, a topic on which I have written a prose book, I shall concentrate here on the instance of some contemporary Scottish poets whose exposure to (and sometimes parody of) the pro-cedures of academia heightens their alertness to issues of value in the information age.

The term 'The Informationists' seems to have appeared in print first in 1991. That year the poet-critic Richard Price, a curator of modern British literary manuscripts at the British Library, wrote in a small Oxford magazine an article dealing with a group of Scottish poets part of whose 're-expressing of Scotland is to do with their fascination with information itself'.[12] The title 'Informationist' has resurfaced elsewhere in discussions of modern Scottish poetry. The 'alternative' British poetry magazine *Angel Exhaust*, in an issue which brought together Scottish poets and Language-related work, commented in its introduction that some of the Scottish poets'

'Informationist' tag indicates their overt interest in the movement of information in society and particularly the information that is prevented from moving. They are creating new senses of social

[11] Robert Crawford, *Spirit Machines* (Cape, 1999).
[12] Richard Price, 'The Informationists', *interference*, 1 (Oxford, 1991), 13.

history and self-critical explorations of national identity – crucially through their fascinating linguistic position.[13]

Here it is implied that 'Informationist' poetry relates to politics as well as to 'information' and that the two may be connected. It is evident from their work that these poets are all, in different ways, part of that wider cultural and democratic shift which led, after the high tide of Thatcherism receded, to the birth to the Scottish Parliament in May 1999. The political as well as visionary dimension of recent Scottish poetry is signalled in the title of Daniel O'Rourke's milestone anthology *Dream State: The New Scottish Poets*, first published in 1994. In his introduction O'Rourke sympathetically mentioned Price's designation of a group called 'the "Scottish Informationists", though it remains to be seen whether the label will stick'.[14] Also in 1994, W. N. Herbert and Richard Price co-edited another Scottish anthology, *Contraflow on the Super Highway*, whose introduction, 'Approaching the Informationists', set out a Scottish Informationist stall, seeing Informationism as building on the work of MacDiarmid and Edwin Morgan.[15] While the term 'Informationism' has become useful, its application often has something of a tongue-in-cheek quality. This is unsurprising and it may be that the academically-nurtured poet always balances an impulse to contribute to academia's hoard (its list of supposedly empowering -isms, its love of pattern and classification) with a countering tendency to spoof its procedures, whether with squibs, full-frontal attacks or absolutely straight-faced book chapters.

Some of the younger generation of Scottish poets, which includes Don Paterson, W. N. Herbert, Kathleen Jamie, John Burnside, Peter McCarey, Alan Riach and the present writer, have invited the label 'Informationist'; others have had it thrust upon them. All tend to recognize some truth in aspects of it, at the same time as being wary about having their diverse, if related, poetries boxed-in together. The term 'Scottish Informationist' more accurately represents a number of tendencies present to varying degrees in the work of several writers than it characterizes any 'school'. Richard Price is at once committed and sceptical in his concern that 'the word "Informationism" is such a preposterous – yet serviceable! – phrase, it seems to undermine itself in the short time the reader takes to get from "In" to "ism"'.[16] If Informationism developed in a way that involved small presses linked to such 1980s and 1990s

---

[13] Scott Thurston and Andrew Duncan, 'Introduction', *Angel Exhaust*, 9 (Summer 1993), 4.

[14] Daniel O'Rourke (ed.), *Dream State: The New Scottish Poets* (Edinburgh: Polygon, 1994), Introduction, p. xxiii.

[15] Richard Price, 'Approaching the Informationists' in W. N. Herbert and Richard Price (eds), *Contraflow on the Super Highway* (London: Souhfields Press, 1994).

[16] Ibid., p. i.

magazines as *Verse* and *Gairfish*, then by the mid 1990s the Scottish poets associated with it were also receiving more mainstream attention. In the 1994 'New Generation Poets' promotion run by the Poetry Society and the Arts Council in Britain, seven out of the twenty poets selected were Scottish and almost all of these linked to the Informationist grouping; by 1996 a feature in *The New Yorker* trumpeted a 'Scottish Efflorescence' of prose and poetry, again including Informationist poets, while in the *Times Literary Supplement* the academic Liam McIlvanney drew attention to a MacDiarmid-related 'resurgence in Scottish poetry' that included Informationist poets.[17] By 1997 Informationism was respectable enough to be the subject of a long, commissioned essay by the present writer in the *Times Literary Supplement*.[18]

As one of the poets involved in this so-called 'Scottish Informationism', I certainly recall discussing 'the Informational' with W. N. Herbert when we were Oxford graduate students and fellow fledgling poets in the mid-1980s, but I have been wary of simply signing up to or supplying a simple prose manifesto. Having expressed, in poems from *A Scottish Assembly* (1990) onwards, a strong interest in informational textures, in heteroglossic assembly and in what O'Rourke has called 'modern communications' and the material of 'knowledge engineers', I wish to make it plain here that I write as a scarcely impartial participant whose work may be aligned with that of a gathering of Scottish 'Informationist' poets.[19] The verse or prose of several of the authors I discuss here manifests an academically-developed self-consciousness which will be apparent in my own writing of this piece. Rather than simply trying to conceal that fact (as MacDiarmid did by reviewing his own work under a pseudonym, for instance), it seems best to acknowledge the position and to come to terms with it as part of the cultural space occupied by the academically-nourished poet at the start of the twenty-first century. For writers who are moulded by academia as well as being suspicious of it, the solution to the constant interaction between critical projects and the creation of poetry surely lies not in pretending there is no connection between the two, but in coming to terms with the fact that such a relationship often exists and in trying to make positive use of the linkage. One sees this happening in practice in earlier centuries, as well as in recent instances as different as Geoffrey Hill and Tom Paulin, Adrienne Rich and Eavan Boland. While no writer is a fully trustworthy critic of his or her work, the modern culture of 'live' readings and interviews encourages self-reflection. The

---

[17] See the New Generation Poets Special Issue of *Poetry Review*, 84:1 (Spring 1994); Alan Taylor, 'Scottish Efflorescence', *The New Yorker*, Double Issue 25 December 1995 and 1 January 1996, p. 97; Liam McIlvanney, 'New Caledonian', *TLS*, 20 December 1996, p. 22.

[18] Robert Crawford, 'The Computer and the Painted Pict', *TLS*, 15 August 1997, pp. 4–5.

[19] O'Rourke, *Dream State*, Introduction, pp. xxiii and xxv.

dangers involved are narcissism and solipsism. The presence of poets on campus can sometimes further such risks, so that it may be necessary to develop defence mechanisms in order to escape inhibiting self-consciousness. On the other hand, there are times when self-awareness must be acknowledged as part of the work in hand. I write this essay not with the aim of boxing-in the interpretation of my own verse or that of my contemporaries, but in the hope of providing hints and provocations that other readers may build on, erode or demolish.

The contemporary Scottish poets who have been called the 'Informationists' all express some hesitation about that label. Yet their poetic personalities have been shaped by a simultaneous awareness of developing in a politically exciting country of parallel texts, of different literatures and languages operating simultaneously as 'Scottish literature' and in an age marked by an informational consciousness that can be related to Scottish antecedents. These might include the eighteenth-century Scottish Enlightenment 'databases' of the *Encyclopaedia Britannica* and *The Statistical Account of Scotland* or the science of James Clerk Maxwell, Alexander Graham Bell and John Logie Baird. At the same time, this new Scottish poetry owes as much to contemporary electronic media and computer technology, the 'spirit machines' of our age.

If Scottish Informationism as an aegis was developed in Oxford where several of these Scottish poets were graduate students in the 1980s, it should be seen as taking, as a crucial point of departure, the work of the poet Edwin Morgan, who taught English Literature at Glasgow University from 1947 until 1980. Morgan's earlier poetry may have influenced the Informationists most strongly, but the title of his 1997 collection *Virtual and Other Realities* indicates how attuned to their concerns he remains. As poet, critic and university teacher, Morgan matured a poetry of knowledge. He had learned from MacDiarmid, yet produced verse which was much more ludic and accessible than the older poet's late work. In such poems as 'Canedolia' (using listings of Scottish place names), 'The Computer's First Christmas Card' (simulating computer-generated text) and 'Pleasures of a Technological University', Morgan hymned the possibilities of a poetry of knowledge in the early information age of the 1960s and 1970s:

> magnesium and Crashaw
> semiotics and ergonomics
> lasers and caesuras
> retro-rockets and peripeteia[20]

---

[20] Edwin Morgan, 'Pleasures of a Technological University', *Collected Poems* (Manchester: Carcanet, 1990), p. 275.

Intellectually-informed, academically-nurtured yet also carnivalesque, Morgan produced a protean body of verse – concrete poetry, sound poems, sonnets, narratives, science fiction poems and translations – which linked MacDiarmid's cerebral adventure to popular concerns. He has been hailed by Daniel O'Rourke as a key figure for the younger generation of Scottish poets; his work has been discussed in detail elsewhere and is seen as crucial in the most recent history of Scottish literature.[21] It is significant, for instance, that Morgan has had a long-standing interest in the work of experimental poets, including those in and linked to the Language poetry movement. This has been accompanied by a strong commitment to the articulation of Scottish identities and of the political aspirations which eventually resulted in the setting up of the Edinburgh Parliament. He has published aleatory pieces which relate to his concern with Jackson MacLow, as well as many poems on explicitly Scottish themes, sometimes deploying experimental techniques but also using such traditional forms as the sonnet or elegy. An accomplished translator from many languages (he has produced dazzling Scots versions of Mayakovsky), Morgan is attracted to the Language poets less because he senses 'a poet-critic bringing both aspects into ... creative writing' than because he recognizes

> a coming together of genuine strangeness, *ostranenie* as the Russian Formalists used to call it, defamiliarization, often in practice the sudden disjunctions of thought or syntax loved by the 'language' poets, and at the same time an interest in prodding at new boundaries of subject-matter which seems refreshing and forward-looking.[22]

The features to which Morgan here responds are characteristics of his own poetry, and of the verse of Hugh MacDiarmid. They are also aspects to the fore in the Informationists' work. The younger Scottish poets, though, tend to follow Morgan's lead in linking experiment to popular tradition, producing a poetry that is often intellectually ambitious but also more accessible, not to mention funnier, than that of most Language poets.

Don Paterson (b. 1963) did not study at university, though he worked in the mid-1990s as Writer in Residence at the University of Dundee. He writes a poetry that is both acutely self-conscious and preoccupied with mixing kinds of knowledge or information. When, in his first book, *Nil Nil* (1993), he opens 'The Alexandrian Library' with a quotation about

---

[21] O'Rourke, *Dream State*, Introduction, pp. xvi, xxiii, xxix; Robert Crawford and Hamish Whyte (eds), *About Edwin Morgan* (Edinburgh: Edinburgh University Press, 1990); Marshall Walker, *Scottish Literature since 1707* (London: Longmans, 1997).

[22] Edwin Morgan, *Language, Poetry, and Language Poetry* (Liverpool: Liverpool Classical Monthly, 1990), p. 15.

'retrieval' (a term now increasingly linked with 'information' and computing) from the *Pensées* of Francois Aussemain, he is attuned to Informationist strategies:

> Nothing is ever lost; things only become irretrievable. What is lost, then, is the method of their retrieval, and what we rediscover is not the thing itself, but the overgrown path, the secret staircase, the ancient sewer.[23]

What follows is an amazing spoil-heap of a poem when, in a second-hand bookshop in the small Scottish town of Cowdenbeath, the speaker discovers a hilarious information overload of lost texts, ranging from '*The Story of Purfling*' to '*16 RPM – a Selective Discography*' and '*Urine – The Water of Life*'.[24] From one angle, this is a parodic replay of the bibliographies that form part of MacDiarmid's late poetry. Yet this huge, fading book-hoard is also akin to the kind of spoil-heaps found in other Scottish Informationist poets' work. So 'Mr and Mrs Scotland are Dead' from *The Queen of Sheba* (1994) by Kathleen Jamie (b. 1962) offers us a rubbish tip in which artefacts and bits of text are strewn together:

> old ladies' bags, open mouthed, spew
> postcards sent from small Scots towns
> in 1960: Peebles, Largs, the rock-gardens
> of Carnoustie, tinted in the dirt.
> Mr and Mrs Scotland, here is the hand you were dealt:
> *fair but cool, showery but nevertheless,*
> *Jean asks kindly; the lovely scenery;*
> in careful school-room script –
> *The Beltane Queen was crowned today.*
> But Mr and Mrs Scotland are dead.
>
> Couldn't he have burned them? Released
> in a grey curl of smoke
> this pattern for a cable knit? Or this:
> tossed between a toppled fridge
> and sweet-stinking anorak: *Dictionary for Mothers*
> M:– Milk, *the woman who worries . . . ;*
> And here, Mr Scotland's John Bull Puncture Repair Kit . . . [25]

---

[23] Don Paterson, 'The Alexandrian Library', *Nil Nil* (London: Faber and Faber, 1993), p. 25.

[24] Ibid., p. 29.

[25] Kathleen Jamie, 'Mr and Mrs Scotland are Dead', *The Queen of Sheba* (Newcastle-upon-Tyne: Bloodaxe, 1994), p. 37.

Presented in the period before the struggle for political devolution was successful, Jamie's heaped fragments, like Paterson's yellowing second-hand books, speak of a Scotland dated, in danger of becoming a provincial backwater, crammed with a glut of texts and information that appears useless, yet has an oddly persisting fascination. This may be related to the slightly earlier poems of Paterson's fellow Dundonian W. N. Herbert (b. 1961), such as 'The Anthropological Museum', written in the 1980s:

> 'mye ham dila' ... 'ghost mucus': a stone tusk;
> a leathern belt is worn by girls during 'tsaranche'
> ... 'active flirtation', dangling with 'iayoyi':
> incantations to prevent conception ... seed capsules
> of *martynia sp.*: a charm against snakebites, on
> the principle of 'the doctrine of signatures' ... [26]

Here, in a poem partly in thrall to James Fenton's 'The Pitt-Rivers Museum, Oxford', Herbert presents yet another spoil-heap, this time not an explicitly Scottish one. Yet in a Scottish context it can be related to concerns about pre-Parliamentary Scotland as a museum-culture and to a number of poems with museum and anthropological resonance which Herbert and the present writer were then writing. These poems appeared in such collections as *Other Tongues* (1990), *Sharawaggi* (1990), *A Scottish Assembly* (1990), *Talkies* (1992), *Forked Tongue* (1992) and *Cabaret McGonagall* (1996).[27] As some of their titles indicate, these works involve not only spoil-heaps of (often dated) information, but also sharawaggies or assemblies of unusually varied language. Herbert, who has half-seriously defined Informationism as *'the aesthetic of the definition'*, in particular revels in the dictionary trawling carried out by MacDiarmid (the subject of Herbert's Oxford DPhil thesis and his 1992 critical book *To Circumjack MacDiarmid*), yet does so with a media-saturated postmodern edge.[28]

[26] W. N. Herbert, 'The Anthropological Museum' in Robert Crawford (ed.), *Other Tongues: Young Scottish Poets in English, Scots, and Gaelic* (St Andrews: Verse, 1990), p. 35.

[27] James Fenton, 'The Pitt-Rivers Museum, Oxford', *The Memory of War and Children in Exile: Poems 1968–1983* (Harmondsworth: Penguin, 1983), pp. 81–4; Robert Crawford (ed.), *Other Tongues*; Robert Crawford and W. N. Herbert, *Sharawaggi* (Edinburgh: Polygon, 1990); Robert Crawford, *A Scottish Assembly* (London: Chatto and Windus, 1990); Robert Crawford, *Talkies* (London: Chatto and Windus, 1992); W. N. Herbert, *Forked Tongue* (Newcastle-upon-Tyne: Bloodaxe, 1992); W. N. Herbert, *Cabaret McGonagall* (Newcastle-upon-Tyne: Bloodaxe, 1996).

[28] W. N. Herbert, 'A Defence of Noetry' in W. N. Herbert and Richard Price (eds), *Contraflow on the Super Highway* (London: Southfields Press and *Gairfish*, 1994), p. xiii; W. N. Herbert, *To Circumjack MacDiarmid: The Poetry and Prose of T. S. Eliot* (Oxford: Clarendon Press, 1992).

In Herbert's earlier Scots work, glossaries threaten to overwhelm the poems. This seems part of the game: an intertextuality both dated and postmodern, English and Scots running in parallel, mutual interference as branches of a 'forked tongue'. In his more recent poems, the demotic edge is stronger, the street beating the dictionary in a Scots poetry which nonetheless remains a postmodern linguistic spoil-heap. Like most of the other poets who can be called Scottish Informationists, Herbert is happy to be humorous in both his poetry and his prose. Yet, after virtually denying that the movement exists, the definition of Informationism which he supplies is as good as any:

> Although Informationism is just something everybody does (as John Ashbery remarked, 'Everybody's a Surrealist now'), the Informationists as a unit are Scottish, male, and generally suffering from Post-Academic Trauma (not so Post-, in some cases). So that means we have a particular heritage, and a particular agenda. The heritage is, in a nutshell: Davidson, MacDiarmid, Morgan; writers who all establish that it is vital to examine what we mean by, as well as what we feel about, knowledge. ... Davidson laid down that agenda in his *Testaments* and his magnificent posthumous volume, *Fleet Street and Other Poems*: an urban poetry, a scientific poetry, a poetry that engages with contemporary metaphysics, and a poetry that can manipulate a prose voice.[29]

Herbert's words apply with varying degrees of appropriateness to the poets here discussed. All have worked in academia. Several have produced substantial critical volumes. All seem determined to make use of voices and subject matter which may include the academic, yet which also go beyond it. Herbert's poetry can have a donnishness about it which puts off some readers, just as Don Paterson's sly and hard donnishness (which partly Scotticizes Paul Muldoon's work) can be rebarbative. Alert readers will soon come to realize that Paterson's favourite philosopher, Aussemain, is his own invention, as are several of the poets whose work he claims to translate. This Ossianic game-playing happens quite a lot in modern Scottish poetry. It may be related to the uncertain status of Scotland itself, existing as a nation but not as a state, a name without full substance. This is Scotland the 'Dream State' of O'Rourke's anthology, whose punning title comes from a poem by Stuart Paterson about Scotland as 'a massive upset dustbin'.[30] The 'Dream State' is also the Edinburgh reflected and

---

[29] Herbert, 'A Defence of Noetry', p. xv.
[30] Stuart Paterson, 'Dream State' in O'Rourke (ed.), *Dream State*, p. 218.

made spectral in Robin Robertson's poem-and-document sequence 'Camera Obscura' or the 'Virtual Scotland' jokily explored by Herbert, a national 'Never Never Land'.[31] Such neverland notions were a frequent topic of conversation among several of the younger Scottish poets throughout the 1980s and early 1990s. In 1991, for instance, an interview between Herbert and John Burnside (poet and computer systems expert) included a discussion of Palestine which, as Burnside pointed out, 'existed and it didn't exist'; Herbert soon picked up on this as 'a real Scottish theme … you recreate your country, you create an independent space for your country in fiction'.[32] Informationist poems are full of cultural uncertainty and displacement. Jamie writes poems in Scots about her travels in Tibet; her book *The Autonomous Region* (1993) refers to that land, yet is shaped by her own Scottishness, while her unScottish-sounding collection *The Queen of Sheba* (1994) is preoccupied with the articulation of Scottish identity. In the Scottish and extra-Scottish hybrid text *Paris-Forfar* (1994), David Kinloch (b. 1959, a poet, founding editor of *Verse* and a teacher of French literature at the University of Strathclyde) writes of the strangeness of old Scots words in postmodern Paris:

> These words are as foreign as the city they have parachuted into, dead words slipping on the sill of a living metropolis. They are extremes that touch like dangerous wires and the only hope for them, for us, is the space they inhabit, a room veering between dilettantism and dynamite.[33]

The political and cultural situation of Scotland during the 1990s in the period culminating in the successful struggle for the establishment of a Scottish Parliament certainly conditions such Informationist concerns. They are also moulded surely by an increasing awareness of technologies of information – Sony Walkmen, televisions, semiconductors are not hard to spot in this poetry which can be both streetwise and moving, as well as cerebrally adventurous. Paterson, whose 'failure' at school meant university was not an option, describes the demanding intellectuality of his poetry as to some extent an outsmarting of academia – 'the autodidact's

---

[31] Robin Robertson, 'Camera Obscura', *A Painted Field* (London: Picador, 1997), pp. 59–93; see the series of 'Virtual Scotland' pieces by Herbert in the magazine *Gairfish* between 1991 and 1993; Robert Crawford, 'Scotland in the 1890s', *A Scottish Assembly* (London: Chatto and Windus, 1990), p. 22.

[32] John Burnside, interviewed by W. N. Herbert in Robert Crawford, Henry Hart, David Kinloch and Richard Price (eds), *Talking Verse: Interviews with Poets* (St Andrews and Williamsburg, 1995), p. 41.

[33] David Kinloch, *Paris-Forfar* (Edinburgh: Polygon, 1994), p. 30 ('Dustie-Fute').

revenge. You throw in stuff when you know that no one will know what you are on about.'[34]

The title of Paterson's *God's Gift to Women* (1997) balances between vaunt and self-laceration. It signals his concerns with themes of sex and gender variously treated by the Scottish poets of his generation in such works as Carol Ann Duffy's *The Other Country* (1990), Jackie Kay's textual assembly *The Adoption Papers* (1991), David Kinloch's dictionaried and lyrical *Paris-Forfar* (1994), Kathleen Jamie's *The Queen of Sheba* (1994), the present writer's *Masculinity* (1996), W. N. Herbert's 'Featherhood' and 'The Informationist's Love Song' (1996), not to mention recent Scottish novels, like Duncan MacLean's *Bunker Man* (1995), and the prose fictions of Janice Galloway, Jackie Kay and A. L. Kennedy. It would be hard to argue that these works were unconnected to the preoccupation with gender in modern higher education. Scottish literary academia in the same period was producing such works as *Tea and Leg-Irons: New Feminist Readings from Scotland* (1992), edited by Caroline Gonda, the 'gender issue' of the interdisciplinary critical magazine *Scotlands* (1994), *Gendering the Nation* (1995), edited by the poet, novelist and academic Christopher Whyte, and the *History of Scottish Women's Writing* (1997), edited by Douglas Gifford and Dorothy McMillan. Few who were present at the conference on 'Scottish Masculinity' at St Andrews University in 1994 will forget Kathleen Jamie's injunction to Scottish men to 'go away and rethink yourselves'. Some commentators might be inclined to suggest that poetry and 'theory' should be seen as antagonistic. They would do well to reflect on the close relationship between the two in this area of Scottish writing. Gender, at least as much as nationalism, has become an important theme for the new generation of Scottish writers. The poets who may be grouped as Informationists bring to it a postmodern consciousness of living in a technological information-saturated society, whether that of Jamie's 'Ultrasound' sequence, Paterson's camcorder sex in 'Postmodern' or Herbert's 'starin thru a screen' and 'lukean fur the sonar ding' of a foetal scan.[35] These poets delight in incorporating into their poetry advanced technologies as well as basic emotions and imaginative refashionings of the way assumptions about gender assign value to people. Characteristically they produce an amalgam of, on the one hand, traditionally poetic and popular forms (including some derived from as familiar Scottish sources as Robert Burns and the Ballads) with, on the other hand, a revelling in mixing or remixing kinds of Scottish language in

---

[34] Paterson in Sally Kinnes, 'Poet with Mission to Bring Lonely Words into Contact', *Scotsman*, 24 January 1998, p. 15.
[35] Herbert, 'Featherhood', *Cabaret McGonagall*, p. 19.

a fashion consciously attuned to the information age and the technologies of academia. Their ideal poet is a shaman with a PhD.

Historically Scots has been a form of language repressed in Scotland by the academic system as 'barbarian'. These poets' use of it can be viewed sometimes as a gesture of sophisticatedly calculated 'primitivism' and, in a British context, their explicit Scottishness might be seen as a claim to a kind of empowering 'marginalization'. Yet, rather than being self-marginalized, the Informationist poets tend to be confidently Scottish, even in their criticisms of Scotland, while maintaining an alert internationalism. This is evident in the principal Scottish-international magazine in which they have published, the university-based *Verse*, as well as in other periodicals sympathetic to the group, such as *Southfields* and *Gairfish*. Their Scotland is sometimes one reflected back from London, Oxford, even from Strasbourg (base of Iain Bamforth), Geneva (base of Peter McCarey) or New Zealand, where the poet and MacDiarmid editor Alan Riach worked before his recent return to Scotland. Yet this assembly of poets, some based outside Scotland, some in that country, projects clear Scottish accents. Geographically, there is a concentration around the St Andrews-Dundee area, home either as birthplace or residence to Burnside, Herbert, Jamie, Paterson and the present writer. Cultural incest, a phenomenon common to many literary groupings, might be seen as a threat here, and there are plenty of signs not only of stylistic and thematic links between these poets, but also other ley lines and publishing matrices which connect them. Whether such relationships should be seen as criminal inbreeding or as the kind of network of mutual stimulation, friendship and rivalry, not unfamiliar among writers of verse or among academics, remains to be seen.

Certainly the connections among these authors, their links with universities and the conversations observable between their books mean that they exist as modern poets in a particularly self-conscious sense. They are well aware of their own status as Scottish, as heteroglot, as marginal yet cosmopolitan, as attracted to the textures of information as well as lyricism. Such self-consciousness may be the lot of postmodern poets everywhere. Around the world verse is alert not only to poetic heritages but also to a multiply-reflecting screen culture of information which surrounds it and of which it is a part. In recent Scottish poetry, though, self-consciousness both inhibits and encourages an involved scrutinizing of the grounds of political and cultural identity, linguistic identity, gender identity and poetic style. The poets may attempt to escape from interrogating these, yet to these they continually return. Scottish Informationist work exists not simply in some institutional and denationalized informational cyberspace. It often burns most brightly where such a zone intersects with and is embodied in figures, voices and accents with a strong Scottish cultural resonance. Media and information-intensified self-consciousness is the lot of the new millennium's poets, bound up with and exploiting, though also suspicious of, marketing and academic or straightforwardly commercial commodification.

The critically-trained, often academically employed, writer observing the creation of his or her own work seeks simultaneously a sophisticated mastery over the creative process and a blind, no-questions-asked surrender to it. A balancing of academic participation and calculating evasiveness (preserving, in the institutional corridors, what Edwin Morgan has called the poet-academic's 'certain modicum of unassimilability') is a necessary juggling act for the poet in today's classrooms.[36] For some in our postmodern age, academically-tinged knowledge and what it was once conventional to call inspiration seem frequently indissoluble. Informationism may be a striking manifestation of this. Particularly if he or she works in academia, the poet cannot simply contend that the age of information with all its computers, databases, televisions and technology did not happen but can seek to locate, in that informational world, a sense of spirituality which maintains an apprehension of the human and the spiritual among the machines that humans invented.

That very notion of invention, so important to the poetic imagination and often touched on by the Informationists, may be a way of signalling in a machine world the persistence of spirit. The introduction to *The Penguin Book of Poetry from Britain and Ireland since 1945*, which I co-edited with Simon Armitage, champions a belief in poetry's ability to trip its readers into 'an otherworld potent with spiritual experience'.[37] MacDiarmid, Morgan and other modern Scottish poets have been attracted to seeing a common ground in the imagination which links the scientific to the poetic, each being a form of creativity. What the contemporary poet may need to do is develop this vision of creativity to locate a sense of numinous presence in the cyberworld of information or show how such a cyberworld can function as a symbol, metaphor or token of spiritual life. Increasingly the sophisticated and intelligent seem more and more bound up with electronics and machines, with information that is digitally or genetically encoded. We need to articulate what it is that both marks out the human spirit from the machine and leads the two towards convergence. To present refreshingly a sense of such issues and sensations would seem a good way in which to be a poet who had learned from as well as inhabited the big machine of the academy.

---

[36] Edwin Morgan, *Nothing Not Giving Messages: Reflections on Life and Work* (Edinburgh: Polygon, 1990), p. 194.

[37] Robert Crawford and Simon Armitage (eds), *The Penguin Book of Poetry from Britain and Ireland since 1945* (Harmondsworth: Penguin, 1998), 'Introduction: The Democratic Voice', p. xix.

5

The Rhetoric of Value in Recent British Poetry Anthologies

Andrew Michael Roberts

I

Anthologies are liable to claim that they represent the literary values of a particular culture at a certain moment in history. However, they are also sites for the definition and propounding of new values. Anthologists usually register, in their introductions, some tension between the two alternatives: the claim to present work which is indicative of prevailing values and the impulse to create new standards of value and, thereby, bring to public notice new talents or new versions of literary history. The roles of cultural historian and promoter of a particular group or movement sit uneasily together, and editors often seem obliged, perhaps against their will or at least against their better judgement, to attempt to square the two by making implausible or tendentious claims for the unique historical significance of the particular literary or aesthetic values with which their selection of poets is associated. In post-war British poetry such attempts begins with Robert Conquest's *New Lines* (1956), with its sweeping if vague claim that 'a general tendency has once again set in, and ... a genuine and healthy poetry of the new period has established itself'.[1] Several anthologies continued this rhetorical stance – Alvarez's *The New Poetry* (1962, 1966), *The Penguin Book of Contemporary British Poetry* (Morrison and Motion, 1982) and *The New Poetry* (Hulse, Kennedy and Morley, 1993) – in a sequence which is part apostolic succession, part a series of what Alvarez called 'negative feed-backs' (reaction against one's predecessors).[2] These anthologies and their claims have been subjected to analysis and critique and even a

---

[1] Robert Conquest, Introduction to *New Lines: An Anthology* (London: Macmillan, 1956), p. xi.

[2] A. Alvarez, 'The New Poetry, or Beyond the Gentility Principle', Introduction to *The New Poetry* (Harmondsworth: Penguin, 1962; revised edition, 1966), p. 21; Blake Morrison and Andrew Motion (eds), *The Penguin Book of Contemporary British Poetry* (London: Penguin, 1982); Michael Hulse, David Kennedy and David Morley (eds), *The New Poetry* (Newcastle-upon-Tyne: Bloodaxe, 1993).

certain amount of derision. Other anthologists have sought, by various strategies, to evade the double bind of typicality and novelty: *A Various Art* (Crozier and Longville, 1987), *The New British Poetry* (Allnutt, D'Aguiar, Edwards and Mottram, 1988), *Conductors of Chaos* (Sinclair, 1996) and *Other: British and Irish Poetry since 1970* (Caddel and Quartermain, 1999) are marked, rhetorically or structurally, by the wish to disavow some of the impositions of value associated with anthology-making.[3] Broadly speaking, the anthologies in the first sequence are committed to an idea of a mainstream, while those belonging to the second sequence are hostile to it (though in some sense tied to the concept by that very hostility). The primary locus of value in the first sequence is that of the generation or movement; in the second sequence it is that of oppositionality or self-definition *against* a cultural dominant. Secondary criteria of value are, however, also evoked in these anthologies, reinforcing or at times lying athwart these primary loci. There exists a standard repertoire of value criteria upon which most anthologists draw, with varying degrees of explicitness: novelty (the 'new' poetry), innovation (the technically new poetry), traditionalism (the organic line of value), representativeness (the poets of a social group, a geographical area or a generation), oppositionality (the poetry of dissent), centrality (the 'mainstream'), marginality (in opposition to the mainstream), inclusiveness (range and variety), exclusiveness (*not* some particular style or aesthetic, usually presented as superseded). The awareness of this repertoire generates a second double bind for the anthologist: that of multiple versus singular value, which, in this context (the context of selection), acts as the key manifestation of the general philosophical antinomy between relative and absolute value. Anthology introductions therefore also register the tension between recognising and responding to diversity and the claim to be operating some universal, neutral criteria of quality equally applicable, at least in principle, to all poetry. On the one hand, the aim of offering the reader as much as possible and the wish to assert the wealth and range of poetry encourages the deployment of multiple forms of value, an openness to varieties of poetry which may ask to be read according to differing protocols of reading, with differing forms of evaluation attached. On the other hand, the implicit claim of cultural authority imposed by the act of selecting, editing and publishing, together with the persistent dominance of an ideology of singular value in public literary debate (masked but not effaced by a supposed 'postmodernist'

[3] Andrew Crozier and Tim Longville (eds), *A Various Art* (Manchester: Carcanet, 1987; London: Paladin, 1990); Gillian Allnutt, Fred D'Aguiar, Ken Edwards and Eric Mottram (eds), *The New British Poetry 1968–88* (London: Paladin, 1988); Iain Sinclair (ed.), *Conductors of Chaos* (London: Picador, 1996); Richard Caddel and Peter Quartermain (eds), *Other: British and Irish Poetry since 1970* (Hanover and London: Wesleyan University Press/University Press of New England, 1999).

ideology of multiplicity and plurality), creates an inertial drag towards a singular hierarchy between the good and the bad. Few anthologists can resist the implication that, whatever other criteria of selection they have applied, some notion of pure 'quality' is in operation.

Anthology editing, and especially the composing of introductions, therefore, implicitly raises theoretical and philosophical issues of literary and cultural value which, however, cannot generally receive much discussion in an anthology, given the nature of the genre and the imperatives of space and publishing strategies. Partly for this reason, it is very easy to attack or deride anthologies (a fact which reviewers often exploit): almost any anthology can be attacked for its omissions and most anthology introductions are obliged to make claims which are readily open to challenge. While the anthologies which I shall discuss vary considerably in their aesthetic allegiances, their cultural politics and the subtlety and cogency of their claims, the same tensions between novelty and typicality and between multiple and singular value tend to recur, albeit with differing degrees of obliquity. My purpose in pointing this out is not to attack anthology-making in general, nor to deride particular anthologists. Neither would I seek to reduce the important divergences between these various anthologies. Rather I am interested in the ways in which the wider cultural meanings attached to poetry, especially the paradoxical tendency of our culture simultaneously to overvalue and to undervalue it, are registered in these competing accounts of poetry 'now' (since any anthology which is not historical always seems to assert some special relation to the moment of the contemporary).

I shall discuss first some of the more recent of the 'generational' anthologies that I have listed, then consider their relationship to some of the anthologies based around ideas of oppositionality, before concluding with reference to three recent anthologies with a wider historical scope, *The Penguin Book of Poetry from Britain and Ireland since 1945* (Armitage and Crawford, 1998), *The Firebox: Poetry in Britain and Ireland after 1945* (O'Brien, 1998) and *Anthology of Twentieth-Century British and Irish Poetry* (Tuma, 2000).[4] The similarity of many of the titles, particularly of the more mainstream anthologies, is often integral to their rhetorical strategies. To avoid confusion, anthologies will here in general be referred to by the names of the editors.

The idea of generations as a locus of value in poetry requires a certain simplification and homogenization of poetry, both synchronically (at a

---

[4] Simon Armitage and Robert Crawford (eds), *The Penguin Book of Poetry from Britain and Ireland since 1945* (Harmondsworth: Penguin, 1998); Sean O'Brien (ed.), *The Firebox: Poetry in Britain and Ireland after 1945* (London: Picador, 1998); Keith Tuma, *Anthology of Twentieth-Century British and Irish Poetry* (New York and Oxford: Oxford University Press, 2000).

given cultural moment) and diachronically (over time). It tends to rely upon some sense of a single 'mainstream' of poetry, within which a succession of generations arise, each displacing the previous one. A real sense of the multiplicity of overlapping, diverging, competing or mutually indifferent strands in poetry would make generations, as such, of limited importance. Poets come to maturity at different ages, have different phases in their work, have long or short writing careers and may respond to successors as well as to predecessors. Sometimes, of course, a number of poets of similar age move in a similar direction at the same time, in a way which seems responsive to what is going on in the culture around them, but, to show the significance of such a phenomenon, one would need to deploy the poetic equivalent of Raymond Williams's trilogy of the residual, the dominant and the emergent.[5] The generational approach is more or less committed to the cultural hegemony of the young (though 'young' in this context might mean as old as forty).

The tensions produced by this approach are evident in the rhetorical manoeuvres used by editors to justify their choices. For example, the first sentence of the preface to Hulse et al.'s *The New Poetry* (1993) contains a crucial ambiguity: 'This anthology represents what we believe to be the best poetry written in the British Isles in the 1980s and early 1990s by a distinctive new generation of poets.'[6] Does this mean that the editors believe *all* the best poetry written in the British Isles in this period was written by this generation or merely that they have selected the best work of this generation, even if it is less good than other work written at the same time? Presumably the latter must be the real meaning but the former is sufficiently present to make it sound as if all of the 'best' poetry is being included. The way in which the sentence finesses the distinction between absolute and relative value and between the values of typicality and novelty is a common response to the dilemma faced by any editors wanting to make their selection representative of some cultural or literary change or moment: what to do about all the poetry which doesn't fit? The claim by Hulse et al. to represent poetry which is indicative of changes in wider culture rests in part on the idea of plurality itself:

> Throughout the century, the hierarchies of values that once made stable poetics possible have been disappearing. In the absence of shared moral and religious ideas, common social or sexual *mores* or political ideologies, or any philosophy on the conduct of life, plurality has flourished.[7]

[5]   See Raymond Williams, *Culture* (Glasgow: Fontana, 1981), Chapter 6, 'Forms', pp. 148–80.
[6]   Hulse et al., *The New Poetry*, p. 14
[7]   Ibid., p. 15.

Like other generalisations in the introduction, this is both overstated and soon contradicted: the next paragraph mentions Thatcherism, hardly evidence for the disappearance of political ideologies (Thatcherism was of course not universally 'shared' – but which ideology ever has been?). Leaving aside issues of historical plausibility, though, one might wonder, if hierarchies of value have dissolved into plurality, what is the hierarchy of value which enables the editors to determine their choice as simply 'the best'? Hulse et al. go on to explain their criteria for inclusion in their 'new generation': a poet has to be born in or after 1940 and *not* to have been included in *The Penguin Book of Contemporary British Poetry*, edited by Morrison and Motion. This repeats the tactics of that earlier volume, which excluded poets who had been in Alvarez's *The New Poetry*, as well as 'work by poets … who belong to older poetic generations than those we wish to represent', exclusions which Morrison and Motion gloss, slightly evasively, as dictated by 'various practical considerations' (presumably cost and space). At the same time, Morrison and Motion claim that their anthology 'illustrates what [they] believe to be the most important achievements and developments in British poetry during recent years'.[8] So, for both Morrison and Motion and Hulse et al., the need to claim the centrality of their poets, based on the 'universal' value of what is 'important' or 'the best', rather than merely representativeness of a particular aesthetic, when combined with the claim for novelty underlying their systematic exclusions, locks them into the indefensible implication that no older poets and no poets who were selected by their predecessors have produced significant recent work. These policies of exclusion mean that poets such as Michael Hamburger, Christopher Middleton, Charles Tomlinson, Iain Crichton Smith, Thom Gunn, Jon Silkin and Geoffrey Hill, having been included by Alvarez while in their thirties, with much of their oeuvre as yet unwritten, are automatically excluded from Morrison and Motion, while a poet such as Paul Muldoon, whose work might have given more substance to Hulse et al.'s allusions to postmodernism, is absent from their selection, though cited prominently in the introduction.

The tactic of frankly admitting exclusion while claiming representativeness can be traced back another step to Alvarez, who asserts that 'I am … simply attempting to give my idea of what, that really matters, has happened to poetry in England during the last decade'. However, he begins by stating that his is a 'personal anthology' not 'a sample of every kind of verse now being written in Great Britain', citing the more modest aim of 'trying to represent what I think is the most significant work of the British poets who began to come into their own in the fifties'.[9] Though he

---

[8] Morrison and Motion, *The Penguin Book*, p. 10.
[9] Alvarez, *The New Poetry*, 'Prefatory Note', p. 17.

excludes 'new work by poets whose reputations were made before 1950', he includes poets who had been in the Movement anthology, *New Lines*, such as Philip Larkin, Donald Davie, D. J. Enright, Kingsley Amis and Thom Gunn, and this despite his famous polemical introduction attacking the 'gentility' of Movement poetry.[10] This allows him a greater honesty about the tricky relationship between cultural generalizations and aesthetic judgements on individual poems. If Alvarez is sweeping with the former ('Once upon a time, the English could safely believe that Evil was something that happened on the Continent'), he is more careful with the latter.[11] Setting Philip Larkin's 'At Grass' alongside Ted Hughes's 'A Dream of Horses' in order to assert the greater power and depths of the latter, he nevertheless notes some lack of control and pretension in Hughes's poem and some elegant, unpretentious beauty in Larkin's.

Tracing the gestures of inclusion and exclusion back through this sequence of 'generational' anthologies, there is a sense of repeated attempts to square claims of novelty and centrality, attempts which becomes increasingly strained and only sustain themselves, ironically enough, through reference back to the earlier anthologies. Hulse et al. allude to the same Larkin poem ('At Grass') as does Alvarez, one of a number of ways in which they rerun Alvarez's gestures, thus seeming to register the inevitable repetitiveness and circularity of the generational approach. This replication begins with the title, which they 'make no apology for using', continues in their Alvarez-like reckless cultural generalisations ('the hierarchies of value ... have been disappearing') and becomes slightly uncanny when they ask, rhetorically, how British poetry can 'escape [its] negative inheritance ... its ironies, its understatements, its dissipated energies'.[12] For these are more or less standard terms in which to describe and denigrate the Movement. Surely the new young poets of the nineties were not still trying to escape from the conventions (if such they were) of over thirty years earlier? What of the 'decisive shift of sensibility' which Morrison and Motion had claimed for the early 80s?[13] What of Heaney and Hughes, surely the dominant older generation by the early 90s? One can accuse Hughes's poetry of many things but understatement and dissipated energies are not amongst them; nor are these terms applicable to Heaney's poetry. Hulse et al. counterpoise to this supposed negative inheritance, Glyn Maxwell's poetry which they state is 'instantly recognisable as something that has its roots in everyday urban speech'.[14] Yet the same could be said of much of Larkin's poetry, even if it is 50s middle-class urban speech, rather than 90s working-class

[10] Ibid., p. 17.
[11] Ibid., p. 27.
[12] Hulse et al., *The New Poetry*, p. 22.
[13] Morrison and Motion, *The Penguin Book*, p. 11.
[14] Hulse et al., *The New Poetry*, p. 22.

urban speech. The comment on Maxwell is a simplification in any case, since he uses words like 'encircled' and 'bibulous'.[15] Next Hulse et al. cite Peter Reading, praising his 'provocatively ironic demands', even though ironies are one of the things from which the new poetry is supposed to be escaping.[16] It is notable that one of the editors of Hulse et al., David Kennedy, has published a very different and more inflected account of the work of Maxwell and Armitage as representing a poetry of the 'rhetorical imagination' in succession to the 'auditory imagination' of Hill, Heaney and Larkin. This would suggest that the argument of the anthology introduction was dictated less by the editors' real understanding of literary history than by a decision to define the identity of the anthology in terms of a rerunning of Alvarez. One might even detect a certain male Oedipal desire to efface the previous generation, with Hulse et al. bypassing Morrison and Motion to claim continuity with Alvarez, while Morrison and Motion are rather casually dismissive of Alvarez but echo Conquest, who noted that no anthology representing a group had appeared for ten years and claimed to detect a 'general tendency' and 'a genuine and healthy poetry of the new period'; Morrison and Motion begin by claiming a 'shift of sensibility' and suggest that 'it is now twenty years since the last serious anthology of British poetry was published'.[17] If one sought for explanations in the wider culture for these tensions surrounding claims of value, one might well attribute them in part to anxiety in the face of cultural divergences since the Second World War: the erosion of the so-called 'post-war consensus' in politics, the multi-cultural society produced by immigration since the late 1950s and the blurring of state boundaries associated with the European community, with globalization and with devolution. Alvarez writes of what 'really matters' in 'poetry in *England*', Morrison and Motion of 'the most important achievements and developments in *British* poetry', and Hulse et al. of 'the best poetry written in the *British Isles*' (emphases added in each case). That sequence from 'England' (in an anthology which included Iain Crichton Smith and Norman MacCaig) to 'British' (in an anthology which, notoriously, gave central place to Seamus Heaney), to 'the British Isles' tells its own story of increasing self-consciousness about the complexity of cultural identity in the late twentieth century.[18] Hulse et al. do address precisely those questions of multiculturalism, Scottish internationalism, and so on and allude to 'the death of the national consensus'.[19] Certainly, pluralism is the central value espoused by their

---

[15] Glynn Maxwell, 'Helene and Heloise' and 'Love Made Yeah', in Hulse et al., p. 324.

[16] Hulse et al., *The New Poetry*, p. 23.

[17] Conquest, *New Lines*, p. xi; Morrison and Motion, *The Penguin Book*, p. 11.

[18] Heaney famously riposted in verse, 'Be advised! My passport's green'. *An Open Letter* (Field Day Pamphlet no. 2, 1993).

[19] Hulse et al., *The New Poetry*, p. 16.

introduction, while their selected poets are, indeed, reasonably diverse in cultural background. Nevertheless, the repetitiveness of the founding gesture, of the 'new' which is also the 'best' in the culture as a whole, reflects the traditional idea of poetry as a discourse of shared national value. The increasingly desperate insouciance with which such claims are made, the sense that the editors feel obliged to make assertions in which they don't entirely believe, surely reflects the difficulty of maintaining such a discourse. In this respect the rhetoric of anthology introductions comes to resemble that of politics and advertising (which is one reason anthologies attract so much scorn from a certain type of reviewer). Both the ideology of contemporary democratic capitalism and the exigencies of marketing under consumerism require the frequent assertion of what is self-evidently untrue (with a sense that it doesn't matter if most people know it is untrue) and the construction of either false singular shared value or spurious choice and diversity. As an instance of false singular shared value, one could cite politicians who feel obliged to assert that 'parents' want a particular policy or that the country is united in a particular mood or view, whilst desperately trying to maintain votes by straddling divergent interest groups, regions and classes. An instance of spurious diversity would be advertising executives who try to get con-sumers all to buy similar products by stressing that the products are an expression of individuality and difference. Such procedures are indicative of what Steven Connor terms 'the bad paradox of the era of exchange-value, in which diversity acts in the service of uniformity'.[20] In this (present) era, the value of all objects, acts, properties is held by many to be determinable on a single scale of value (money). Poets and critics from certain aesthetic positions (notably that of the avant-garde, of which more shortly), would probably hold that 'mainstream' poetry is all essentially similar, like Gap clothing, that the diversity or plurality invoked by Hulse et al. is spurious. This is itself a simplification – there is considerable diversity there, though within certain limits. The *sense* of a certain uniformity arises less from the characteristics of the poetry than from institutional placing, from conventions and protocols of reading and from the singular terms of exchange which operate within the dominant aesthetic-cultural realm, via those seeming neutral value terms, such as 'important', 'best' and so on. Such terms, like money, serve to 'deny ... the possibility of value while seeming to multiply it'.[21] This effect also extends to certain evacuated and commodified values such as

[20] Steven Connor, *Theory and Cultural Value* (Oxford and Cambridge, MA: Blackwell, 1992), p. 4.
[21] Ibid., p. 4.

'self-expression'.[22] Some critical responses to Hulse et al. asserted the need for singular value in opposition to their stress on multiplicity. John Lucas, in a lively but tendentious essay on 'Value and Validity in Contemporary Poetry', suggests that diversity undermines value itself:

> This is why we can sense a very real anxiety lurking beneath [the editors'] apparent confidence: if the new poetry is remarkable for its diversity, who is to say what, if any of it, is any good? Can aesthetic, or moral, or political or social value have any meaning in a world of poetry which is so emphatically democratic?[23]

Lucas is right, I think, to identify a lurking anxiety on this point, but his conception of its cause involves the assumption that real value has to be singular and absolute, and that, if you allow diverse forms of value, then value itself disappears. Barbara Herrnstein Smith argues for an idea of literary value, as 'not the property of an object *or* of a subject but, rather, *the product of the dynamics of a system*', going on to suggest that 'as readers and critics of literature, we are within that system' and hence we assess the value of a literary work from a particular perspective. However, such an assessment is neither illusory, nor necessarily inaccurate. While 'our experience of "the value of the work" is equivalent to *our experience of the work in relation to the total economy of our existence*', 'our estimate of its probable value for other people may be quite accurate ... [because] the total economy of *their* existence may, in fact, be quite similar to that of our own'.[24] In other words, cultural value is constructed and variable, but it is neither constructed by isolated individuals nor variable in a random and unstable manner. Herrnstein Smith seeks to confront the powerful evidence of the relativity of aesthetic value judgements, while retaining the sense of their importance and insisting that 'relative' or 'contingent' (the two terms which she favours) do not mean subjective and arbitrary. Values are the product of systems involving our own way of being as well as that of others; systems which are deeply embedded in social practices and in human psychology. Anthology-makers are 'within the system' to a notable

---

[22] Geoffrey Hill makes the crucial distinction between 'creative expression of personality' and 'commodity exploitation of personality'. *Viewpoints: Poets in Conversation with John Haffenden* (London: Faber and Faber, 1981, pp. 76–99), p. 87. In publicity and the more superficial forms of criticism, 'self-expression' is often short-hand for commodity exploitation.

[23] John Lucas, 'Value and Validity in Contemporary Poetry', *Critical Survey*, 10.1 (1998), 4–16 (p. 10).

[24] Barbara Herrnstein Smith, *Contingencies of Value: Alternative Perspectives for Critical Theory* (Cambridge, MA and London: Harvard University Press, 1988), pp. 15–16.

degree, participating in the reproduction and modification of cultural value even as they make assertions about it. The tension, which I mentioned at the start of this chapter, between presenting values as culturally given and constructing or changing poetic values, underlies the anxiety detectable in many anthologies, and this is particularly so when plurality is explicitly evoked, because of the reflexive paradox set up when one seeks to assert the multiplication of values *as* a value. But to see this as the destruction of value, as Lucas does, is to miss the point, made by Connor, that there exists an 'imperative to value', an inescapable process in which 'we continue evaluating in the face of every apparently stable and encompassing value in particular', which means continuing 'evaluating values themselves, or value itself'.[25]

I have as yet only mentioned in passing the most systematic exclusion from Morrison and Motion, and Hulse et al., that of what I will for convenience term 'the avant-garde tradition'.[26] Morrison and Motion identified as a period of 'lethargy', when 'very little ... seemed to be happening', the 60s and 70s, a time of exuberant and diverse innovation in avant-garde poetry.[27] Hulse et al. claim to have 'worked with total openness to what is being written', a claim which Robert Sheppard has rightly termed credulous.[28] Despite their optimistic assertion that 'the new poetry highlights the beginning of the end of British poetry's tribal divisions and isolation ... its constituent parts "talk" to one another readily, eloquently and freely while preserving their unique identities', Hulse et al. demonstrate the opposite by their failure to include a whole field of avant-garde work.[29] Yet there are points of congruence with

[25] Connor, *Theory and Cultural Value*, p. 3.

[26] There is, and probably could be, no satisfactory single term to the designate the whole diverse field of poetry (overlapping with performance, music, installations and other art forms), sometimes known as experimental poetry, 'open-form' poetry, LIPS (linguistically-innovative poetry) or avant-garde poetry, a field which has evolved in Britain since the 1960s in parallel to, and influenced by, developments from and around Language poetry in the United States. I use the term 'avant-garde' because, despite the problematic nature of the concept of an avant-garde 'tradition', this work seems to me to share most characteristics of the historical twentieth-century avant-garde in various arts: an emphasis on testing the boundaries and conventions of the medium, a self-reflexive questioning of the concept of art, an anti-establishment political engagement and an inclination to *épater le bourgeois*, a fluid and experimental interaction of different media and art forms, an anti-traditional, anti-conventional rhetoric and a dependence on self-organized performance/display or self-produced and self-distributed publication.

[27] See Robert Hampson and Peter Barry (eds), *New British Poetries: The Scope of the Possible* (Manchester and New York: Manchester University Press, 1993), especially the Introduction (pp. 1–11) and Chapter One, Eric Mottram, 'The British Poetry Revival, 1960–75' (pp. 15–50).

[28] Hulse et al., *The New Poetry*, p. 14; Robert Sheppard, 'Elsewhere and Everywhere: Other New (British) Poetries', *Critical Survey*, 10.1 (1998), 17–32 (p. 19).

[29] Hulse et al., *The New Poetry*, p. 16. See Sheppard, 'Elsewhere and Everywhere, p. 19.

avant-garde positions in their introduction. In a crucial 'alternative' or oppositional anthology, *The New British Poetry* (Allnutt et al.) of 1988, one can find the irony of the Movement, as in Hulse et al., invoked as something to be deplored.[30] In the introduction to the third section of the anthology, Eric Mottram characterises 'the British Poetry Revival of the 1960s and 1970s' as resisting 'past metrics, self-satisfied irony, the self-regarding ego and its iambic thuds'.[31] For Mottram and the other poets and critics of the avant-garde from the 60s to the present, the 'mainstream', represented by Conquest, Alvarez and Morrison and Motion, is a limited, regressive, conservative establishment, against which all that is adventurous in contemporary poetry must set its face, and Hulse et al. would tend to be seen as a continuation of this line.[32] Allnutt et al.'s *The New British Poetry* achieves a form of structural pluralism by its use of four sections, with separate editors and separate (brief) introductions. The volume as a whole is prefaced only by an even briefer 'Publisher's Note' which nevertheless includes some of the standard manoeuvres of anthology introductions. The 'Publisher's Note' offers the collection as an alternative to 'a narrowly-defined orthodoxy', in place of which it offers examples of the 'vitality and strength ... amongst younger poets across the entire spectrum of British poetry now'.[33] This is the more or less obligatory claim to the general application of neutral or universal value-criteria ('vitality', 'strength'), although the purpose and achievement of Allnutt et al. is very clearly to represent certain parts of the spectrum: selections from the avant-garde, women's poetry and black poetry. Its overlap with Morrison and Motion (published a mere six years earlier) is zero and its title a riposte and reproof to their arch and secretive-sounding claim to be representing what 'a number of close observers have come to think of as the new British poetry', though it also alludes to an influential American anthology of 1960, *The New American Poetry*.[34] Allnutt et al. share nine poets with Hulse et al. (published five years later) and the overlap poets are all Scottish or female or black (or more than one of these): Eavan Boland, Tom Leonard, Selima Hill, Liz Lochhead, Michèle Roberts, Grace Nichols, Linton Kwesi Johnson, David Dabydeen, Jackie Kay. This is less indicative of any willingness on the part of 'mainstream' editors to accommodate avant-garde poetry than of the willingness of the avant-garde to accept forms of social marginality or under-representation in establishment culture as conferring honorary membership of the

---

[30] It was preceded by Michael Horovitz's *Children of Albion: Poetry of the Underground in Britain* (Harmondsworth: Penguin, 1969).

[31] Allnutt et al., *The New British Poetry*, p. 131.

[32] See, for example, Sheppard, 'Elsewhere and Everywhere', pp. 18–19.

[33] John Muckle, 'Publishers Note' to Allnutt et al., p. vi.

[34] Morrison and Motion, *The Penguin Book*, p. 12; *The New American Poetry*, ed. Donald Allen (New York: Grove Press, 1960).

'opposition'.[35] The work of the overlap poets is, in technical terms, mainstream, in that it generally retains conventional narrative, syntactical and semantic structures. The dilemma for the avant-garde is that it faces continuing marginalization by an ideology of the 'mainstream', which dominates many publishing outlets and critical forums, privileging a poetry of the mainstream that is increasingly diverse and hard to define. Also, the aesthetics of the mainstream might be seen as replicating aspects of avant-garde rhetoric in a form of protective mimicry. Thus Hulse et al. claim to be representing the marginalized but express scepticism about the idea of a centre:

> A multicultural society challenges the very idea of a centre, and produces pluralism of the poetic voice.
> The idea of a centre is particularly fraught for those who feel marginalised. Arguably it is now more an idea than a reality ... But the need of those traditionally on the periphery to define themselves against 'the centre' continues.[36]

They allude to the influence of Language poetry on Scottish writers such as Robert Crawford and W. N. Herbert but make no mention of the many avant-garde poets more closely allied to the Language inheritance. They deploy familiar avant-garde critical gestures ('Doubts about the authenticity of self and narrative authority') but in relation to poets such as John Ash, whose questioning of such authenticity is relatively trivial.[37] They cite Paul Muldoon, whose work might feature in some bridging of 'tribal divisions' such as they claim to detect, but only as authority for a rather simple version of postmodernism, as 'a realisation that ideas of meaning, truth and understanding are in themselves fictions determined by the rhetorical forms and linguistic terms used to express them'.[38]

An anthology which appeared the year before Allnutt et al. took a very different approach to the representation of alternative poetries. Entitled *A Various Art*, it is, nevertheless, a much tighter selection of seventeen poets (compared to the eighty-five in Allnutt et al.). One of the editors, Andrew Crozier, has written a cogent analysis of issues of value

---

[35] The American avant-garde poet and critic Charles Bernstein explains something of the rationale for such a link: 'I want to acknowledge the significance of group-identified poetries (ethnic, racial, linguistic, social, class, sexual, regional) in shattering the neoconventionalist ideal of fashioning by masterly artifice a neutral standard English, a common voice for all to speak.' Charles Bernstein, *A Poetics* (Cambridge, MA: Harvard University Press, 1992), p. 120.

[36] Hulse et al., *The New British Poetry*, p. 18.

[37] Ibid., p. 23.

[38] Ibid., pp. 16, 24,

and the post-war poetic canon, with particular reference to the debates surrounding Conquest and Alvarez, so it is perhaps not surprising that the anthology shows itself as being peculiarly sensitive to the risks of anthology-making and particularly concerned to avoid the sort of 'incoherent and question-begging' arguments that Crozier had found in Conquest.[39] The results, though, are curious. The manner in which Crozier and Longville present their poets represents a sort of degree-zero of anthology-making: the poets are in alphabetical order, there is no biographical information (as one reviewer noted, only a poem by one in memory of another betrays the fact that not all are still alive) and the introduction gives only a minimal sketch of their allegiances: the 'formative moment' of the 60s, a reaction against a 'depthless version of the [English] past', an enthusiasm for American poetry and publication organised by poets themselves. Reviewers have associated many of the poets here with a 'Cambridge school' but the editors would concede only that 'in various places, in Birmingham, Bristol, Cambridge, London and Manchester, for example, several of them became aware of one another's presence and a shared reaction to current taste'.[40] One might contrast such an approach with the Bloodaxe anthology *Poetry with an Edge*, edited by Neil Astley, which appeared the following year.[41] Unashamedly a celebration of a particular publisher's 'stable', this volume headed each selection of a poet's work with a photograph and brief biography (including suggestions as to theme or approach and quotes from reviewers), bringing personality and life history to the fore where *A Various Art* scrupulously eschews them.[42] The difference points up the dilemmas of anthology-making. Neil Astley's use of photographs plays straight into the media tendency to see the value of poetry as lying in the commodification of personality and the representation of personal experience. The headnotes make the poems more accessible, though within necessarily limited frameworks: where they were written or the poet's upbringing or a one-sentence account of their aesthetic. The refusal of Crozier and Longville to name a 'school' is scrupulous: to have proclaimed a

---

[39] Andrew Crozier, 'Thrills and Frills: Poetry as Figures of Empirical Lyricism', in Alan Sinfield (ed.), *Society and Literature 1945–1970* (London: Methuen, 1983), pp. 199–233.

[40] Critics as different in their positioning as Blake Morrison and Robert Sheppard concurred in associating *A Various Art* with a Cambridge school of poets. Blake Morrison, 'Every Three Years', review of *A Various Art* and other volumes, *London Review of Books*, 3 March 1988, p. 14; Sheppard, 'Elsewhere and Everywhere', p. 22.

[41] Neil Astley (ed.), *Poetry with an Edge* (Newcastle-upon-Tyne: Bloodaxe, 1988).

[42] Apparently the selection of poets in *A Various Art* was also influenced by publishing affiliations, though this is not made explicit in the volume; Alan Halsey has commented that the editors' 'brief was to make an anthology based around the publishing activities of Grosseteste and Ferry' (two small British presses). Message to british-poets e-mail discussion group, 13 July 2000.

'Cambridge School' would have been a better marketing strategy but, as is always the case in such proclamations, would have required some simplification and distortion or a much lesser selection (for example, Roy Fisher, so firmly associated with the West Midlands, could hardly be co-opted for such a school). Of the two anthologies, *A Various Art* has a more sophisticated notion of poetic value but offers a somewhat ascetic and discouraging front to the new or relatively uninformed reader. Indeed, the introduction often gives the impression of having been written in code: one can tell what it is saying about contemporary poetry only if one is already familiar with the terms of the debate. It begins with a resounding and very traditional claim of abstract value within a generational framework – 'This anthology represents our joint view of what is most interesting, valuable and distinguished in the work of a generation of English poets now entering its maturity' – only to add the curious qualification, 'but it is not anthology of English, let alone British, poetry'. 'We did not begin with this distinction in mind', continue the editors, while many readers are probably still wondering what the distinction *is*.[43] It gradually becomes clear that they are concerned to avoid any linking of poetic value to national prestige, in reaction against anthologies in which 'the frame of reference of national culture and the notion of quality have been brought into uncomplicated mutual alignment'.[44] However, Astley might reasonably claim that his inclusion of a range of Irish, American and European poets is a more effective way of avoiding the alignment of value with national origin than a statement of principle prefacing a selection of English poets.

In asserting its position, the avant-garde needs to construct a relatively unified mainstream and, to some extent, needs to demonize it. In denying value to this mainstream, the avant-garde is forced into a position, contrary in general to its own principles, of essentializing the value of poetry. Frequently the ideology of the avant-garde stresses community and equality but also generates (or at least is drawn into) a wholesale dismissal of 'mainstream' poetry. The American poet Bob Perelman commented in interview that:

> [i]t's problematic, the notion of value goes against the aspiration to community, the ideology of community ... The traditional sense of value – it's scarce, there are only a few great composers, painters, etc. – is a problematic model for an art community to constitute itself around.[45]

---

[43] Crozier and Longville, *A Various Art*, p. 11.
[44] Ibid.
[45] Interview with Peter Nicholls, *Textual Practice*, 12.3 (1998), 525–43 (p. 526).

The critical and meta-poetical discourse of the avant-garde tends to be very wary of hierarchies of value within the hugely various but nevertheless identifiable field which it embraces but, at the same time, tends to assert strongly a binary of value between that field and its other, defined as the mainstream and seen as politically and aesthetically conservative. Connor proposes this as an inescapable feature of any avant-garde: 'The paradoxical structure of value enacts itself in avant-garde art, which can be truly new only by means of its refusal to abandon what it aims to leave behind', the point being presumably that its cultural meaning as avant-garde depends on the evocation of a mainstream.[46] It is debatable how far what I am calling avant-garde poetry is tied to such a need, since it has developed its own autonomous aesthetic on both sides of the Atlantic and beyond over the last forty years and so is no longer, if it ever was, dependent on effects of radical newness or shocking departure from a cultural norm. But its self-description does tend to involve the mainstream as 'other', although the organizer of a 1999 conference in London opened with the assertion, 'we are the mainstream'.[47]

The 1999 anthology, *Other*, edited by Caddel and Quartermain, inscribes in its very title this positioning of the avant-garde relative to an 'other' (the 'mainstream') and as the other *of* that mainstream. The introduction, while criticizing the cultural domination of the mainstream, disclaims any intention of dismissing it as 'devoid of worth'.[48] In common with Hulse et al., Caddel and Quartermain invoke the value of pluralism but, in this case, as grounds for rejecting a mainstream tradition which they see as suppressing pluralism and which would include most of Hulse et al.'s poets: 'About the only thing that is not possible in such a pluralistic, fragmenting, evolving society is a unitary, closed-system approach to culture, an insistence on a single "great tradition".' Nevertheless, Caddel and Quartermain fall into the temptation of constructing a monolithic and homogenized other against which to specify their pluralist alternative. They identify this mainstream as including 'the narrow lineage of contemporary poets from Philip Larkin to Craig Raine and Simon Armitage, and encompassing their attendant "collectives" (Movement, Martians, New Generation)'. While admitting that '[g]eneralisation ... is fraught with difficulties', they assert that 'in each case the typical poem is a closed, monolineal utterance, demanding little of the reader but passive consumption'.[49] The problems with such a formulation become evident when, for example, they note that '[m]ost of the poets in this anthology are English, but each will understand this in a

---

[46] Connor, *Theory and Cultural Value*, p. 3.
[47] Lawrence Upton (organizer), *Third Sub-Voice Colloquium*, 12 January 1999, University of London Institute of English Studies.
[48] Caddell and Quartermain, *Other*, p. xv.
[49] Ibid.

different context, and most will reject the stylised anglophilia of, say, Geoffrey Hill or Philip Larkin'.[50] Presumably we are to understand from this that Hill is part of the 'mainstream'. It could certainly be argued that he practises 'stylised anglophilia' but to bracket him with Larkin is reductive and simplistic, given that Hill is very much a European poet and a late modernist, whereas Larkin was notoriously unenthusiastic about both 'foreign poetry' and modernism.[51] Hill and Larkin clearly understood 'being English' in different contexts, no less than do the poets of *Other*. It is difficult to imagine a poet *less* prone than Hill to 'demand little of the reader but passive consumption', since his work is highly dense, multilayered and difficult. Furthermore, Hill eminently fits the prescription which Caddel and Quartermain derive from Basil Bunting: 'an (urgent) felt need to turn to foreign-language models (and a re-evaluation of "classical" literatures), and an insistence ... on the worth of the local and regional.'[52] The problems here go beyond the specific instance of Hill: what of 'mainstream' poets who might also fit this prescription, such as Tony Harrison or Don Paterson? What of all the other poets who, though their work may have been temporarily harnessed to 'collectives' by editors, publishers or marketing executives, have their own trajectories? Caddel and Quartermain, though their account of 'other' poetries is rich and scrupulous in its sense of plurality and complexity, simplify that Other's other (the 'mainstream' but, in fact, a wider range of poetry not within their field of interest) by trying to match up poetic technique, political stance and media success, when actually these things are connected in complex (though structured) ways.

Two anthologies of 1998 (Armitage and Crawford; O'Brien) avoided some of the risks and impositions associated with a generational approach by taking a broader historical sweep and surveying British and Irish poetry since the end of the Second World War. This strategy, which has, of course, its own antecedents, notably Edward Lucie-Smith's *British Poetry since 1945* (1970/1985), depends on a publisher being willing to extend to a considerably larger volume.[53] Armitage and Crawford echo certain aspects of the rhetoric of the sequence of generational anthologies, such as Conquest's dismissal of the New Apocalyptic movement, Alvarez's evocation of the Nazi death camps of World War Two as the moment of a change in aesthetics, Morrison's and Motion's

---

[50] Ibid., p. xviii.

[51] On one occasion Larkin famously claimed never to read any foreign poetry. *Four Conversations: Philip Larkin* (interviewed by Ian Hamilton), *London Magazine*, 4.8 (November 1964), p. 73. Larkin's strictures on modernism are found in *All What Jazz: A Record Diary 1961–68* (London: Faber, 1970), p. 17.

[52] Caddel and Quartermain, *Other*, p. xvii.

[53] Edward Lucie-Smith (ed.), *British Poetry since 1945* (London: Penguin, 1970; revised edition 1985).

talk of widening the franchise, and Hulse et al.'s claims of a breakdown in hierarchies and stress on pluralism and diversity as key values.[54] However, their historical scope allows such gestures to be more inflected and grounded, while their comments also signal that they have noted some of the vicissitudes of anthology introductions. In place of Alvarez's sweeping claims of a belated English discovery of evil, we have a sense of the War and the subsequent dismantling of Empire as a crux of social and linguistic change.[55] In place of the vague 'imaginative franchise' of Morrison and Motion, we have 'the educational franchise', alluding to the Butler Education Act of 1944 and thus identifying a specific institutional factor influencing 'the constituency of readers and writers'. Where Hulse et al. become enmeshed in paradoxical generalizations about margin and centre, and the implausibly deterministic claim that a 'multicultural society ... produces pluralism of poetic voice', Armitage and Crawford anchor their idea of the 'democratic voice' in a claim which, while still general, is easier to sustain: that poets, since 1945, tend to show 'an awareness of inhabiting one voice that is among others, part of a vernacular community surrounded by further vernacular communities'.[56] Thus their claim is not that pluralism is necessarily integral to all the poetry (which maps the socio-political straight on to the aesthetic) but rather that most of the poetry, in some way, registers the plurality that surrounds it (which acknowledges the pressure that the socio-political exerts on the aesthetic). The tension between the value of the typical or indicative and a notion of absolute quality weighs less heavily on Armitage and Crawford because the parameters of their anthology remove the obligation to be remorselessly 'new'. However, that tension is still present since a historical account implies certain emphases which need to be supported by poetic instances. Armitage and Crawford register this tension and ultimately come down on the side of absolute value, stating that 'all anthologies must face up to questions of poetic value' and that, while their 'introduction may set out a trajectory in terms of cultural and political currents', 'the editors were determined to include only writing of high poetic worth'.[57] They specifically disavow the generational idea, 'the notion that there is one straightforward, quasi-monarchical line of succession in this period of the democratic voice'.[58]

---

[54] See Armitage and Crawford, *The Penguin Book*, pp. xx–xxi.

[55] The direct allusion in Armitage and Crawford ('Poetry *was* possible after Auschwitz', p. xxi) is to Adorno's famous comment, 'To write poetry after Auschwitz is barbaric'. Theodor Adorno, *Prisms: Cultural Criticism and Society*, trans. Samuel and Shierry Weber (London, 1967), p. 34.

[56] Hulse et al., *The New Poetry*, p. 18; Armitage and Crawford, *The Penguin Book*, pp. xxi–xxii.

[57] Armitage and Crawford, *The Penguin Book*, p. xxviii.

[58] Ibid., p. xxvi.

The title of Sean O'Brien's *The Firebox* gestures to a Romantic conception of poetry, as a form of mythic and therefore universal value: 'It re-creates and renews itself, replenishing the fire which by tradition Prometheus stole from the gods – the fire of creation, understanding and language itself'.[59] The introduction, however, is simply a summary history of mainstream poetry in Britain and Ireland since 1945, though it is weakened by its reliance on enervated definitions of modernism and postmodernism. Though O'Brien is far less explicit than Armitage and Crawford in addressing issues of value, he broadly shares with them a dissent from unitary or centralized models of cultural value: he begins by referring to the new insecurity of 'ideas of nation and nationality', to devolution within Britain and to the multiple cultural identities and 'openness to other literary cultures' which he feels characterize his own generation of poets and the next.[60] It remains to be seen, then, whether the 'new poetry' and 'new generation' rhetoric has, in some sense, had its day and what value will succeed that of pluralism, which currently seems to be dominant in the discourse of poetic value. The notion of pluralism requires some putative unity within which or against which the plural is to be defined. Recent anthologies tend to define their pluralism through gestures of disengagement from earlier ideas of the Englishness of 'English literature' and by the denial of any intention of offering singular, shared cultural values. As the disavowals of any simple anthologizing of Britishness indicate, the alignment of poetry with the nation state becomes ever more difficult to sustain. Increasingly it seems as if plurality is, in effect, plurality within English as a world language. However, an adequate anthology of poetry in all the world varieties of English seems unlikely as a practical publishing proposition, except in electronic form (which may, of course, be the future of anthologies).

Neither Armitage and Crawford nor O'Brien embrace the avant-garde tradition to any great extent: both anthologies include Roy Fisher (often regarded as the acceptable face of the avant-garde), while the Armitage and Crawford volume extends to Denise Riley and Ian Hamilton Finlay, but neither volume includes Tom Raworth, Bob Cobbing, Maggie O' Sullivan, Robert Sheppard or Allen Fisher (to name but a few). [61] These anthologies continue to inhabit a parallel poetic universe to that represented in collections such as *Other* or the defiantly eccentric

[59] O'Brien, *The Firebox*, pp. xxvii–xxviii.
[60] Ibid., p. xxvii.
[61] Roy Fisher's status in this respect is humorously alluded to by Ken Edwards, in his Introduction to his section of *The New British Poetry*: 'Oh alright, perhaps Roy Fisher, but *nobody else*' (p. 266).

Conductors of Chaos (edited by Iain Sinclair).[62] Although pluralism figures as a value in anthologies of both the 'mainstream' and the 'alternative' or avant-garde, in neither case does this pluralism extend to any significant inclusion of the work of the other, nor to any full recognition of its possible values. This situation seems to pose two questions. First, is pluralism itself a value or is it the acceptance of multiple values? In other words, are we faced with the paradox of anthologies which include only that poetry which accords with the editors' particular conception of pluralism and actually excludes other poetry, on the grounds that it is not plural enough, or plural in the wrong sort of way, not 'the best poetry'? Second, how can we find terms of exchange between radically different sorts of poetry other than a single standard of value which collapses pluralism back into battles for places in a hierarchy?

An anthology which appeared when the present chapter was almost completed, Keith Tuma's *Anthology of Twentieth-Century British and Irish Poetry*, has a historical range which places it in a somewhat different category from the other anthologies discussed here, making it a successor to Philip Larkin's *Oxford Book of Twentieth-Century English Verse* (1973). Nevertheless, it represents a crucial intervention in the anthologizing of contemporary British poetry because it has the best claim of any so far to span the 'mainstream'/'alternative' divide. Going back as far as Hardy, it nevertheless finds space in the post-war period for Larkin, Davie, Hughes, Heaney, Raine, Boland and Duffy, on the one hand, and Bob Cobbing, Asa Benveniste, Gael Turnbull, Roy Fisher, Tom Raworth, Veronica Forrest-Thomson and Alan Halsey, on the other (to name only a few from Tuma's selection in each category). In the matter of multiple as opposed to singular value, Tuma's explicit allegiance is to the multiple. He notes the 'many modes of poetry that informed readers, critics and poets have found more or less valuable' and espouses 'critical pluralism' or 'whatever negative capability allowed me to take poems and their advocates on their own terms'. [63] At the same time, he confronts directly one version of the tension which I have identified between the value of the indicative or typical and a purely qualitative criterion of selection. His evaluative process as he describes it privileges the 'history of artifice' rather than 'history per se', in that he chooses not to 'subordinat[e] questions of aesthetic value to questions of representation'. [64] This need not mean a singular scale of aesthetic value but, rather, an attempt to represent a diversity of aesthetic and technical possibilities at their most intense level; the idea of representativeness is still present but what is to be

---

[62] Sinclair's *Conductors of Chaos* draws its own longer perspectives through the striking technique of inviting 'a number of the poets to nominate [and discuss/anthologize] significant figures from previous generations' (p. xix).

[63] Tuma, *Anthology*, p. xxi.

[64] Ibid., p. xx.

represented is not history or cultural tendencies but the development of an art form through its 'exemplary poems'. [65] There is a certain circularity in the argument here. What one judges to be a poem exemplary of the form must depend on one's conception of poetry as a form – and that conception is presumably a product of one's reading of particular poems, as well as one's reading of critical discourses which in turn carry their own freight of values (aesthetic and other). Tuma suggests that 'some poems seem alive as possible resources for those who seek to know something or to write poetry', a statement which more or less reduces the criterion of a poem's value to whether interested parties find it valuable. The circularity is acknowledged: 'the significance of poetry ... depends upon discourses prepared to argue for particular poems and modes of facture as exemplary or flawed, on judgments determining what is groundbreaking or perfected or worn and boring'.[66] Tuma is only being honest here about the way in which aesthetic judgments emerge out of contingent processes of mutual influence between responses to individual works and the arguments by which we justify, reinforce or even create those responses in ourselves and others. Nevertheless, these elements of circularity and uncertainty represent an aporia (an irresolvable doubt or hesitation) arising from that structure of value which Connor identifies: the inescapable imperative to assert and justify values, and the vulnerability of those values to challenge by the processes of evaluation. [67] The cautious tone and many qualifications of Tuma's preface, as he thinks through his own evaluative processes as editor, are a more sophisticated and interesting response to this aporia than defiant reassertion of firm values or gestures towards the determining effects of cultural change or cultural diversity. Tuma is, nevertheless, forced back at certain points upon some of the traditional humanist place-markers for pure literary value (such as Leavisite metaphors which equate literary value with vitality) and upon the acknowledgement that tastes and judgments differ: 'this anthology [is interested in] ... the history of poetry as a living, serious, vital artform'; 'some poems seem alive'; 'which leaves us to quarrel about which critical opinion has been and should be influential'; 'You will choose your own terms'.[68] One hint of an fixed criterion of value lies in Tuma's allegiance to 'love of poetry' as against other (presumably more mercenary) motives: 'I have paid little attention to awards and titles and searched instead among the publications and opinions of those who have got little at stake beyond their love of poetry and hope for its future.'[69]

[65] Ibid., p. xix.
[66] Ibid., p. xxi.
[67] See Connor, *Theory and Cultural Value*, pp. 2–3
[68] Tuma, *Anthology*, pp. xx, xxi, xix, xxi.
[69] Ibid., p. xxi.

In a critical study published three years before his anthology, Tuma gestures tentatively towards a utopian international aesthetic community:

An aestheticist internationalism can proffer an image of freedom ... An international 'republic of letters' or 'international avant-garde' might name the possibility of a world with fewer boundaries and contingencies, an as yet nonexistent democracy, or perhaps one should say that one hopes it might name such a world. [70]

Taken together, these remarks suggest a Kantian ethical valuation of disinterested aesthetic judgment. Terry Eagleton describes Kant's conception of the cultural domain as one in which 'aesthetic intersubjectivity adumbrates a utopian community of subjects, united in the very deep structure of their being'. [71] Tuma is an enthusiast for the avant-garde, for modernist experiments and for small-press publication, and his sense of an ideal aesthetic community springs, one senses, from the particular devotions and dynamics of that international literary subculture. Hence Tuma's other key value term is 'modernism': he is concerned to remedy the neglect in British anthologies of 'contemporary poetry ... indebted to an international modernism', a neglect which he sees as symptomatic of anti-modernist insularity in Britain. [72] One should not deny the very real existence of dedicated enthusiasts – poets, publishers, booksellers and editors – who continue to champion poetry which is unlikely to make their fortune or their careers. But, as a grounding for value, the gesture to disinterested love of the art is problematic. Without dismissing the concept of aesthetic disinterestedness as 'vacuously idealist', I would doubt that such a concept can be used to divide sheep from goats in a culture where emotional, intellectual, professional and financial investments in the value of poetry co-exist and intertwine. [73] Be that as it may, Tuma's anthology is a major step towards an exchange between the parallel poetic universes of 'mainstream' and 'alternative', an exchange which might render those terms obsolete.

In probably the fullest discussion to date of issues and theories of cultural value, Steven Connor proposes the desirability of multiplying values and multiplying 'the standards or registers of value'.[74] He argues that *both* 'the impulse ... towards stable or absolute forms of value'

---

[70] Keith Tuma, *Fishing by Obstinate Isles: Modern and Postmodern British Poetry and American Readers* (Evanston, IL: Northwestern University Press, 1998), pp. 9–10.

[71] Terry Eagleton, *The Ideology of the Aesthetic* (Oxford and Cambridge, MA: Blackwell, 1990), p. 97.

[72] Tuma, *Anthology*, p. xxi.

[73] Eagleton, *The Ideology of the Aesthetic*, p. 39.

[74] Connor, *Theory and Cultural Value*, p. 4.

and (more surprisingly) 'the relativizing desire to recognize and tolerate the maximum of competing values' should be seen as imposing unwelcome restrictions on the dynamics of value and evaluation.[75] The first privileges fixed values over evaluative processes, while the second does the reverse. Each constrains the endless and paradoxical play of value, 'the simultaneous desire and necessity to affirm unconditional values and the desire and necessity to subject such values to continuous, corrosive scrutiny'.[76] Anthologies of contemporary poetry seem haunted by these contrary desires and necessities, in ways which reflect the wider problematic of ethical, political and aesthetic values in contemporary culture. Connor suggests that:

> almost more of an ethical curtailment than these two forms of constraint in themselves ... is the limiting exclusiveness of the binarism they form together, in which it proves impossible to imagine a theory of value which does not propose either some absolute closure or some absolute openness, fixation or difference.[77]

A less constrained assessment of poetic value might require critics and editors to think, and work, beyond this binary.

[75] Ibid., p. 16.
[76] Ibid., p. 17.
[77] Ibid., p. 197.

6

Recent American Poetry Anthologies and the Idea of the 'Mainstream'

Alan Golding

I

'There's nothing that can be called a mainstream movement in our poetry – or an avant-garde'; 'there is no need for any anthology to choose sides'.[1] These two statements from editors of American poetry anthologies, the first by Edward Field in 1979, the second by J. D. McClatchy in 1990, summarize one widely shared 'poetic positioning', to use Pierre Bourdieu's term, of the last twenty years. But for all the alleged inclusiveness that would destabilize ideas of 'mainstream' and 'margin' in our age of anthologies, a mainstream in recent American poetry can indeed be located and described.[2] This mainstream reveals itself especially at those points where its existence is most energetically denied or its inclusiveness most energetically touted – and those points include anthologies.

In this essay I will examine patterns of editorial rhetoric and self-representation in a particular body of anthologies: survey-style collections of recent (or in a few cases, of post-World War II) American poetry, designed for the college creative-writing and literature classroom, that appeared mostly from trade and university presses in the 1970s, 1980s and into the early 1990s. Although boundaries between 'centre' or 'mainstream' and 'margin' are more porous than in the times, say, of the early 1960s anthology wars, we can still derive, from these mainstream contemporary poetry surveys, a reliable picture of current aesthetic ideology, especially at those points where ideology and its conflicts are denied. Reading these anthologies, that is, makes it possible to construct a picture of the period's aesthetic centre. I lack the space here to discuss the

---

[1] Edward Field (ed.), *A Geography of Poets: An Anthology of the New Poetry* (New York: Bantam, 1979), p. xli; J. D. McClatchy (ed.), *The Vintage Book of Contemporary American Poetry* (New York: Vintage, 1990), p. xxi.

[2] Fred Moramarco and William Sullivan conclude their critical survey of post-1950 American poetry with a chapter-length characterization of the 1980s as a latter-day 'age of anthologies', in Randall Jarrell's well-known formulation. Fred Moramarco and William Sullivan, *Containing Multitudes: Poetry in the United States since 1950* (New York: Twayne, 1998).

relationship between editorial claims and actual content in individual texts – an important factor in assessing any anthology fairly. Nevertheless, describing the rhetoric of such anthologies still provides a concrete example of the circulation of poetic value within the period and an instructive case study in cultural politics. It involves reading anthologies as cultural artefacts, products of a particular cultural formation – and a hardy one too, given that the vast majority of the collections to be discussed here, including one published as early as 1969, remain in print.[3] Less clearly delineated than it once was, obscured by editorial assertions of its benignly amorphous inclusiveness, some kind of mainstream in recent American poetry still flows on.

These recent mainstream surveys typically project a bogus tolerance, a denial that 'sides' have to be taken when in fact they always already have been. As Eliot Weinberger points out in the introduction to his openly avant-gardist anthology *American Poetry Since 1950: Innovators and Outsiders* (1993), what he calls (from the poetic 'outsider's' point of view) ruling-party rhetoric 'insists there is no ruling party, and thus no opposition'.[4] Such a denial evades the social and the institutional factors that shape editorial decisions and ultimately canons. It pervades, for instance, J. D. McClatchy's introduction to his *Vintage Book of Contemporary American Poetry* (1990), the beginning of which I cited in my opening sentence: 'There is no need for any anthology to choose sides'.[5] In a contradictory move, McClatchy lists historical examples of 'sniper fire from the poets themselves' but then goes on to dismiss such conflicts as 'merely sibling rivalries and territorial imperatives'. He claims to separate the purity of poets from the tainted interests of readers and critics: 'Though angry ideologies have been built of such flimsy stuff, it's usually done not by poets but by their dull readers.'[6] Given the role of twentieth-century poets and poet-critics in debates that have been simultaneously, and inseparably, both literary and ideological, this stance is both disingenuous and not even close to being historically accurate. Belatedly perpetuating the separation of the aesthetic or private and the social in terms derived from Harold Bloom, McClatchy argues that only weak poets are concerned with superficial issues of social conflict; strong poets work privately, 'alone with their art', their apparent differences

---

[3] The fact that these anthologies also are all male-edited is subject for a separate essay in itself.

[4] Eliot Weinberger, *American Poetry Since 1950: Innovators and Outsiders* (New York: Marsilio, 1993), p. xi.

[5] For a related treatment of some of the issues I am addressing here that focuses on McClatchy's anthology as a sustained example, see Chapter 5 of Jed Rasula's *The American Poetry Wax Museum: Reality Effects, 1940–1990* (Urbana, IL: National Council of Teachers of English, 1996).

[6] McClatchy (ed.), *Vintage Book*, p. xxi.

mystically reconciled by subterranean, non-ideological streams of sympathy that unite them under the surface 'landscape of trends and schools and movements'.[7] Not surprisingly, the assertion that a deeper inclusiveness has really existed all along works to deflect more ideologically charged writing. That is, claims to a false pluralism help suppress or deflect emergent poetries that are part of a real pluralism (socially, if not always aesthetically):

> Of the claims made that new literary movements – black, feminist, gay – have emerged, it would be better to say that new audiences have developed; weaker poets play to them, stronger poets ... attend to their art and work to complicate the issues.[8]

Like McClatchy, William Heyen in *The Generation of 2000* (1984) is baffled by the idea of an 'enemy' in poetry but immediately goes on to dismiss 'quasi-surrealist[s]', 'dadaists', 'faddists', 'stand-up comics' and 'aestheticians tripletalking ethereal voices' – quite a long list of 'enemies'.[9] Daniel Halpern is equally eager to argue that the camps and groups of 1950–1965 no longer apply but less than eager to include much of the poetry that stems from them, either of the formally traditional or more innovative variety – this in the context of an allegedly heterogeneous collection offered as *The* (not *An*) *American Poetry Anthology* (1975).[10] In Ronald Wallace's *Vital Signs: Contemporary American Poetry from the*

---

[7] Ibid., pp. xxx, xxii. Compare Rasula, *American Poetry Wax Museum*, p. 451:

> McClatchy's non- or antipartisan position is of course the dominant style of advocacy today. It replicates liberal ideology by declaring the romantic efficacy of the person, the centered subject whose artistic proclivity bestows (on 'us') that indubitable icon of value, the work of art.

Despite his pretence in the *Vintage* anthology to a kind of Whitmanian connectiveness, McClatchy's 1989 collection of critical essays, *White Paper*, shows both the mutually reinforcing relationship of criticism and anthologies and his fundamental commitment to a New York and Ivy League-centred canon. *White Paper* devotes three essays to Lowell and one to Bishop, with whom McClatchy begins his *Vintage Book* and whom he calls there 'the strongest poets of their generation', 'towering models' (p. xxviii). *White Paper* also contains essays on Penn Warren, Berryman, Plath, Snodgrass, Merrill, Howard, Hollander, Clampitt and Hecht. On the matter of 'inclusiveness', one of the most egregious *exclusions* in the *Vintage Book* is that of the three most explicitly homoerotic pages of Allen Ginsberg's 'Howl', suggesting that the genteel tradition, paradoxically instantiated in a gay editor and perhaps in alliance with a publisher's reluctance to risk maximum marketability, is far from dead.

[8] McClatchy (ed.), *Vintage Book*, p. xxviii.

[9] William Heyen (ed.), *The Generation of 2000: Contemporary American Poets* (Princeton: Ontario Review, 1984), p. xxi.

[10] Daniel Halpern (ed.), *The American Poetry Anthology* (New York: Avon, 1975), pp. xxxi–xxxii.

University Presses (1989) too we find the common conjunction of three points: explicit commitment to a mainstream aesthetics; claims to 'richness and diversity' in representation; and the denial of 'warring "schools"'.[11] Like McClatchy, Wallace collapses difference in the image of a 'great ongoing dialogue' among poets, just as Heyen links his denial of opposition to his 'aim to reach that level where "the most divergent intelligences" ... may come together'.[12]

This rejection of 'schools' – that highly charged term – recurs throughout mainstream anthologies. Contrary to what Stuart Friebert and David Young argue in their *Longman Anthology of Contemporary American Poetry* (1983), however, 'dislike of schools and dogmas'[13] is not an intrinsic generational trait of poets who started publishing between 1950 and 1980 but rather a trait constructed through the editors' representation of that 'generation'. In effect, an anthology compiled on this basis reinforces an aesthetic ideology that privileges the figure of the individual artist – an issue to which I will return later. For one could equally construct a picture of the period precisely *in terms of* schools, movements and dogmas – though more positive and accurate terms might be 'communities', 'networks', 'affiliations', 'principles'. Further, the poetic mainstream, despite its wariness of schools, can itself easily be seen as one. Admittedly the creative-writing workshop that has produced so many of the poets in recent mainstream anthologies does not, on the surface, look like a 'school'. Affiliation with a workshop does not tie the poet to a particular time and place (Black Mountain College in the early- to mid-1950s, New York or San Francisco at the same time or in the 1970s and early 1980s); it does not suggest an overt coherence of poetic concerns; it does not issue in manifestoes or distinctive little magazines. The workshop is not easily identified as a 'movement', then – until it issues an anthology. But, when it does, uniformity of background and of shared but *unstated* assumptions work against the eclecticism and 'school-less-ness' that mainstream editors often assert. John Koethe argues that 'writing programs are not usually "schools"' in the sense of proposing an explicit and exclusionary poetics. However, he continues,

in the absence of explicitly articulated theoretical principles regarding the nature and purpose of poetry, [these programs]

[11] Ronald Wallace (ed.), *Vital Signs: Contemporary American Poetry from the University Presses* (Madison: University of Wisconsin Press, 1989), p. xix.
[12] Wallace (ed.), *Vital Signs*, p. xix; Heyen (ed.), *Generation of 2000*, p. xx.
[13] Stuart Friebert and David Young (eds), *The Longman Anthology of Contemporary American Poetry 1950–1980* (New York: Longman, 1982), p. xxix.

articulate, by default, a poetics of the 'individual voice' that valorizes authenticity and fidelity to its origins in prepoetic experience or emotion.[14]

The close relationship between creative-writing programs and university press publishing further shows how mainstream anthologies end up representing a de facto 'school' or at least a more specific point on the literary political spectrum than they claim. One sub-set of the mainstream survey, the collection of university press poetry, uses just this institutional conjunction allegedly to 'cover' American poetry. As Michael Collier puts it in *The Wesleyan Tradition* (1993), 'a program such as Wesleyan's arrived to meet the future publishing needs of university creative-writing programs'.[15] Both Collier and Wallace, in *Vital Signs*, see creative writing programs as promoting the decentralization of literary power. The growth of these programs could equally be seen, however, as a relocation of power in an institution (rather than in a place, a handful of critics and reviewers or a magazine). How does this relocation work? Wallace praises the poems in his collection for having survived evaluation by numerous different readers: 'The poems included here have been judged excellent by magazine editors, press editors, and reviewers, as well as myself, over a period of time'.[16] More accurately, however, these poems have been praised at different stages by similar *kinds* of reader, those within the university poetry publishing network.

In principle, all this is not especially blameworthy; it operates no differently from most kinds of self-authenticating literary network. In practice, however, it is different because it pretends to neutrality, not partisanship.[17] Without thinking of this network as monolithic, one can assume some consistency of taste and principle throughout it, especially given Wallace's own admission of the university presses' commitment to

---

[14] John Koethe, 'Contrary Impulses: The Tension Between Poetry and Theory', *Critical Inquiry* 18 (1991), 60–75 (p. 70). The terms of this debate over 'schools' are anticipated in Paris Leary and Robert Kelly (eds), *A Controversy of Poets* (Garden City, NY: Doubleday, 1965).

[15] Michael Collier (ed.), *The Wesleyan Tradition: Four Decades of American Poetry* (Hanover, NH: University Press of New England, 1993), p. xxvi.

[16] Wallace (ed.), *Vital Signs*, p. xvii.

[17] As Jed Rasula rightly points out, in contrast, what distinguishes a collection like *In the American Tree* is precisely the explicitness with which Ron Silliman presents the anthology 'as an exercise in community development': 'Many anthologies are of course gatherings of associates, but few are *articulated* that way, so any clarification about community becomes latent' (p. 447 n. 18).

mainstream poetry and to the dissemination of a period style.[18] As Wallace says, 'university presses tend to preserve the conservative mainstream. There is little radical experimentation, little extreme political poetry, little ethnic dialect, little of the avant-garde, little of the flamboyance associated with the great modernists'. Later he adds 'most poets publishing with university and trade presses today reject modes of disruption, discontinuity, inconsistency, erasure, and incoherence'.[19]

Like Wallace, Collier relates university press publishing to 'the democratization of poetry that was taking place through the creative writing programs in American universities and colleges'. At the same time, and again like Wallace, Collier admits that historically Wesleyan has stayed 'solidly within the mainstream and normative in contemporary American poetry', even while remaining 'alive to the widespread possibilities of the newest work being written' – an aliveness that has been more evident at Wesleyan over the last few years in its publication of writers such as Susan Howe, Joan Retallack and Leslie Scalapino.[20] Jack Myers and Roger Weingarten similarly attribute 'pluralism and decentralization of aesthetic-political power' in large part to creative-writing programs.[21] By constructing a democratized mainstream (which, to be fair, has indeed become more heterogeneous), its spokespersons can paradoxically claim for it both normative status and 'aliveness to the widespread possibilities of the new'.

Despite the impossibility of an inclusive or representative anthology for the post-war period, many editors still claim to produce just that. Most claims of this kind occur, however, in mainstream survey anthologies that nearly always *exclude* aesthetic extremes (from Language writing to New Formalism). While mainstream poetics has, indeed, grown more pluralist, it is important to realize the limits of that pluralism in the face of editors purporting to offer 'eclecticism regarding styles, concerns, and forms'; 'a representative array of some of the best and most exciting poetry being

---

[18] The closer one approaches the present, the more necessary it becomes to acknowledge exceptions to this generalization about university press poetry. In the 1990s, books of poetry, poetics and theory by writers working in various 'alternative' modes have appeared or are forthcoming with numerous university presses: California, Wesleyan, Chicago, Harvard, Princeton, Alabama, Northwestern. As the publisher of major collections by, for instance, Charles Olson, Robert Creeley and Louis Zukofsky, California has also significantly supported poets in the Objectivist-Black Mountain line. At the same time, among these presses, only Wesleyan maintains a genuinely eclectic *contemporary poetry* list open to non-mainstream work – a tendency whose beginning, interestingly, more or less coincides with the moment of Collier's retrospective *The Wesleyan Tradition* in 1993.

[19] Wallace (ed.), *Vital Signs*, pp. 20, 32.

[20] Quotations all derive from Collier (ed.), *Wesleyan Tradition*, pp. xxii, xxv, xxiv.

[21] Jack Myers and Roger Weingarten (eds), *New American Poets of the '90s* (Boston: David R. Godine, 1991), p. xv.

written today'; 'an enormous range of styles and perspectives'; 'an eclectic book', 'a gathering ... of various aesthetics'; 'richness and diversity'; or 'diversity and richness', 'heterogeneity ... of form, attitude, and treatment of content'.[22] 'This book is pluralistic,' insists McClatchy.[23] Mark Strand asserts that: 'it is part of the character of American poetry since 1940 to have made friends with everyone. Many different sorts of poetry seem to have existed more or less peacefully.'[24] Writing in 1969, at a time of intense social conflict over the Vietnam War, one can understand Strand's wishful thinking about peaceful coexistence at home and abroad. But, at home especially, that peaceful coexistence is hardly all-embracing; at the end of the Civil Rights decade, Strand's 92 poets since 1940 include precisely two African-Americans. In a rhetoric that uses military metaphor to suppress literary ideological conflict, Strand dismisses the '50s and '60s anthology wars as 'a brief skirmish' rather than as a charged symbolic moment.[25] I do not mean to argue the impossibility of inclusiveness and then indict these editors for not being inclusive. My point is to comment on their baseless *claims* to breadth and representativeness. Despite Wallace's and Collier's admissions in their collections that university presses tend to stick with 'the mainstream and normative', editors will still argue that the products of a single university press can provide, in Wesleyan's case, 'a definitive record of American poetry written since the late fifties' or, in Pittsburgh's case, 'as valid a cross-section of contemporary American poetry as we know'. [26]

Another feature by which we can recognize the mainstream survey as such is that it foregrounds a contrast between, on the one hand, 'poets' and, on the other, 'poems' or 'poetry'. Some sample statements: 'any anthology is finally a gathering of poems rather than of poets'; 'it is hoped ... that more concern will be given the poems than the poets'; 'the

---

[22] Sources for the quotations in this sentence are as follows: Myers and Weingarten (eds), *New American Poets of the 1980s* (Green Harbor, MA: Wampeter, 1984), p. xiv; Myers and Weingarten, *Poets of the '90s*, p. xv; Robert Pack, Sydney Lea and Jay Parini (eds), *The Bread Loaf Anthology of Contemporary American Poetry* (Hanover, NH: University Press of New England, 1985), p. v; Heyen (ed.), *Generation of 2000*, p. xx; Wallace (ed.), *Vital Signs*, p. xix; Halpern (ed.), *American Poetry Anthology*, pp. xxix, xxxi.

[23] McClatchy (ed.), *Vintage Book*, p. xxvii.

[24] Mark Strand (ed.), *The Contemporary American Poets: American Poetry Since 1940* (New York: Meridian, 1969), p. xiii.

[25] Strand (ed.), *Contemporary American Poets*, p. xxiii. One might expect a canon as all-inclusive as that claimed by mainstream editors to be somewhat flexible, mobile, open to change. As evidence of the mainstream canon's inertia, however, consider that forty of the first forty-six poets in McClatchy's 1990 anthology overlap with those in Strand's 1969 anthology.

[26] Collier (ed.), *The Wesleyan Tradition*, p. xxii; Ed Ochester and Peter Oresick (eds), *The Pittsburgh Anthology of Contemporary American Poetry* (Pittsburgh: University of Pittsburgh Press, 1993), p. xv.

preface to this book directs the reader's attention to contemporary *poems* and suggests that it is less than useful to consider them chiefly in the light of school or coterie'; 'the generation [of 2000] is in the poems themselves, of course, or it is nowhere'; '*Poetry* [magazine] publishes not poets but poems; this surely is what a magazine, or anthology, of verse exists to do'.[27]

This proposed emphasis on the poem would seem, on the surface, to imply a proportionately reduced focus on individual careers. Despite such protestations, however, mainstream editors more often construct texts that privilege the category and identity of the 'poet'. These editors contradict the pretence of stressing poems over poets by their overwhelming focus on a poetry of the self and by an idealizing of the individual (sometimes reinforced by *American Poetry Review*-style photo portraits) that connects, I think, to the widespread mistrust of 'movements' and the imagined loss of self that they bring. (This mistrust drives William Heyen's remark, in attempting to define the generation of 2000, that 'I've needed to feel part of something, not necessarily a "movement" or "group" or "school" with cloned characteristics, but of a community'.)[28] Thus Mark Strand identifies as a recurrent concern of American poetry since 1940 'the self, a self defined usually by circumstances that would tend to set it apart' and notes 'the energetic pursuit of an individual manner that would reflect a sense of self-definition'.[29] McClatchy sees 'the hazards of the self as the primary focus' for his poets' work. 'All of them have put the private life on public view', he continues, in 'the lyric [that] has continued to dominate our poetry'.[30] Self, individual, the poet – these are the concepts that betray what Jed Rasula calls the mainstream '*anxiety of contact*, a neurosis about collaboration as much as confrontation'.[31]

In this way, anthologies buttress the cult of the individual 'voice' that came to define the centre of American poetry starting in the mid-1970s. In the revealingly titled *Singular Voices* (1985), Stephen Berg gathers 'a wealth of original voices ... Each poet in this book writes his or her own kind of poem'. Poets in *The Bread Loaf Anthology* (1985) must each have 'a well-developed voice'. Stuart Friebert and David Young's

---

[27] Sources for the quotations in this sentence are as follows: McClatchy (ed.), *Vintage Book*, p. xxviii; Strand (ed.), *Contemporary American Poets*, p. xiv; Leary, 'Postscript I', *A Controversy of Poets*, p. 559; Heyen (ed.), *Generation of 2000*, p. xix; Daryl Hine, 'Introduction' to Daryl Hine and Joseph Parisi (eds), *The Poetry Anthology 1912–1977: Sixty-Five Years of America's Most Distinguished Verse Magazine* (Boston: Houghton Mifflin, 1978), p. xlvii.

[28] Heyen (ed.), *Generation of 2000*, p. xix.

[29] Strand (ed.), *Contemporary American Poets*, p. xiii.

[30] McClatchy (ed.), *Vintage Book*, pp. xxvi, xxviii.

[31] Jed Rasula, 'The Empire's New Clothes: Anthologizing American Poetry in the 1990s', *American Literary History* 7 (1995), 261–83 (p. 277).

'primary emphasis is on the poets as individual artists', poets whose 'dislike of schools and dogmas [is] concomitantly high'. Dave Smith and David Bottoms's *Morrow Anthology of Younger American Poets* illustrates vividly the felt tension between the claims of representativeness and individuality that shapes the rhetoric of many mainstream survey editors. In the space of a little over one page, Smith and Bottoms assert the 'vigorous, rich, and diverse' nature of recent American poetry, paint a generic, composite portrait of the young American poet-professor who produces such diversity and propose that 'the assertion of an individuality' lies at the heart of this composite poet's work.[32] (One could compare the second edition of Friebert and Young's *Longman Anthology* for a similar wariness of any politics beyond a fetishizing of the 'ordinary'.)

Also governing the mainstream survey is an ideology of the unmediated or self-evident that again suppresses the evaluative criteria involved in selection and removes the poetry from the circumstances or site of its

---

[32] Sources for the quotations in this paragraph are as follows: Berg (ed.), *Singular Voices: American Poetry Today* (New York: Avon, 1985), p. ix; Pack, Lea and Parini (eds), *Bread Loaf Anthology* p. vi; Friebert and Young (eds), *The Longman Anthology of Contemporary American Poetry 1950–1980*, 2nd edn, (New York: Longman, 1989), p. xxix; Dave Smith and David Bottoms (eds), *The Morrow Anthology of Younger American Poets* (New York: Quill, 1985), p. 17. On the issue of the 'individual' poet, Jed Rasula observes how, in paradoxical violation of its editors' intentions, the *Morrow*'s 'tight juxtaposition of 104 poets ... renders the poetic voice anonymous and collective as perhaps no previous anthology has done', and Geoffrey O'Brien comments on how the *Morrow* reduces the range of its poets' work in other contexts to an 'overwhelming unity of tone', so that 'you start to feel that you're reading the work of a single author'. See Rasula, *American Poetry Wax Museum*, p. 432, and Geoffrey O'Brien, *Bardic Deadlines: Reviewing Poetry, 1984–95* (Ann Arbor: University of Michigan Press, 1998), p. 35. In a collaborative 1988 essay, six Bay Area Language writers responded to Smith and Bottoms's individualist wariness of a phantasmatic 'card-carrying group member' as follows:

> If such poets avoid 'card-carrying' explicit aesthetics, it may be because they provide an ideology of no ideology, a plausible denial of intention in their work. However, it's easy to read intention in such a project. In these examples, the maintenance of a marginal, isolated individualism is posited as an heroic and transcendent project.

(See Ron Silliman, Carla Harryman, Lyn Hejinian, Steve Benson, Bob Perelman and Barrett Watten, 'Aesthetic Tendency and the Politics of Poetry: A Manifesto', *Social Text* 19/20 (1988), 261–75 (p. 264).) In *The Future of Memory* (New York: Roof, 1998), p. 11, Bob Perelman parodies the Smith/Bottoms position pointedly in observing that his recent '. . . writing seems pretty normal: // complete sentences; semicolons; yada yada. I / seem to have lost my avant-garde // card in the laundry'. Compare also Walter Kalaidjian's critique of this aspect of the anthologies as marking 'the period's political limit: one that actively led readers to invest in ideologies of bourgeois individualism' (*Languages of Liberation: The Social Text in Contemporary American Poetry* (New York: Columbia University Press, 1989), p. 14).

production, collection and consumption: 'the work of the poets speaks best for itself'. Such statements echo throughout the introductions to these texts: 'the poetry ... speaks for itself' or 'defines its own excellence'.[33] But, as Jed Rasula observes, 'that poems "speak for themselves" is an editorial pretension, deflecting attention from the ventriloquial ambience'.[34] Speaking for itself, the poetry apparently just talks its own way into the mainstream anthology. That to anthologize a poem is already in some sense to speak *for* it rather than have it speak for itself; that 'excellence' is widely argued now to be historical, institutional and contingent rather than self-defining: these are issues that the mainstream editors tend to finesse. Sometimes they seem to do so out of a knee-jerk 'resistance to theory' that puts 'art' and 'theory' at odds: 'Editing is an art, and we don't intend to theorize our position.'[35] This rhetoric extends to anthologies that once looked far more adventurous than they do now, such as Stephen Berg and Robert Mezey's *Naked Poetry* and *The New Naked Poetry*. In *Naked Poetry* (1969) Berg and Mezey assert that 'the poems certainly don't need interpreters', and immediately follow this exercise of the self-evidence principle by recording their resistance to theorizing the work in their anthology: 'We soon grew bored with our original plan to discuss the theory and practice' of what they called 'open form' poetics.[36] In their 1976 revision, *The New Naked Poetry*, this resistance emerges even more strongly, as they invoke the over-determined opposition between theorist and poet: 'In any case, we are not theoreticians. We write the stuff.'[37] This opposition anticipates that inscribed in Smith and Bottoms's now-notorious figure of the composite individualist, 'rarely a card-carrying group member, political or aesthetic', who 'seems to jog more than to write literary criticism'.[38]

The disavowal of conflict and the denial of sides that have already been taken; the related distaste for 'schools'; dependence on the

---

[33] Sources for the preceding quotations are as follows: Myers and Weingarten (eds), *Poets of the '80s*, p. xiv; Halpern (ed.), *American Poetry Anthology*, p. xxxiii; Ochester and Oresick (eds), *Pittsburgh Anthology*, p. xvi.

[34] Rasula, *American Poetry Wax Museum*, p. 466. Rasula also argues that anthologists of alternative poetries, like Eliot Weinberger, Paul Hoover and Douglas Messerli, share McClatchy's position 'that letting [poems] "speak for themselves" is the editor's primary obligation'. While these editors do little to question the basic structural format of the anthology *as a form*, however, so that admittedly they 'showcase isolate poems' (*American Poetry Wax Museum*, p. 466), they do not propose as explicitly as their mainstream counterparts this position about the poem's self-articulating value.

[35] Ochester and Oresick (eds), *Pittsburgh Anthology*, p. xvi.

[36] Stephen Berg and Robert Mezey (eds), *Naked Poetry: Recent American Poetry in Open Forms* (Indianapolis: Bobbs-Merrill, 1969), p. xi.

[37] Berg and Mezey (eds), *The New Naked Poetry: Recent American Poetry in Open Forms* (Indianapolis: Bobbs-Merrill, 1976), p. xix.

[38] Smith and Bottoms (eds), *Morrow Anthology*, p. 19.

creative-writing program as a primary site of poetry's production and consumption; untenable claims to eclecticism; the university presses' reinforcement of the 'normative'; the alleged privileging of 'poems' that conflicts with the actual privileging of 'poets' and the reifying of 'voice'; an ideology of the unmediated or self-evident: all these features combine to make up the mainstream contemporary survey of American poetry and to maintain the structure of the current mainstream anthologizing machinery. As Rae Armantrout puts it in her review of the *Morrow Anthology*, 'it is worthwhile to examine claims to naturalness and objectivity carefully to find out what is being suppressed'.[39] Examining these claims allows us to understand and de-naturalize these texts' efforts to claim a centre in the guise of decentralization.

As I have suggested, the term 'mainstream' in reference to poetry conflates the social and the aesthetic, describing both a location within a range of publishing, grant-giving and degree-granting networks and a set of formal features associated with that location. In mainstream anthologies, social and intellectual background, academic training and aesthetics tend to meet and perpetuate each other. To discuss a poetic mainstream in this way runs some risk of circularity: I choose what I have already decided are mainstream texts in order to generate a pseudo-inductive account of mainstream texts. However, the apparent problem of circularity – picking mainstream anthologies as a way of defining the mainstream – is itself a problem *within* mainstream poetics, where social and formal considerations are hard to separate even as their connectedness is persistently either denied or dismissed as coincidental. While it is hard to agree with Jed Rasula that we lack a critical vocabulary for discussing what is commonly called the workshop lyric – there are plenty of accounts of it available by now – I *would* agree 'that such a vocabulary necessitates a shift from the aesthetic to the sociological and the political'.[40] This vocabulary becomes especially necessary when claims about the distinctive aesthetics of individual writers are used to efface or evade the social components of mainstream poetics.

One other possible objection to the kind of analysis that I have conducted here is that it risks collapsing distinctions among poets, to whom, as readers and critics, we owe our attention on a case-by-case basis. From this point of view, the mainstream proves a chimera once one starts to ask how or where given poet X fits; how the work of X manifests allegedly 'mainstream' features; or how two poets as different as A and B can both meaningfully be described as 'mainstream'. It is true that (by definition) attention to individual cases foregrounds differences, distinctiveness. But, at the same time, an anthology often puts individual poets

---

[39] Rae Armantrout, 'Mainstream Marginality', *Poetics Journal* 6 (1986), 141–4 (p. 144).
[40] Rasula, *American Poetry Wax Museum*, p. 427.

and their individual(ized) poems in a context that *de*-individualizes them.[41] The irony of this situation for a poetics of fetishized individualism is especially acute. Furthermore, objections to the notion of a 'mainstream' that rest on the distinctiveness of the individual poet can equally be seen not as the refutation of the idea of a mainstream poetics but as a tactical *example* of it. In other words, the critical strategy of dismissing 'mainstream' as a meaningful category by reference to the work of individual poets replicates the strategy among anthology editors of denying similarities among the hardy individualists whose work they gather. Indeed, the mainstream's denial of its own existence as a socio-poetic formation parallels, in Althusser's terms, the workings of ideology, one attribute of which is to maintain its own invisibility in order to do its regulatory work.

The notion of a 'mainstream' exists in relation to various other terms within critical discourse – a discourse of 'margin' and 'centre', of 'avant-garde', 'experimental' and 'oppositional'. Sceptical as one might be of the terms' precise usefulness, they have, in the period under discussion, continued to provide ways of mapping the poetic field – for poets, not just for critics. Language writing, for instance, arose in the context of – though not necessarily *in reaction to* – a hegemonic poetic ideology of anti-theoretical lyric individualism: a setting of 'mainstream poetic "individuality"', as Charles Bernstein puts it, in which 'the prevalent phobias against groups and against critical thinking encouraged us to make our opposing commitments specific and partisan'.[42] Furthermore, these mainstream 'phobias' were represented and circulated in anthologies coincident with the planning (from 1976 onwards) and eventual founding of L=A=N=G=U=A=G=E magazine: in Halpern's *The American Poetry Anthology* (1975), for instance, or Berg and Mezey's *The New Naked Poetry* (1976). Comments from Language writers such as Bob Perelman or Rae Armantrout on a poem like William Stafford's 'Traveling in the Dark' reflect a genuine and active

---

[41] From this point of view, it may well be that the very phenomenon of the anthology conflicts with the aura of individual and asocial creativity that the mainstream collection projects. Ann Lauterbach suggests as much in a recent essay:

> There still attaches to the *idea* of the poet a belief that poetry should be, is, exempt from market forces, from brute commerce and commodification. And yet, into this abstract, distilled sanctity, the protected solitude of Rilke's Beloved, comes the Angel of History with his Anthology under his Wing.

(See 'The Night Sky IV', *American Poetry Review* 26 (July/August 1997), 35–42 (p. 36).)

[42] Charles Bernstein, 'An Autobiographical Interview with Charles Bernstein', with Loss Pequeno Glazier, *Boundary 2* 23.3 (1996), 21–43 (p. 42). For an effective exposition of this aspect of Language writing's coalescence as a movement, see Bob Perelman, *The Marginalization of Poetry: Language Writing and Literary History* (Princeton: Princeton University Press, 1996), pp. 12–13 and Silliman et al., 'Aesthetic Tendency'.

cultural conflict.[43] In the decade 1975–1985, what came to be tagged so notoriously as the 'workshop lyric' was getting established as mainstream contemporaneously with the development of Language writing, as the period saw not only a rush of anthologies but also a sudden increase in the number of poetry prizes and trade and university press publication series (some of which, admittedly, are now defunct)[44] and a dramatic expansion in the credentializing reach of creative writing as an institution: according to D. G. Myers, 'between 1971 and 1989 the number of degrees awarded in the field more than tripled – from 345 to 1107'.[45]

The decades of the creative-writing workshop's expansion were also the decades of the anthology – ninety-two of them published between 1970 and 1989, according to Jed Rasula, who includes in his count textbooks devoting substantial space to poetry but excludes topic-based and identity-based anthologies.[46] Given the claims to newness proposed in a number of these collections, it is worth noting that only Halpern's *American Poetry Anthology* – as the first of its kind, the mainstream survey – really served the function of introducing new poets. Sixteen of Halpern's poets received their first anthology appearance in his text. Ten years later, by contrast, the *Morrow* served more of a retrospective or consolidating function: only eight of its 103 poets were new to anthologies, as were only ten of Jack Myers and Roger Weingarten's allegedly 'new' poets of the 1980s. In line with these figures, Jonathan Holden reads the *Morrow* and Myers/Weingarten collections as what I would call

---

[43] See Bob Perelman, 'The First Person', *Hills* 6/7 (1979), 147–65 (pp. 156, 160–2) and his further comments in *The Marginalization of Poetry*, pp. 113–14; also Armantrout's parody 'Traveling in the Yard', *Precedence* (Providence: Burning Deck, 1985), p. 18.

[44] For example, the Academy of American Poets' Walt Whitman Award, the Associated Writing Programs award series and the National Book Critics Circle Award all started in 1975; 1976 brought the Princeton University Press and Houghton Mifflin poetry series (now both defunct); the Elliston Award was founded in 1977 and the National Poetry Series (far more diverse than most such series) and the Poetry Society of America's William Carlos Williams Award in 1979. The L. A. Times Book Award was first granted in 1980 and, in 1981, the first MacArthur Fellowships; see Rasula, *American Poetry Wax Museum*, pp. 519–47 and Jonathan Holden, 'American Poetry 1970–1990', in Jack Myers and David Wojahn (eds), *A Profile of Twentieth-Century American Poetry* (Carbondale: Southern Illinois University Press, 1991), pp. 254–74 (p. 261). (Only the years 1945–6 have seen a comparable eruption of award series.) Details from the Devins Award's history provide concrete examples of how institutional networks in poetry sustain themselves. Gerald Constanzo used his 1974 prize money to publish the first Carnegie Mellon University Press poetry books in 1975; Jonathan Holden's award earned him his first academic job (Gerald Constanzo (ed.), *The Devins Award Poetry Anthology* (Columbia: University of Missouri Press, 1998), pp. 5–6). The point here is not to demean Constanzo's labor and generosity or to begrudge Holden his employment. It is to make concrete the claim that mainstream publishing series and rewards tend to generate more

[45] D. G. Myers, *The Elephants Teach: Creative Writing Since 1880* (Englewood Cliffs, NJ: Prentice-Hall, 1996), p. 166.

[46] Rasula, *American Poetry Wax Museum*, p. 485.

'career' anthologies, sequels to Halpern's (which Holden too credits for instituting a new mainstream) in so far as they gather poets first appearing in Halpern's text and document their ongoing achievement.[47] Thus the mainstream anthology, while certainly foregrounding a particular aesthetics, can also be thought of as occupying a crucial place in a self-sustaining socio-poetic network.

Data on academically sponsored poetry readings further illustrate how the anthologies under discussion here have functioned as part of a larger network of legitimation. Hank Lazer finds that in the period 1985–87 – which saw the publication of two anthologies of the same poetic generations, the *Morrow* and Ron Silliman's *In the American Tree* – forty of the one hundred and four *Morrow* poets delivered academically sponsored readings, while nine of the forty *Tree* poets did so. This disparity is heightened by the fact that most of these *Tree* readings took place at a single local outlet for these writers, San Francisco State University. (The figure of almost forty per cent from the *Morrow* also represents a kind of shared mainstream canon between that anthology and *New Poets of the 1980s*: thirty-eight of Smith and Bottoms's poets reappear among the ninety-five of Myers and Weingarten's anthology.) To come at Lazer's data from a different angle, the poets from one single anthology accounted for close to twenty per cent of the four hundred campus readings that he surveyed. In the face of these data, it is hard to argue with Lazer's conclusion that 'the academic poetry reading circuit is a narrowly constituted prop for the dominant craft of the workshop' and as such 'is condemned to a non-self-reflective act of formal repetition'.[48]

The anthologies described here have exercised their influence as part of a wider cultural field that has tended to sustain the same values via literary histories, interviews and other, more specifically focused anthologies. In his critical book *The Fate of American Poetry*, for instance, *Morrow* contributor Jonathan Holden praises that anthology for demonstrating 'the depth and strength of the mainstream, "centrist", realist mode'.[49] In *The Columbia History of American Poetry*, post-war experimental

---

[47] Holden, 'American Poetry', p. 273. I have cited this version of a discussion that appears also as part of Holden's *The Fate of American Poetry* (Athens: University of Georgia Press, 1991) because the book version drops any mention of the Myers and Weingarten anthology.

[48] Hank Lazer, *Opposing Poetries*, 2 vols (Evanston, IL: Northwestern University Press, 1996), vol. 1, *Issues and Institutions*, pp. 53–4.

[49] Holden's praise of the *Morrow Anthology* echoes the terms, cited earlier in this essay, in which Smith and Bottoms describe their representative younger American poet:

> The mainstream of American poetry . . . has continued to be, whether narrative or meditative, in a realist mode that is essentially egalitarian, university-based, middle-class, and to be written in a free verse that has, by and large, vastly improved since the sixties.

(See Holden, *Fate of American Poetry*, pp. 47–8.)

movements such as the New York School, Black Mountain and Language writing are barely mentioned (and mostly in the context of one essay, by Lynn Keller, who is also the only writer in the book to consider innovative writing by women) and the Objectivists as a group are not mentioned at all. In a remarkable revival of nineteenth-century gentility, Longfellow enjoys a full single-author chapter, while Louis Zukofsky and Charles Olson get a total of four pages combined.[50] Meanwhile, the mainstream workshop lyric gets its own chapter (Gregory Orr's 'The Postconfessional Lyric'), as does confessional poetry itself.

This category of the 'postconfessional' had already provided the title for a 1989 collection of interviews that, in the words of co-editor Stan Sanvel Rubin, 'represents what might be termed the "mainstream" of American poetry during the seventies and eighties' – which means that 'many of [the poets] are included' in Smith and Bottoms's and Heyen's anthologies, have won prizes, 'published at least one major book' and appear regularly in 'the major journals'.[51] (Rubin's invocation of prizes is one of the many places in the mainstream's self-valorization where one sees at work the circular premise that the prizewinners must be the best poets because only the best poets win the prizes.) In turn, those 'major journals' have made their own contribution to maintaining the mainstream by producing their own historical anthologies, from *Poems from the Virginia Quarterly Review, 1925–1967* (1969) up to anthologies from *Poetry* (1978), *Antaeus* (1986), *Georgia Review* (1987), *Ploughshares* (1987) and *The Paris Review* (1990). (A category of anthology related both to the magazine and to the university press collection would include those published by university presses to commemorate academic poetry awards – the University of Michigan's *Hopwood Anthology* (1981), the University of Missouri's *Devins Award Poetry Anthology* (1998), *The Yale Younger Poets Anthology* (1998).)[52]

---

[50] My point here is not so much to argue the merits or demerits of the Longfellow revival that Dana Gioia's quite compelling chapter proposes; rather, it is to point out the price of that revival in this publishing context, the exclusions with which it is associated in an academically sanctioned construction of American literary history that cannot imagine a parallel tradition of formal investigation running alongside the bland centrism that it unspokenly promotes.

[51] Stan Sanvel Rubin, 'Introduction', in Earl G. Ingersoll, Judith Kitchen and Stan Sanvel Rubin (eds), *The Post-Confessionals: Conversations with American Poets of the Eighties* (Rutherford, NJ: Fairleigh Dickinson University Press, 1989), pp. 11–24 (pp. 15, 11).

[52] A list of counterexamples, of anthologies based on alternative publications and awards, would include Clayton Eshleman (ed.) *A Caterpillar Anthology: A Selection of Poetry and Prose from Caterpillar Magazine* (Garden City, NY: Doubleday, 1971); Cid Corman (ed.), *The Gist of Origin 1951–1971* (New York: Grossman, 1975); J. J. Phillips, Ishmael Reed, Gundars Strads and Shawn Wong (eds), *The Before Columbus Foundation Poetry Anthology: Selections from the American Book Awards 1980–1990* (New York: W. W. Norton, 1992); and Douglas Messerli's series of volumes for the years 1993–1996, *The Gertrude Stein Awards in Innovative American Poetry*, 3 vols (Los Angeles: Sun and Moon, 1995–97).

As a relational term, 'mainstream', not surprisingly, is used much more commonly by those who see themselves on the margins of it than by those who might be described as occupying it. Less established poets, working in 'alternative' modes, still turn to the familiar structuring binary as a way of locating themselves socio-poetically. In 1960, Donald Allen made his now-famous claim that the New American Poetry 'has shown one common characteristic: a total rejection of all those qualities typical of academic verse'.[53] In 1998, Lisa Jarnot prefaced a co-edited *Anthology of New (American) Poets* by arguing that 'what all these writers share' is, among other things, 'their marginalization from mainstream literary culture'.[54] Both at the levels of editorial rhetoric and aesthetics, versions of this binary retain some force. What can look, from one point of view, like a binarized and dated 'war of the anthologies' looks different if one views anthologies in toto, as a genre, as a site of ongoing conversation, debate and struggle over literary and social values. Anthologies and their editors are constantly measuring themselves against their market competition and their predecessors; the texts have their meaning partly in relation to other anthologies. Thus it is unsurprising to find Dennis Barone and Peter Ganick couch the poetics of their *Art of Practice* in explicitly anti-mainstream terms: 'poetry is not the place for expression of common or authentic voice' and their anthology is 'opposed to the so-called natural free verse poem'.[55] Setting one stated criterion of the mainstream anthology against what can often appear an actual criterion, Barone and Ganick claim that 'the poem – not degrees, hobbies – is primary'.[56] What constitutes 'the poem' here, however, is one thing that further separates *The Art of Practice* from more mainstream anthologies. That is, the latter generally preserve the generic stability of the poem, while gatherings like *The Art of Practice* and other experimental anthologies (Douglas Messerli's *From the Other Side of the Century* is a prime example) 'challenge rigidity of genre', in Barone and Ganick's words.[57] Over half the writers in *The Art of Practice* (twenty-five out of forty-five, including seventeen women) are represented partly or wholly by prose, as are thirteen out of sixty-three in Leonard Schwartz, Joseph Donahue and Edward Foster's *Primary Trouble*, which explicitly 'seeks to elevate a

---

[53] Donald Allen, *The New American Poetry* (New York: Grove Press, 1960), p. xi. For discussion of the category of the 'academic' in Allen's influential anthology, see Alan Golding, 'The New American Poetry Revisited, Again', *Contemporary Literature* 39 (1998), 180–211, especially pp. 200–7.

[54] Lisa Jarnot, 'Preface', in Lisa Jarnot, Leonard Schwartz and Chris Stroffolino (eds), *An Anthology of New (American) Poets* (Jersey City, NJ: Talisman House, 1998), pp. 1–2 (p. 1).

[55] Dennis Barone and Peter Ganick (eds), *The Art of Practice: Forty-Five Contemporary Poets* (Elmwood, CT: Potes & Poets, 1994), pp. xiii–xiv.

[56] Ibid., 'Foreword', p. xv.

[57] Ibid., 'Foreword', p. xiii.

certain poetics into view against the mainstream poetics that might obscure it', even as it complicates the usual binary by expressing considerable ambivalence toward Language writing.[58] In another context, one of the editors (Edward Foster) shows comparable ambivalence about the terms 'avant-garde', 'experimental' and 'alternative' but still situates the poets who interest him 'outside the poetic mainstream as defined in standard classroom anthologies and histories of American poetry'.[59]

While I have not organized this essay around particular collections, Smith and Bottoms's *Morrow Anthology* has been widely taken as the most influential and representative anthology of those under discussion. That is, the poetic mainstream became widely noticed as such with the *Morrow*'s publication. Commenting on the Associated Writing Programs' institutionalization of creative writing, Jed Rasula argues that 'while there has been no *official* anthology, the hefty *Morrow Anthology of Younger American Poets* (1985) has, in its fidelity to the workshop mode, preempted the need for one'.[60] Vernon Shetley shares this judgment, describing the *Morrow* as 'very much an anthology of mainstream poetic practice, the mainstream that flows through the creative writing programs'; as such the *Morrow* is an anthology of a (one might even say, *the*) period style.[61] Smith and Bottoms begin their preface to this representative text with a revealing slippage, as they implicitly compare their situation as editors with 'Emerson greeting Whitman at the beginning of a new poetry'. If we recall Emerson's actual phrasing, however, he greeted

---

[58] Leonard Schwartz, 'Introduction', in Leonard Schwartz, Joseph Donahue and Edward Foster (eds), *Primary Trouble: An Anthology of Contemporary American Poetry* (Jersey City, NJ: Talisman House, 1996), pp. 1–4 (p. 3).

[59] Edward Foster (ed.), *Postmodern Poetry: The Talisman Interviews* (Hoboken, NJ: Talisman House, 1994), p. vii. Characterizations and critiques of the mainstream anthology, however, by no means all stem from its self-designated experimental Others. From a formally traditional perspective, R. S. Gwynn finds that *The Pittsburgh Book of Contemporary American Poetry* symbolizes 'what the center holds' – 'a marked uniformity of style and subject' ('What the Center Holds', *Hudson Review* 46 (1994), 741–50 (p. 741). Vernon Shetley, who has written on poets as uncontroversial as Bishop and Merrill, argues, as I have here, the false pluralism of mainstream poetics:

> Though a rhetoric of pluralism obscures the underlying conformity, the range of stylistic options and models employed in the mainstream is in fact quite narrow; differences in outlook and approach are rarely so dramatic as to involve fundamental disagreements of principle that would be worth arguing publicly.

(See *After the Death of Poetry: Poet and Audience in Contemporary America* (Durham, NC: Duke University Press, 1993), p. 137.)

[60] Rasula, *American Poetry Wax Museum*, p. 417.

[61] Vernon Shetley, 'The Place of Poetry', *Yale Review* 75 (1986), 429–37 (p. 434). Compare Geoffrey O'Brien's characterization of the *Morrow* as a textbook of 'academically respectable verse', 'a display of officially sanctioned art, a veritable *poesie de salon*' (*Bardic Deadlines*, p. 34).

Whitman 'at the beginning of a great career'.[62] Smith and Bottoms's unspoken conflation of 'poetry' and 'career' seems as symbolic a moment as any of the forces driving mainstream American poetry anthologies in the 1970s and 1980s.

[62] Smith and Bottoms (eds), *Morrow Anthology*, p. 15; Ralph Waldo Emerson, *Selections from Ralph Waldo Emerson: An Organic Anthology*, Stephen F. Whicher (ed.), (Boston: Houghton Mifflin, 1957), p. 362.

7

The Progress of the Avant-garde: Reading/Writing Race and Culture According to Universal Systems of Value

Romana Huk

We live, we tell ourselves constantly, in a pluralizing world. Much recent work in critical theory has tended to assume that value lies entirely on the side of opening, expansion, alterity and invention, and not on the side of fixity, conservation, tradition and repetition. This book assumes that these are not clear or continuous opposites. The paradoxical structure of value enacts itself in avant-garde art, which can be truly new only by means of its refusal to abandon what it aims to leave behind in its past, or in a deconstructive philosophy that can avoid re-enacting tradition only by a repetitive working through of that tradition. Only an institution can dissolve itself, only an identity can know plurality, only the same is vulnerable to alterity, only a kind of consciousness can embrace the unthought, only tradition can beget newness; in sum, only the commitment or imperative to value can effect any kind of transvaluation.[1]

I

In his 1993 book *Culture and Imperialism*, Edward Said warns that ours is a necessary and dangerous time of 'surpassing theoretical elaboration', when 'universalizing techniques' of rethinking thinking, according to postmodern philosophical paradigms, have both illumined the way of the world's cultural impositions and occluded specific responses to specific histories of imposed thought.[2] Like Steven Connor in my epigraph, Said splices the two imperatives – to universalize and to particularize – in a paradoxically suspended grammar of 'progress'; in its 'good'

---

[1] Steven Connor, *Theory and Cultural Value* (Oxford: Blackwell, 1992), p. 3.
[2] Edward Said, *Culture and Imperialism* (New York: A. A. Knopf, 1993), p. 60.

version, according to Connor, the paradox plays itself out in our invention of new thinking or new art practice via the imperative to construct
value

> as the Derridean *différance* of value, not only because it defers the
> arrival of ultimate value (though it is always necessarily orientated
> towards it), as *différance* defers the arrival of meaning, but because
> of [its] reflexive structure ... in which every value is itself subject to
> the force of evaluation.[3]

The problem that arises in this utopian model of progress, and is studied
in Connor's concluding chapter, 'Beyond Cultural Value: The Writing of
the Other', is that in even the most current re-evaluations of art – or art-
culture systems, such as the one James Clifford drew up in his seminal
work, *The Predicament of Culture* – the unrepresentability of the values
that *underlie* such new valuation often causes assessment to remain
'ethically underspecified, because [it is] unable to bring the imperatives
which motivate it to evaluative visibility'.[4] If we import this description of
the dilemma into current debates concerning postmodern poetry/poetics
and race – a field of writing/righting dependent upon the notion of
pluralizing values/meanings, or even the post-pluralization of them, as I
will try to describe it – the question becomes: *whose* identity is being
pluralized in the quest for avant-garde unravellings of past value systems
(see epigraph above), and how does that starting point for departure
regulate the valuing of the distances achieved? Which universalizing
systems of value are (inadvertently) active in the articulation of a 'postmodern' aesthetic for poetry, and how do such underlying systems affect
the reading/writing/categorization and ultimately the subsidization of

---

[3] Connor, *Theory and Cultural Value*, p. 3.
[4] James Clifford, *The Predicament of Culture: Twentieth-Century Ethnography, Literature
and Art* (Cambridge, MA and London: Harvard University Press, 1988). Connor uses the
language of ethics to describe the 'responsibility' of the ethnographer (and by extension,
the critic) to 'fully occupy' the paradox of value as he sees it; the inability of

> Clifford's postmodern ethnography ... to bring the imperatives which motivate it
> to evaluative visibility ... is not so much a failure to escape the paradox of value
> whereby it is necessary to affirm in absolute terms the contingency of all such
> absolutes, but a failure properly and fully to inhabit it, to acknowledge fully one's
> own necessary imperatives and value-investments. (Connor, p. 255)

'particular' cultures of poets – say, new generations of black writers working in the 1980s and '90s in the UK and America?[5]

The British black poetry scene will be my primary focus here (particularly in the second section below) because of its shorter history within white boundaries, dating back, as it does, fifty years from the time of writing (which coincides with the black community's 'Windrush celebrations').[6] At the beginning of the new millennium, this history leaves the British black poetry scene in a much more fluid state, one of constant 're-evaluation' of its own projects. It can also be seen as facing cultural situations and issues that differ greatly from those of its counterparts across the 'Black Atlantic'.[7] The latter have found ways to connect their work to the American theorizing that has, by virtue of its prolific energy and comparatively numerous publishing outlets, dominated postmodern aesthetics for poetry. If postcolonialist theory shares many of its premises with the postmodern philosophy that undergirds those aesthetics, should avant-garde work done by black poets in Britain be valued according to its adherence to the same methods and modes of departure? Can the supplementation of a diasporic model for black writing within those aesthetics clarify the workings of what Connor calls 'the paradox of value' by offering specifications that allow for difference in practice beyond the constraints of particular continental and racial identities that underlie the theorized 'pluralization' of worldwide postmodern poetries? Patrick Williams argues that since the term 'post-colonial'

---

[5] When I refer to 'postmodern' poetry I think of key anthologies that have begun to articulate the category, such as Paul Hoover's *Postmodern American Poetry: A Norton Anthology* (New York and London: Norton & Co., 1994), Maggie O'Sullivan's *Out of Everywhere: Linguistically Innovative Poetry by Women in North America & the UK* (London and Suffolk: Reality Street Editions, 1996), Iain Sinclair's *Conductors of Chaos* (London: Picador, 1996), Jerome Rothenberg's and Pierre Joris's *Poems for the Millennium*, Volume Two (Berkeley, CA and London: University of California Press, 1998) and others in the same vein. I should also explain, in what has perhaps become a kind of obligatory gesture given the long arguments that have evolved around the issue, that I use the term 'black' British only because 'Anglo-African' cannot work in the same way that 'African American' does (wrongly at times) in the States – all inclusively; in the United Kingdom, 'black' often covers a number of different communities aside from the African one.

[6] This anniversary commemorates the June 1948 landing of the first boat of immigrants (the *SS Empire Windrush*) from the Caribbean, when the freeing of former colonies was running apace and reconstruction in the UK required a larger, inexpensive workforce. Waves of immigration followed from not only the West Indies, but also the South Asian subcontinent and Africa. 'Black' in the United Kingdom often includes reference to Chinese immigrants as well – though my own references must not, as I have too little acquaintance with that particular field of work.

[7] I refer with 'Black Atlantic' to Paul Gilroy's book by that name which suggests a diasporic model rather than a national one in appreciating the innovations of 'postcolonial' black art. *The Black Atlantic: Modernity and Double Consciousness* (London: Verso, 1993).

refers to more than three quarters of the world, and ... one of the major contemporary phenomena in relation to which post-colonialism has to situate itself is that of globalization, any avoidance of totalizing methods which attempt some understanding of the overall workings or significances involved would be sheer irresponsibility.[8]

That drive toward re-evaluating artistic dynamics in light of world dynamics – or rather, toward making one illumine the other – finds compelling company not only in postmodern poetics as a whole but also in the advocacy of diasporic models for reading such as those proposed by Gilroy, who also argues that black cultural practices 'indicate a more substantive "postmodern" vision when they have stepped outside the confines of modernity's most impressive achievement – the nation state'.[9] In that postmodern space, he suggests, they display more readily the 'cultural syncretism' as opposed to acculturation that he associates with black aesthetics; that distinction is an important one to which I will return below.

But does that space hover in transcendence of cultural boundaries or does it become entangled in the 'unrepresentable values' that guard a text's entry into readability within a specific cultural (which includes the concept of 'national') terrain?[10] The intercultural/international comparisons of projects, among not only black artists specifically but also avant-garde poets more generally, often disregard such questions, longing as they do for 'the arrival of ultimate value' that Connor argues is never expected to happen in his utopian model of progress, though desire for it must remain operative nonetheless. Therefore, we also get unselfconscious identifications *between* aesthetic and raced projects, such as the

[8] Patrick Williams, 'No Direction Home? Futures for Post-Colonial Studies', *Wasafiri: A Journal of South Asian, Caribbean, and African Writing* 23 (Spring 1996), 3–6 (p. 3).

[9] Paul Gilroy, *'There Ain't No Black in the Union Jack': The Cultural Politics of Race and Nation* (1987; rpt. London: Routledge, 1998), p. 219.

[10] Writers such as Gayatri Chakravorty Spivak have been using this understanding to warn of certain invisible classifications of power that have been building beneath what seem to be levelling conceptualizations of the world, such as those of 'transnationalism' or transculturalism. In 'Diasporas Old and New: Women in the Transnational World', where she discusses the discrepant economic base to such theorization, Spivak argues that:

> as important as the displacement of 'culture' – which relates to the first word in the compound, 'nation', and is an ideological arena – is the exchange of state, which is an abstract area of calculation.... And the mechanisms of civil society, although distinct from the state, are peculiar to it. And now, in transnationality, precisely because the limits and openings of a particular civil society are never transnational, the transnationalization of global capital requires a post-state class-system.
>
> *Textual Practice* 10: 2 (1996), 250

one Peter Quartermain makes in his important book, *Disjunctive Poetics*, which begins with the suggestion that:

> [t]he situation of the American writer in the first thirty or forty years of this century bears distinct resemblances to the situation of the writer in the postcolonial world, where the grand hegemonic authority of rule by imperial standard is giving way to a frequently bewildered and more often than not anarchic series of disagreements.[11]

Yet how do we begin to discuss the *differences* here in terms of response – or the *différance* of value involved in appreciating the two projects' many varied responses? Whereas avant-garde or 'Language' poetry (originally spelled analytically as 'L=A=N=G=U=A=G=E' to suggest poetry issuing in tandem with poststructuralist theories of language) in the States has become, as Quartermain argues, extremely 'disjunctive' in confronting its cultural situation, most postcolonial work outside the States has not – though it has, as he claims, responded to the same general sets of stimulants. Do we find ways of valuing those differing responses as anything but 'other' – situated yet again outside what we have learned to read and wish to see as our pluralized response to the postmodern landscape? What happens when the 'identity' which, according to Connor, can 'know plurality', is exceeded by others outside that dominant starting point for departure into the 'avant-garde'?

The dominant mythos of identity, as it has evolved in the States, offers a differing illusion from that which has evolved in Britain, or its former colonies, as well as a differing set of forces to oppose and, therefore, differing strategies of opposition – all of which must contribute, however inadvertently, to the disposition of a radical poetic, as well as to possible constructions of raced responses within the same. As Patricia Waugh writes, '[b]ecause "nation" exists in imaginative space ... the founding origins of its narratives of identity tend to be buried and, though constructed as pragmatic fictions, may come to take on the essential and unchanging aspect of myth'.[12] Grown up around cultural narratives of America's immigrant identity – which counteract its short history by valorizing instead its unhampered newness or supposed escape from 'traditional baggage' (theorized most famously in twentieth-century poetry by William Carlos Williams) – is the celebration of a kind of oxymoronic collective atomization that, at every level, enables the

---

[11] Peter Quartermain, *Disjunctive Poetics: From Gertrude Stein and Louis Zukofsky to Susan Howe* (Cambridge: Cambridge University Press, 1992), p. 12.

[12] Patricia Waugh, *Harvest of the Sixties: English Literature and its Background 1960 to 1990* (New York and London: Oxford University Press, 1995), p. 151.

individual to imagine herself/himself reassembling dissociated fragments of pooled cultures into new formations independent of historical constraints. Similarly, potent democratic rhetoric equalizes access to that pool, so that 'difference', though so much at issue in the last forty years, remains notionally erasable in the mix – an ideational inheritance that has survived *both* the melting pot image's later denunciation *and* theory's critiques of the subject in dominant bourgeois ideology. It continues to structure the imagination of a kind of unlimited identity achieved, ironically, *through* difference (as one goes *through* history to its teleological end), even in current writings by African American poststructuralist theorists like Michael Awkward, who argues that '[o]n our American shores of knowing, there is no racial or gendered purity, no space to which we can locate an untainted state of being, no irreducible difference'.[13] The critique of essentiality in America still tends, in other words, to be inflected in such a way that particular histories are melted down, reduced according to an earlier national imagination of reconstructable identity; as Gilroy warns, such postmodern theorizing can lead to what I would describe as an inverted form of absolutism rather than pluralism – characterized by some permutation of the statement, 'we are all not different' – which encourages increasingly vague responses to 'the lingering power of specifically "racial" forms of power and subordination'.[14]

The position of the American subject as self-creator located in an equalizing mesh of differences that ironically obviate difference has had an enormously powerful impact on the relationship drawn in postmodern poetry between artists and materials – the latter including 'race' and 'history' – which Language poet Bruce Andrews recently described as one that has insisted upon attentiveness to 'the particular, the concrete, the present' in a way that atomizes the artist and 'de-specifies' her/his stance, as well as the work, at the same time.[15] 'It is almost a commonplace amongst twentieth-century American writers,' Quartermain writes,

> to notice, as Stein did in her 1935 lectures on narration at the University of Chicago, that in American writing, words 'began to detach themselves from the solidity of anything' ... [and] that American language exhibits a 'lack of connection' with material daily living

[13] Michael Awkward, *Negotiating Difference: Race, Gender and the Politics of Positionality* (Chicago: University of Chicago Press, 1995), p. 13.

[14] Paul Gilroy, *Small Acts: Thoughts on the Politics of Black Cultures* (London: Serpent's Tail, 1993), p. 123.

[15] Bruce Andrews, *Paradise & Method: Poetics and Praxis* (Evanston, IL: Northwestern University Press, 1996), p. 62.

– so much so that Laura Riding could make her famous comment about Stein's material for poetry: 'None of the words Miss Stein uses . . . has ever had any history . . . They contain no references, no meanings' (*Disjunctive Poetics*, p. 14). Charles Bernstein, a leading apologist for Language poetries, incorporates such thinking into his work on the avant-garde poetics of 'ideolects' – a linguistic construct that revises the notion of ethnic and regional dialects to make way for a less group-based, more interactive/intertextual view of language's gerrymanderings that dislocates them from ownership, sets them afloat, accessible, nomadic – which allows language to become a sort of sea that erases any 'trace of [specific] consciousness', in which '[t]here are no terminal points (me → you)', only 'a sounding of language from the inside'.[16] Starting from that sublimated construct of collective identity that idealizes the notion of movable parts, Bernstein's project of a kind of post-pluralization involves incorporating variously marginalized poetries' projects into the Language poetry project rather than critical self-evaluation from plural points of view. In calling for 'writing . . . that pushes the limits of what can be identified, that not only reproduces difference but invents it, spawning nomadic syntaxes of desire and excess that defy genre (birth, race, class) in order to relocate it',[17] postmodern poetry's poetics can be seen to participate in the same – or rather self-perpetuating – erasure of particular national and raced histories that began with melting pot ideology and that now, as with most unexamined motivating dynamics, finds support in its apparent opposite: those few edges of postmodern thinking that have been criticized for bordering on the nihilistic, though their flipside is often culturally conservative. In the writings of American Language poetics, the works of 'others' are allowed their difference in a contradictory, because temporalized, sense. They are treated as having contributed *historically* to unlocking repressions of difference in a 'grand narrative', but that narrative, ironically, is now rejected in favour of a *dehistoricized* linguistic landscape. It seems that 'others' may speak with a 'voice' in the old style but only by temporal dispensation, because they need to reach a point of acquiring equivalent starting points of identity before they can join the ranks engaged in the fully fledged losing of it:

I want to acknowledge the significance of group-identified poetries (ethnic, racial, linguistic, social, class, sexual, regional) in shattering

---

[16] Charles Bernstein, 'Comedy and the Poetics of Political Form', in Charles Bernstein (ed.), *The Politics of Poetic Form* (New York: Roof, 1990), p. 238; 'Writing and Method', first collected in Ron Silliman (ed.), *In The American Tree* (Orono, ME: National Poetry Foundation, 1986), p. 594; 'Language Sampler', *The Paris Review* 24/86 (Fall 1982), 75.

[17] Charles Bernstein, *A Poetics* (Cambridge, MA: Harvard University Press, 1992), p. 120.

the neoconventionalist ideal of fashioning by masterly artifice a neutral standard English, a common voice for all to speak ... But groups are composed of sub-groups, which are composed of fractionate differences that can be recombined into other formations incommensurable with the first ... In practice, the poetic force of expressing what has been repressed or simply unexpressed – whether individual or collective – has been considerable. Yet there is also the necessity of going beyond the Romantic idea of self and the Romantic idea of the spirit of a nation or group (*volksgeist*) or of a period (*zeitgeist*), a necessity for a poetry that does not organize itself around a dominant subject, whether that be understood as a self or a collectivity or a theme ... [one that engages in] the negative totalization of many separate chords, the better heard the more distinct each strain ... so that there *is* an acentric locus to English-language poetry.[18]

'The ideal of an absolute dialogism of peoples, or, as it were, a pure interference of voices, is self-contradictory to the extent that it occludes the questions of agency, commitment and responsibility,' writes Connor; '[w]ho holds to and assumes responsibility for realizing the ideal of the collective decentred writings of culture? Who sustains or justifies the absolute value of the dispersal of absolutes?'[19] In the same way that Clifford's postmodern ethnography is, as Connor describes it, ultimately underwritten by its own unacknowledged imperatives of value, the above post-Marxist, utopian vision of a new sort of democratically accessible linguistic 'base' in the cultural production of 'meaning', so key to the politics of the avant-garde, has reproduced, with ironic helplessness, the 'neutral, common language' that the quote suggests it repudiated at the beginning of its project. In these formulations, race becomes just another 'generic' syntax entering into the process of recombination and new production – a model of race that Gilroy objects to, given that its effect upon material history is blurred or diffused by the too simple unravelling of it as a floatable construction. Moreover, as with 'race', the 'subject' in avant-garde poetic theory is also too often pre-emptively dismantled or deconstructed as being, from the outset, a shifting, pronominal illusion that vanishes into the larger cultural text rather than studied as, at the very least, a *functional* illusion connected to and productive of *particular* material conditions, different in every case, due to differing, particular histories, all of which undergo changes within successive power relationships – in other words, as being exactly what

---

[18] Ibid., p. 120.
[19] Connor, *Theory and Cultural Value*, p. 253.

Bernstein dismisses above as that complex site of 'fractionate differences' 'recombining into other formations incommensurable with' original or even incremental ones: that is, traces of 'history' as we might newly define them through our postmodern focus on language. Gilroy laments that European theory is 'persistent in dealing with the problem of the subject exclusively in terms of its formation rather than through the fundamental issues of agency, action, reason and rationality inherent in considering the relationship between master and slave'.[20] In Language poetics theory, the intricate movement of thought is such that fractionate differences – pluralized – *seem* to be exactly that which is initially pursued in lieu of coherent theories of the subject or of collectives, but by dispensing with supposedly 'Romantic' recourse to ideas of the self as a particular site, a new culturally-specific, yet universalized, conception of (non)selfhood is born – a photo-negative of the bourgeois one, operant in a 'negative totalization of many chords', whose role in this oppositional poetics is as *centralizingly* envisioned as was that of its predecessor, according to theories concerning subject *formation* rather than the study of its historical functioning.

The potent influence of this model of identity is apparent in the particular lean of work by key African American experimentalists such as Nathaniel Mackey, whose important book, *Discrepant Engagement,* is rightly celebrated for drawing connections between experimental 'authors not normally grouped under a common rubric'.[21] These include white Americans such as Robert Creeley and Charles Olson; Anglo-Caribbean writers such as Wilson Harris (who moved to Britain in 1958) and Kamau Brathwaite (now living in America); and African Americans such as Amiri Baraka and, of course, himself. In the development of his argument, Mackey reminds readers of the case which Martiniquan writer Edouard Glissant made in the '70s against imperatives describing the only valuable oppositional strategy for black writers as the 'shout' that somehow rediscovers 'the innocence of primitive ethnos' – an argument that importantly warned, as Mackey notes, against 'universalizing and reductivity' and described the need for a theory of 'particular opacities'. However, he then stretches that crucial argument along a levelling horizon, one similar to Bernstein's, concluding that:

> [i]f language generally, not just a particular language, is catastrophic rather than grounded, ... [and i]f, as Maurice Blanchot

---

[20] Gilroy, *Small Acts*, p. 107.

[21] Nathaniel Mackey, *Discrepant Engagement: Dissonance, Cross-Culturality, and Experimental Writing* (Cambridge: Cambridge University Press, 1993), from the unnumbered, pre-preface blurb to the book.

says, 'to stay within language is always to be already outside,' then Césaire and Senghor are no more exiled in French than Jabès or Blanchot.[22]

His work on Wilson Harris emphasizes 'the American yet-to-be-inhabitedness' of Harris's Guyana, quoting C. L. R. James who wrote that Harris, in his novels, participates in the Heideggerean Dasein, or profoundly present-tense 'being there' of the Caribbean, where 'there has never been that fixed assumption of things, that belief in something that is many centuries old and solid'.[23] Such brokenness from continuities allows Harris – whose work, as Mackey notes, begins to become more syntactically disjunctive with time – to tap into 'the status of cosmogonic truth'[24] whose premises include 'suggestions of a universal condition of exile' in language itself.[25] Mackey's own form of syncretism gathers the particular into the universal by understanding disconnection from past, 'solid' things as the human condition; he describes his works' operations by invoking Spanish poet Federico García Lorca's figure of the duende which 'always presupposes a radical change of all forms based on old structures'.[26] 'The hope throughout' Mackey's long poetic sequence, *Song of the Andoumboulou*, as Jerome Rothenberg and Pierre Joris put it in their 'Commentary' on the fragment of it that appeared in *Poems for the Millennium*, 'is that rhapsodic song will stitch together all those othering threads – & do so by grounding itself in a duende that can be found in Coltrane, say, or in Bedouins' poetic traditions – here – as much as in Lorca's'.[27] Sympathetically, in the practice of African American poet Erica Hunt, even writing poems focused on 'Local History' means that '[o]ne arrives in the zone of detachable parts, dangerously soft, ripe for collision',[28] like the excerptable pieces of negative representations that Harryette Mullen 'recycles', as she puts it in a conversation with several Canadian writers in *Boo* magazine, going on to explain that 'I wouldn't want anyone to learn something about me, or black people, necessarily [from these representations]; [i]n some way, I don't accept them at face value; instead, I use them as material, I shred and recycle them'.[29]

---

22 Ibid., p. 263.
23 Ibid., p. 163.
24 Ibid., p. 177.
25 Ibid., p. 179.
26 The figure of the duende was made available in an essay of Lorca's anthologized in Donald Allen and Warren Tallman, *The Poetics of the New American Poetry* (Grove, 1974). Mackey, *Discrepant Engagement*, p. 163.
27 Rothenberg and Joris (see note 5 above), *Poems for the Millennium*, p. 782.
28 Erica Hunt, *Local History* (New York: Roof Books, Segue Foundation, 1993), p. 26.
29 Harryette Mullen, 'Harryette Mullen: In Calgary, Alberta', an interview compiled by Louis Cabri, *Boo* 7 (July 1996), p. 2, effectively, of the unpaginated magazine.

It is particularly this latter approach to history as text and to representations and language as products of universal processes and as recyclable material – a postmodern version of the Steinian conception of 'words with no history' – that differs in key ways from that of black British poets, in part because their relationships to other cultural pasts are more immediate, whereas, as Mullen puts it, '[m]ost of my access to so-called Black oral tradition is books, or possibly records, tapes or films . . . [t]here I was in this class learning my oral tradition mainly through textbooks.'[30] There is less possibility of 'migratory subjects', fashionably dislocated in current post-colonial theory, crossing borders such as these and choosing to 'syncretize' – or make, by transculturalized racial connections, similar responses from materials with which they have very different conceptual relationships. This is so not because of essential differences at work, obviously, but because of historical differences and the impact that history has in creating not only one's 'particular opacities', as Glissant so aptly put it, but also *one's modelled position in language* and perception of self versus other: that is, one's imagination of the opposition itself. An African American's position in American English is different from a former West Indian's in British English – despite adherence to certain Amerindian visions – and both differ a good deal from the new black British generation's in the UK. Often at issue for the latter is not whether one or the other, Césaire or Jabès, is, as Mackey puts it, in *theory*, more 'truly' exiled in language – but rather what the practice of these positionalities within discursivity makes possible for a particular user, whose linguistic 'possessions' (in the sense of 'subject foreign territory', and rather than dispossessions) reveal the workings of language in history. This is in part due to dispositions inculcated from their new home culture as well as their particular disconnections from and positions within it. Whereas in America, the exemplary postmodern poem often takes universalized theory about the problems of writing as its 'subject' (in the senses of both topic and speaker) organizing and deploying radically disjunctive phrases/words within a 'yet-to-be-inhabited' frontier zone, many have noted that Irish and UK experimentalisms, white *and* black, appear less 'radical' to Americans because they most often foreground recognizable discourses rather than textual/semantic fragments, a tendency that can be understood, in part, as arising out of a group-oriented social mythology built less powerfully on early models of self-reliance, transcendence and agency. Some influential American avant-gardists have had difficulty seeing their own in relationship to such differently-formed experiment, even when (or, perhaps, particularly when) it is work produced within the same country. Bruce Andrews, for example, illustrated this when he rejected Erica Hunt's observation that some group

---

[30] Ibid.

projects have oppositional strategies, appropriate to reaching their own readers, 'that are analogous to a more textual project'. 'Why would the project they set for themselves be less textual?' he asked, continuing by saying:

> transparency ... [is] a problem ... [b]ecause if the fundamental building blocks of sense reside at a lower level in the fundamental structure of the sign, and how that functions systematically – if that's not addressed first, the power of the work to address the nature of the social order evaporates.

He rejects such projects in favour of 'this other more totalizing, perspectival approach that [he's] trying to work out',[31] which is best accomplished from the position of atomized transcendence his culture's poetics afford.

But their context's differing cultural models of identity and personal agency do not allow for the construction of such a diffuse opposition for black British poets. Most immediately, it is not the individual before the universal, melted down 'fundamental building blocks of sense' that radicalism tends to envision as its mise-en-scène in an historically hierarchical, traditional and formerly-imperialistic, rather than democratic/evangelistic, tradition-eroded and diffuse, society. Beginning simply, the very conception of how ethnic identity and race operate in culture differs in the UK due to the historical shapes and shaping properties of its own imaginary models. Instead of the mighty expanding/dissolving dynamic of identity created early on in America by the drive westward toward 'manifest destiny', complemented by its potent melting pot imagery, Britain, 'in the stress and turbulence of [national decline and] crisis', as Gilroy writes, *and* in the wake of its first significant waves of postcolonial immigrants arriving in the late '40s, has been 'induced ... to clarify its own identity' and thereby force the discriminating question – the 'Enoch Powell question', as Gilroy specifies it provocatively – 'What kind of people are we?'[32] The forces that confer identity are less contourless in a post-imperial culture such as Britain's – one now caught, too, in the struggle of self-definition and preservation that accompanies entering into the European union – and, therefore, the language against which postmodern critique is deployed is also less generalized in that it is less

[31] Bruce Andrews, *Paradise & Method: Poetics and Praxis*, pp. 62, 63.

[32] Gilroy, *Small Acts*, p. 23. For a sample of the inflammatory remarks made by Powell (a senior Conservative politician), see the extract from his speech 'Still to Decide' in *Empire Windrush: Fifty Years of Writing About Black Britain*, Onyekachi Wambu (ed.), (London: Victor Gollancz, 1998), pp. 139–45. In the prefatory comments to this section, the editor writes that this excerpt 'brings together ... the three key issues that obsessed [Powell]: Who rules? On what principles? What sort of people?'.

abstractly or cosmically at work than it is in America. Social discourse is striated more overtly according to station, and regional accents still bear class-marks; the laundering of such power-strata in the US and the 'MacDonald's' effect of its levelling discourse present a different sort of moving oppositional target as well as a formational point of departure/identification for Language poetry.

As a result of such differences, the dangers of absolutism in black British aesthetics seem to arise out of an alternate set of tendencies that defend identity – both national and cultural – in a space where dominant forces are doing the same. These tendencies are not to be seen as continuances of the kind of 'Civilization of the Universal' espoused by writers like Léopold Sédar Senghor during formulations of the Négritude movement in the '30s; these are local tendencies that have to do with both the racial climate in the UK and the influence of British constructions of identity. The climate includes potent levels of overt racism, which are perhaps the product of that crisis mentality of decline being confronted by the mid-century's sudden 'colonization in reverse', to quote Louise Bennett's famous poem; they seem to have been deepening since the 1980s riots and massacres that sign-posted the delayed start of a civil rights movement. Economic factors in the 1990s have justified the narrowing of educational opportunities for school children as well, whose short introduction to a 'multicultural' palette of resources for self-identification has been terminated by a streamlining of priorities and the test-foci of the new National Curriculum. The need for a didactic or 'teaching' poetry – one that once again preserves and passes along cultural identity, often by oral means – is compelling for a number of new writers,[33] and the need for solidarity in such a climate causes any splintering within black ranks to be viewed as a deep threat. In other words, the *seeming* opposite of universalizing tendencies is called into play in the form of absolutist, totalizing gestures, with the same result: the very idea of particularized new responses from black writers causes influential critics and poets to make statements like Fred D'Aguiar's, in the important first book out in Britain on the poetics of the avant-garde: 'I am not sure how much mileage is to be had out of seeing [the] wellspring of black women's writing as so different from what black men are writing that it merits separate treatment'.[34] The theme here is unity, as in the

---

[33] Roger Robinson, a young black British poet and former coordinator of Apples and Snakes (see note 37), suggested to me in conversation (October 1998) that the newest generation of writers, mellowed though they may be in terms of response following the rage of the 1980s in Britain, feel the necessity to learn and teach the traditions that sustained previous generations of writers, the trick being to innovate as well as preserve.

[34] Fred D'Aguiar, 'Have you been here long? Black Poetry in Britain', in Peter Barry and Robert Hampson (eds), *New British Poetries: The Scope of the Possible* (Manchester: Manchester University Press, 1993), p. 69.

quote from Bernstein, but the tone is one of judgement. Similar though milder gender discrimination (which I am equating just for the moment with race discrimination on the grounds that both eliminate difference) goes on in American avant-garde poetics, which still regard women's more self-referential writing as the aberration rather than the rule and leave many of the major female players out when constructing genealogies of Language poetry history.[35] Inversely, too, the stance against poststructuralist aesthetics is very strong in D'Aguiar's camp, which works much more closely along mainstream formal models than other black British contingents. He writes that to be recognized as black and yet working in experimental modes is to buy into the white tradition of British modernism and its 'posts', 'as if Blackness and Britishness were two traditions brought together in this neat coalition bound to give both a new lease of life ... ' when his suspicion seems to be that, despite his own earlier participatory anthologization of black poets in one 'alternative' anthology, *The New British Poetry: 1968–1988*, experimental poetics tend to subsume raced writing rather than create rainbow coalitions.[36] Once again, as in the example of Language poetics, such attempts to present an oppositional poetics through traditional means of discriminating via unexamined, foundational cultural dynamics set up notions of absolute value and shut down pluralizing processes, despite the fact that these may have been at the heart of the original project. New black writers caught between writing in modes of absolute or non-identity – that is, those employing methods of repeatedly working through and re-evaluating such traditional conceptions in the manner Connor described at the beginning of this section – are misread by both, because difference in the repertoire of current evaluative formations is either categorized absolutely or judged by universalizing/erasing principles that vitiate the same processes of making 'the avant-garde'.

II

It has therefore been difficult for critics in both the UK and America to value/evaluate the full spectrum of black British poetry and performance

---

[35] Linda Kinnahan, an important critic of experimental women's writing, draws attention to the fact that '[t]he history and analysis of a feminist avant-garde ... has yet to be included in any full or significant way in considering the reading and writing practices of the current avant-garde'. 'Feminist Experimentalism, Literary History, and Subjectivity: "this lyric forever error" of Kathleen Fraser and Denise Riley', in Romana Huk (ed.), *Assembling Alternatives: Essays on/against Reading Postmodern Poetries Transnation-*

[36] Fred D'Aguiar, 'Against Black British Poetry', in Margaret Butcher (ed.), *Tibisiri* (Coventry, Sydney and Mundelstrup: Dangaroo Press, 1989), p. 114. The anthology referred to came out from Paladin in 1988; its other three sections were devoted to feminist experiment (ed. Gillian Allnutt), post-war experimental writing (ed. Eric Mottram), and young British experimentalists (ed. Ken Edwards).

work beyond those strands committed to absolutist strategies; the latter
tend to be more visible and quite well funded due to efforts on the part of
local and national art boards to support ethnic 'diversity',[37] though such
support is of course not what I mean here by 'valuing'. Monetary
scaffolding often substitutes for the lack of true integration into existing
systems of value (which would necessarily mean altering those systems).
The most immediate reasons for any lack of integrative attention to black
poetry within mainstream poetics are too predictable to rehearse at any
length here; it comes as no surprise that virtually all of the readers/
publishers (who are still almost without exception white)[38] practise what
Caryl Phillips has called 'the missionary approach':[39] meaning that they
expect/encourage raced work to be informative about difference, 'other'
enough to be worth reading, but then ultimately not comparable with
'native' work. It is also not surprising that they find performance poetry's
ephemerality and frequent lack of page-presence to be grounds for
dismissal or that young writers of Britain's new generation of black poets
like Patience Agbabi are forced to put up with the ignorance of reading
circuits that still advertise them as 'rap poets' when their work negotiates
a number of other forms, oral and inscribed.[40] Variations within black
writing may seem less easy to promote, particularly those whose practice
overlaps with white aesthetics and might, therefore, muddy the waters
through the implicit critique they inscribe through their difference, which
can only be comfortably housed within 'plurality' if it remains black/
other by white definition. As Joan Riley puts it by concretizing the same
abstract dynamic:

> It's hardly surprising that the only authors writing in Britain deemed
> worthy of notice were those who concentrated on the Caribbean, or

---

[37] Conversation with John Hampson, Principal Literature Officer, London Arts Board;
October 1998. Hampson was adamant that there are no 'affirmative action' policies at
work at the Board (though Apples and Snakes, a black literature development project in
the city, receives the single largest grant from the Board, and other such development
programs in the city's margins have sprung into being within the last ten years), asserting
that the poetry was judged according to its value. He was also clearly concerned about
the state of black writing, particularly performance work, for which the audiences have,
in the last five years or so, 'levelled off', a fact he attributed to 'their lack of a serious
aesthetic'.

[38] Conversation with John Hampson (see previous note). Hampson raised this issue; he
said that, to the best of his knowledge, there are no commissioning editors for major
presses in the country who are black and that all of the literature officers and chief
executives of the Arts Board and Council are white as well (the one very important
exception in the scenario being Trevor Phillips, then Chair of the London Arts Board).

[39] Caryl Phillips, 'Living and Writing in the Caribbean', in Gordon Collier (ed.), US/
THEM: Translation, Transcription and Identity in Post-Colonial Literary Cultures
(Amsterdam and Atlanta, GA: Rodopi, 1992), p. 221.

[40] Conversation with the poet, 26 October 1998.

wrote in terms of the transient. One wonders if this might not be due to the British refusal to acknowledge the existence of a settled, permanent black presence.[41]

What is less easy to understand is why those who anthologize 'alternative' work also seem – following the successful inclusiveness of *The New British Poetry* – to have lapsed in awareness of the issues underlying raced experimental work, as well as in acquaintance with the work currently being produced by the black community. Neither of the two most recent collections, *Conductors of Chaos* and *Out of Everywhere*, include any black writers at all, though the latter's 'Postscript' from the publishers reminds us to read American poet Erica Hunt. *Poems for the Millennium* includes only one writer of colour who has any contemporary presence in the UK: South Asian poet Sujata Bhatt (who lives in Germany). *Other,* a new anthology of experimental British poetry, includes only the more mainstream (that is, visible) authors such as Grace Nichols and John Agard, whose well-established work is, in some ways, more conventional than others' in terms of identity construction (if inventive in its interrogation of language as the oppressor's instrument).[42] Symptomatically, nothing is said in the introduction about how these works fit into our conceptions of a developing aesthetics for experimental writing in general; no critique of the going aesthetic is investigated through their differing practice, as might be done if postmodern pluralism were to actually work as Connor describes. It is conceivable, of course, that what these poets are doing is simply not perceived to be sufficiently concerned with the same issues that experimental poetry is concerned with: 'the language-reality nexus', as well as the 'turning away ... from totalizing/ authoritarian ideologies and individuals' (if not without relapse) – though much of the work, indeed, seems to this reader to be so engaged, albeit with differing inflections.[43] Consideration of them may be made problematic too because they are, to varying extents, actively disengaged from the poetics of postmodernist theory which, as a largely white western phenomenon, becomes for some the dominant against which they collide.[44] Does a postmodern aesthetics allow for a critique of its

---

[41] Joan Riley, 'Writing Reality in a Hostile Environment', in Collier, *US/THEM*, p. 215.

[42] Richard Caddel and Peter Quartermain (eds), *Other: British and Irish Poetry Since 1970* (Middletown, CT: Wesleyan University Press, 1998).

[43] Rothenberg and Joris, *Poems for the Millennium*, pp. 9, 5.

[44] Objections to theory – postcolonial and other sorts – by scholars and writers from/in the former colonies are commonplace; see, for one recent example, Stephano Harney's *Nationalism and Identity: Culture and the Imagination in a Caribbean Diaspora* (London and New Jersey: Zed Books; Kingston: University of the West Indies, 1996), in which Harney writes that the 'high theory' of postcolonial studies ignores study of the local in favour of a 'world systems theory' of new literatures (p. 5).

central principles through the consideration of such writers? Or are those principles the cordons that protect the limits (and values) of the universal model of identity which that aesthetics claims to pluralize?

It is helpful to approach this question through the disagreements with postmodern aesthetics voiced by theorists and practitioners in black British cultural studies and poetry – particularly those who employ postmodern strategies of articulating such disapproval and, thus, are closest to (even acceptable within) the models they critique; their thoughts provide a view of both the overlaps and departures. What immediately emerges is the difference between models of identity in the two projects, though both have been cast into a state of 'spillage' due to poststructuralist conceptions of language's slippery dynamics in fashioning 'the truth' (an idea that many writers, such as Henry Louis Gates, have linked to age-old conceptions of language and story-telling as involuting illusion in African philosophy).[45] Yet, given starting points based not in mythologies of arrival or conquest but rather disruption and exodus, such spillage from original constructs of identity – which in postmodern theory is the *European* construct of selfhood and its history of progress – must, understandably, be accompanied by a reinvestment in the impossible past with its lacunae that suggest an uninscribed but lived alternative history. Black re-evaluations of identity and their strategies and placement of the writing agent, therefore, involve re-encountering the constraints of history through methods that critique postmodern critiques of history. First off, they invoke history's impact on the speaking subject in ways that challenge avant-garde tendencies to relegate history to the realm of the subjective and then, simultaneously, erase the subject. Gilane Tawadros, in an essay on black British women artists, calls this our 'evacuation of history', a non-re-evaluative process linked to those I have attempted to describe:

> By ignoring the historical exigencies which contributed to the formulation of these concepts [that is, the rise of 'total history' at the end of the eighteenth-century to replace 'general history', which as Foucault describes it meant learning to 'draw all phenomena around a single center' or 'world view' instead of seeing 'discontinuities, differences of level, shifts and chronological specificities'],[46] postmodernism can assert itself as a break or rupture from past tradition and hence fail to recognize the persistence of these notions both *outside* and *within* postmodernism itself. [T]his evacuation of history enables postmodernism to deny the continuing hegemony of

---

[45] See Henry Louis Gates, Jr., *The Signifying Monkey: A Theory of Afro-American Literary Criticism* (New York and Oxford: Oxford University Press, 1988).

[46] Michel Foucault, Introduction to *The Archaeology of Knowledge*, trans. A. M. Sheridan Smith (New York: Tavistock Publications, 1986), quotes from pp. 3–17.

the West, both in the cultural sphere where it still prescribes and legitimates the artistic practice of its choosing ... and also in the political sphere where the dispersion and changing forms of Western hegemony are mistaken for economic and political egality. What distinguishes ... black artistic practice ... from postmodern practice and theory is the assertion of history and historiography unambiguously within the frame of cultural reference, [which is] part of a coherent political and aesthetic strategy based on an interrogation of Western history *through* history.[47]

Tawadros would say that, as soon as one leaves off speaking of group and individual histories, which contribute to that alternative 'general history' made up of discontinuities, boundaries, differences of level, shifts, chronological specificities, dispersion and difference, one is caught in 'Western culture's universalist mode of making transcendental claims to speak for everyone, while being itself everywhere and nowhere'.[48] Her main project, in the piece quoted from above, is to discuss yet another pluralizing force within black art (primarily painting, in this case): women's work, whose links to postmodern theory (whether they actually read it or not) are in some ways doubly strong given their connections with what feminist thought is allowing readers to read within the gendered spaces of texts and visual work. Though her approach and even her vocabulary demonstrate her sympathies with postmodern aesthetics, she insists that black British women artists diverge from avant-garde practice 'at the point where pluralism and heterogeneity [become, as in the earlier quote from Bernstein,] a set of aesthetic or political codes based on negation – negation of coherent identities or the negation of fragmented identities'.[49] Black women artists are working toward

the assertion of the positive and political implications of difference ... Femininity in the space of the diaspora is conceived in terms of an intersection of ... such totalizing discourses as postmodernism and feminism, which remain confined within the perimeters of European consciousness ... draw[ing] their often transcendental and globalizing conclusions in a conceptual field which in many cases has been evacuated of wider historical and economic perspectives.[50]

[47] Gilane Tawadros, 'Beyond the Boundary: The Work of Three Black Women Artists in Britain', in Houston A. Baker, Manthia Diawara, and Ruth A. Lindeborg (eds), *Black British Cultural Studies: A Reader* (Chicago and London: University of Chicago Press, 1996), p. 255.
[48] Tawadros, 'Beyond the Boundary', p. 242.
[49] Ibid., p. 261.
[50] Ibid., pp. 261, 268.

With the same reversed directionality – by which I mean *back* into complex history as well as forward into innovative response – David Marriott, the only black poet in Britain active in the experimental community (though a figure wholly unknown to mainstream readers of black work or to the African American avant-garde), takes issue with certain dominating trajectories in Language poetry theory which he indicts for establishing what he calls an 'aesthetics of disavowal'. Using a psychoanalytic approach to analyse the theoretization of the reduced or erased subject in early 1970s Language work, he argues that it is 'the traumatic excess associated with referential markers of sexual and racial difference' that triggers such disavowal of irreducible difference, creating an inadvertent 'defense against the radically heterogeneous' which foils coherent and universalizing re-conceptualizations of the postmodern subject. His objections directly address the new constructions of (non)selfhood, proposed in the earlier quote from Bernstein, as well as new foci on words as dehistoricized surfaces and materials as one finds them in some versions of Language exploration:

> In reading language poetry, what attracts the gaze is not the making manifest of the ideological operations of language, nor the non-referential complexity of ideolects in the social sphere, but rather the gaze being drawn back to a symbolic and excessive process of spectacle and disavowal – 'I know very well, but all the same . . . '. What I am saying is that there is a fetishism of the signifier in language writing which serves to conceal and guard against something else, and that something else is the encroachment of nameless anxieties and displacements associated with knowledge, power and agency. In this presence-absence process of disavowal the signifier is emptied out of its representational function leaving nothing but a sheen of substitution, i.e., the poetic signifiers hide what is missed, leaving phantasies and symptoms. This overly symbolic investment in signification excludes its own historical-political inscription . . . [and] is designified . . . of any mediation between particularities and the state, of any ethical or principled notion of human autonomy, because of the confused relations between language's meta-discursive claims and the poetry's processed and technologically repeated rationality of disruption . . . This, at a time when representation and historical events are becoming increasingly dislocated, if not segregated.[51]

Marriott's fears echo Gilroy's as he imagines such premature erasure of difference/race-in-history, the 'empt[ying]-out' of 'mediation[s] between

---

[51] David Marriott, 'Signs Taken for Signifiers: Language Writing, Fetishism and Disavowal', *fragmente: a magazine of contemporary poetics*, 6 (1995), 79–80.

particularities and the state' which compose the muddying linguistic traces of the unequal entry of 'others' into the pool of signs available for re-assemblage in avant-garde poetry. In recent poems, he emphasizes the issue by signalling his re-examination of discursive structures of history through lines that seem too fully syntactical – even residually metered – to be immediately recognized as 'experimental', though the sensibility that informs them is fully cognizant of its (non)situation in discursive history, as well as the impossibility/necessity of re-membering those 'fathers' of ambiguous linguistic creation/destruction whose 'light' depends on the unforgivability of 'darkness' – a poststructuralist dynamic of defining oneself against the 'other':

> Lying father, lying ghost – in whose name we speak.
> We need the tomb of the murdered child
> buried beneath ice and fallen snow;
> we need the trauma that predates us
> the issues and the summons,
> weaned into the loving memory of death and nothingness,
> the sacred delirium of our fathers.
> ....
> In this living memorial
> will the long-memoried become an empty husk not to be passed on
> like a lover's remorse
> amid news of the world's end and a black sun,
> doomed to roam the stars in the company of the lost one? ...
> As the last star fades into nothingness
> we are born knowing
> that in my father's house darkness can't be forgiven ...
> Exile is a story not not to be passed on ...
>
> (from 'Names of the Fathers',[52] ellipses Marriott's)

The ghosts of end-rhymes in especially the last nine lines, beginning with the epistemological impasse caused by the indeterminate-because-contra-dictorily-charged meanings of 'passed on', form a kind of unfulfilled set of quatrains (or textual structures) that the 'back sun' ('black son'), in ironic resurrection of 'the murdered child', nevertheless stirs into continued presence through the last line's final double-negative. The unbaptized/unenlightened or the 'dark, unsanctified, unredeemable of 'scripture' – that is, patriarchal text/language which houses the 'names of the fathers' – is not expellable either; to not forgive is to acknowledge and, as in Derridean models of linguistic formation, making meaning

---

[52] The sections of poems by Marriott quoted in this essay were published in *Angel Exhaust*, 15 (Autumn 1997), 29–32.

depends upon such occlusions of the netherside, the other. And yet the opening words – 'Lying father, lying ghost' – recall Hamlet's aporetic situation of 'speaking in the name of' what could be simple illusion, corrupt intrusion or delusional subconscious necessity; the translation of such into 'action' also becomes the focus of Marriott's dilemma as a black writer. Writing about Caribbean-Canadian poet M. Nourbese Philip's disjunctive poems inflected by both oral and scribal remnants (as well as tropes of gendered bodily desire less evident in his own work), Marriott recognizes that there too the traumatic lies like a substrate below the workings of language, where

> absorption of the unintegrated word by figural desire itself passes away into silence of a thing or the 'body-in-pieces' and into every word that intends that thing: the word – or the name – itself cut by a process of negativity by which psychic events come to register in the writing down of a word.[53]

And yet he cautions, speaking of current theorizations of both 'woman' and 'blackness', that rather than 'understand this silence … as a beyond of language' or 'simply reproduce the oral-scribal split of "nation-language"',[54] 'this silence … cannot be dissociated from the working through of memory and mourning in those racial catastrophes of European history' that have rendered them 'an archive of alterity and difference, of loss and violence':

> The question then becomes how one writes and remembers this silence given that it cannot be either easily written or read. Uncovering such silence becomes the work of writing as a process of memorialisation and of the working of the poetic as already other, naming the foreignness of self. This task takes on a particular urgency given the traditional historical excision and exclusion of women and blacks from the archive that is writing.[55]

Such a premise for writing necessitates not only the situated or delimited 'presence' of the poet in history (without romanticizing the writing as unproblematized 'lyric expression' of self) but also a kind of recognition of the 'foreignness' of language or the constructed nature of reality that, in some ways, exceeds that of certain avant-garde poetic practices in

---

[53] David Marriott, 'Figures of Silence and Orality in the Poetry of M. Nourbese Philip', in Joan Anim-Addo (ed.), *Framing the Word: Gender and Genre in Caribbean Women's Writing* (London: Whiting & Birch Ltd, 1996), p. 81.

[54] 'Nation-language' is a term used by writers such as Edward Brathwaite to refer to the creolized English spoken in the West Indies and other former colonies.

[55] Marriott, 'Figures of Silence and Orality', pp. 75–6.

which words, excised of 'history', can be recombined and reassembled by writing agents who, through their very lack of self-referentiality, exhibit belief in the undelimited agency of the poet. In other words, linguistic history *is to be made* in the latter's 'progressive' avant-garde practice, rather than recognized *as having made* the writer. In black British work like Marriott's, where the memory (and continuing effects) of a historically locatable experience of re-entry into cultural and linguistic foreignness is more accessible, one finds a different model of progress. Agency must take another kind of tack when, as Marriott puts it in another poem, writers seem more aware of having been 'the script':

when we stepped off the boat
          the tide, the long imperial gain,
extended to all colonies,
debased by the raw stink,
the world retched in the advocacy, we were the script –

what secret
          emerges from these idylls of nations, at the mercy of ringworm gods
                         arteries open
               wide to the
                    purity of island stories –
do we love the obsession,
          this way of being a blocked wall
screening out more desolate places?
                                   (from 'the "secret" of this form itself'[56])

The 'form' of the poem versus its 'secret', its blackness, or silence in the text provides the tense space for (self)articulation here, a kind of wading between suppressed phenomenal and clear rhetorical lines, as the speaker does, centaur-like, in a later stanza – 'wading through a warm stinking mess to meet my father'. The only freeing to be had from such tense suspension/segregation between textures/texts of being occurs through disruption of the form, which begins to 'open wide' from what in the first stanza preceding those quoted above was a regular indentation of alternate lines. The leverage necessary for such opening requires a foregrounding of language's foreignness, as well as some syntactical wedging to suggest its processes of becoming politicized abstraction, as in juxtapositions of phenomenal experience/history with its rhetorical 'extensions'. For example, the 'tide' is enhanced by its figural translation into 'long imperial gain', illuminating the passively constructed mid-century invitation 'extended to all colonies' as being fully underwritten (with no

[56] Marriott (see note 52), p. 29.

indentation) by its revolted physical response to the actual 'tide' of incoming peoples. The vulnerability of the abstracted/abstracting 'idylls of nations' to revelation of 'the secret' – the vomit that was messy history as opposed to 'the script' – is suggested by the suddenly exploded openness of the third stanza as well. The question that follows is for black artists who might create a supportive wall for those idylls by giving back what is wanted – 'pure island stories' – as opposed to the 'desolation' (both a physical and affective state) or (s)crypt of silence that here is also communicated in part by the spaces on the page. A 'Language' poet to the extent that he focuses on experience as being predicated on the discursive, Marriott, nevertheless, refuses to abandon the affective in his work, even if its dimensions are circumscribed by his characteristically stagey high rhetoric that signals its own limited props. Through it he registers that different – raced *and* nation-specific – trauma of entry into being through language that he describes as elided in avant-garde poetics.

Marriott's willingness to enter into an avant-garde aesthetic, even for the purposes of critiquing it, isolates him in terms of publishing venues from other black British writers; his work becomes 'whitened' or read 'beyond' issues of race as soon as it enters the avant-garde arena. But I have wanted to construct the foregoing overlap in order to visualize a possible extension of similarities within a continuum of 'radicality' as it might illuminate re-evaluations of other black writers – not in order to rate them as 'good' from received avant-garde perspectives, but to facilitate new integrations of black British critique of dominant radical forms as they develop among allied African American and Amerindian artists. On that continuum, one finds overt and politicized moves to retain both the (however compromised) historical and the (all but effaced) affective dimensions of the subject as we once spoke of it – even, at times, overtly mythologizing its 'remains' in acknowledgement of its impossible reality, effecting imaginative reconstructions not so much of 'phantom limbs', as Mackey describes them in Wilson Harris's work,[57] as of prosthetics, perhaps, in a version of the 'syncretism' Gilroy identifies as a connective between black aesthetics on either side of the Atlantic. Phantom limb

---

[57] In his chapter entitled 'Limbo, Dislocation, Phantom Limb', Mackey quotes extensively from Harris's essay 'History, Fable and Myth in the Caribbean and Guianas' (*Caribbean Quarterly*, 16 (1970), 1–32) in which Harris suggests that the artist's imagination can compensate for gutted histories in the Caribbean by 'bring[ing] into play a figurative meaning beyond an apparently real world or prison of history' through regeneration of the 'phantom limb', an allusion to the myths that involve re-assembly of the dismembered man or god which join Egyptian, Christian, Hindu and other religions. The 'vision' required for this act of rememoralization, so unlike Marriott's, plots the artist's position as shamanistic guide to new histories and syncs well with certain modern American strains of experiment from Pound to Olson (who also makes an appearance in Mackey's chapter). (Quoted in Mackey, 168–9.)

thematics suggest by image that there is an origin to reconstruct or return to by imagination and, therefore, a different directionality into 'history', the obverse of which constitutes the continuum upon which a breakdown of something *owned* can occur – that is, the full alienation in/from a sense of identity and means to express it in language that characterized the radical break of early 1970s' Language poetics in America. But the radical black British syncretic response tends not to demonstrate alienation in the same ways, either through imaginative recovery or through linguistic breakdown. There is no apocalyptic separation from meaning, resulting from postmodern philosophy's revelations, for this writing to respond to. As Tawadros and others have made clear, these subjected subjects have never been so situated and, therefore, require no violent disconnection from the past's nostalgic constructs, which serve only as traces of confines between (not within) which their history has been drawn.

8

The Sign of Democracy and the Terms of Poetry

Paul Breslin

My title derives from two lines in Walt Whitman's *Song of Myself*:

> I speak the pass-word primeval, I give the sign of democracy,
> By God! I will accept nothing which all cannot have their
> counterpart of on the same terms.

These words appear in the 1855 edition and remain, apart from two changes of orthography, unaltered in the 'deathbed' edition of 1891–2; they are core Whitman. Can an American concerned with poetry read them unmoved? Can an American with any brains read them uncritically? What if some things worth having cannot be had 'on the same terms' by all people? Whitman seems worried enough by that possibility to include the translation-term 'counterpart of'. But what, in poetry, is an acceptable 'counterpart' and where does 'counterpart' end and impoverishment begin? Can poetry adapt its terms to the demands of 'all' and remain poetry? And who defines the terms of poetry, anyway? Are the verse homilies printed occasionally in Ann Landers and Dear Abby poetry? Those columns reach a larger percentage of 'all' than even our most successful poets: our revolving laureates (such as Robert Pinsky who held the post from 1997–2000), Nobel Prize winners such as Derek Walcott and Seamus Heaney or those, such as Adrienne Rich or the late Allen Ginsberg, whose political commitments have drawn in readers from outside the usual circles. Some highbrow poets do get short poems posted in buses and subway trains now and then, as a part of a civic attempt at cultural edification but, when I ride, I don't see many of my fellow passengers reading these offerings. Most widely disseminated of all are the lyrics of rock and rap that can be heard everywhere: as 'hold music' on the phone, as the ebb and flow of cars in the night, as background ambience at health clubs or restaurants. You hear them whether you want to or not. Are these 'counterparts', to be had by all on the same terms, of the works of the poets such as those I've named, or are they something else altogether, to be had on different terms?

I Poetry and Self-Flattery

It is beyond my ambition to answer this question for 'all', but I hope I can begin to answer it for myself and perhaps for some of the readers of this essay. The winding path from one to 'all' has to pass through the middle ground of 'some' and that's as far as I hope to get just now. I'll begin with a poem from an Ann Landers column that strikes me as typical of the kind of earnest verse that turns up in the advice columns. I passed by a number of examples of narrowly topical, lighter verse that aim at nothing more than a localized observation and a laugh. This one, however, proffers advice and a moral of sorts. Criticizing it, especially to an academic audience, is like shooting fish in a barrel, but the point of the exercise is to be as articulate as possible about why I can't take it seriously. Here it is, complete with its framing prose:

> Dear Ann Landers: I found this verse in a column of yours in my father's desk drawer. It was in a date book from 1974. It's as good today as it was 23 years ago. Please rerun it. *Dixie.*
> *Dear Dixie: I agree. Thank you for asking. Here it is:*
> Forget It
> By Judd Mortimer Lewis
> If you see a tall fellow ahead of a crowd,
> A leader of men, marching fearless and proud,
> And you know of a tale whose mere telling aloud
> Would cause his proud head in anguish be bowed,
> It's a pretty good plan to forget it.
> If you know of a skeleton hidden away
> In a closet, and guarded, and kept from the day
> In the dark, and whose showing, whose sudden display
> Would cause grief and sorrow and pain and dismay
> It's a pretty good plan to forget it.
> If you know of a tale that will darken the joy
> Of a man or a woman, a girl or a boy,
> That will wipe out a smile or the least bit annoy
> A fellow, or cause any gladness to cloy,
> It's a pretty good plan to forget it.[1]

'Dixie' sees this poem as a classic, 'as good today as it was 23 years ago', valued by father and daughter across generational lines. It passes Samuel

---

[1] Ann Landers, *Chicago Tribune*, 17 May 1997.

Johnson's test of pleasing many (or three at least: Dixie, her father and Ms Landers) and pleasing long (though twenty-three years may seem but a moment in Johnson's terms, it is an improvement on the Warhol quota of fifteen minutes). It may please by its insistent meter, anapaestic tetrameter, with a trimeter refrain line. It sounds singable – instantly recognizable as verse, not prose chopped into lines. Each stanza has four consecutive rhymes, and the refrain provides relief not only by varying the meter, but by breaking the pattern of rhyme at predictable intervals. The refrain functions as a punchline, reversing the temptations to indiscretion in the previous four lines.

No poet I know would be caught dead with a poem like that and yet, in the nineteenth century (when famous poets had three names, like Henry Wadsworth Longfellow, John Greenleaf Whittier – or Judd Mortimer Lewis), highbrow poems might still have much in common with this piece. They'd be more gracefully written, with fewer redundancies and clumsy enjambments, but they would rhyme and lilt and point a moral. The once-beloved recitation piece, 'The Village Blacksmith', for instance, with its closing stanzas in earnest praise of humble industry, was written by the first Harvard professor of modern languages, an able translator of Dante, an up-to-date literary intellectual of his time. The conventions of popular and professional verse have drifted apart in the years between Professor Longfellow and Mr Lewis.

Despite the refrain's reversal at the close of each stanza, Lewis's stanzas offer no progression. Each case is parallel to the last and each is presented in well-worn phrases: the second expands the cliché 'skeleton in the closet' into four lines. The poem is full of appositive rephrasings of the same idea and, even where its syntax is hypotactic, it can't resist paratactic add-ons (for example, 'whose showing, whose sudden display'). In order to like 'Forget It', you have to want a poem that develops a helpful maxim in a clear, unmistakable way, rather than a poem that questions its own statements or leaves them to implication. You can't expect pleasure in the supple deployment of syntax. And you can't value economy of means too highly or you will find yourself asking why, when you already know the skeleton is in the closet and guarded, you also have to be told that it is 'in the dark' or 'kept from the day'. Or what significant distinctions require the enumeration of 'sorrow', 'grief', 'pain' and 'dismay', which appear to be virtually interchangeable. (I see that as I discuss the poem, my own prose begins to mimic its redundancy!)

But the moral shallowness of 'Forget It' bothers me even more than its prefab diction and lazy versification. To show what I mean, I tack on a stanza (still doggerel, of course) that would have made a difference:

But suppose the young fellow whose head is so proud
Rides by night with the Klan, though he's never avowed

> The connection, and, afterwards, going home ploughed,
> Starts beating his children until they are cowed:
>   Speak up, or you'll live to regret it!

Or to spell it out: tact is a virtue, but it is not the highest virtue, and there are times when the responsibility to expose evil outweighs its claims. It's one thing not to tell your neighbour about his wife's affair with the milkman five years ago and another to keep quiet when, let's suppose, you see him in his yard frantically burying a bag shaped like a human body. The poem's thought, like its language, grips nothing but its own conventionality, refusing to investigate any counterexamples (and they're not hard to think of) that could cast doubt on its reiterated moral. The implicit assumption is that of course the reader will agree with the poem's judgments, which are, after all, thoroughly conventional. And the reader will be grateful to the poem for confirming what a good person he or she already is, rather than for trying to change the reader's judgments through the experience of reading. I have to admit that, if poetry must be like this in order to be had by all on the counterpart of the same terms, I don't want it.

It would be nice to think that when one picks up the latest issue of, say, *American Poetry Review*, one leaves such banality behind and enters an entirely different sphere. Now I'm not singling out *APR* for abuse – they have published work of mine and I hope they will again. The point is, rather, that differences between the sort of poetry that turns up in places like advice columns and the average run of what turns up in reputable magazines is not absolute but a matter of bands on a spectrum, each shading imperceptibly into the next. The general run of contributions to *APR* is more sophisticated in syntax, more compressed and less predictable in diction than Lewis's 'Forget It'. Nonetheless, rummaging through the January/February 1999 issue, I find some poems that seem, no less than 'Forget It', to rest on a certain complacency, the expectation that certain attitudes will be shared by the poet and the magazine's readers, who will, therefore, appreciate the poem for making them feel that they are the right sort of people. My example (winnowed from a short list of four, each by a different poet) is far more skilfully written than 'Forget It' but its way of claiming a bond with the reader – a reader of a different social class and level of education, to be sure, but a reader expected to respond very much as a loyal member of a class – is not terribly different. Robin Becker's 'Why We Fear the Amish' sets out to answer the title's question with reasons such as

> Because they smell us in fellowship with the dead works
> of darkness and technology

and concludes that

We know their frugality in our corpulence. We know their sacrifice
for the group in our love for the individual. Our gods are
cross-dressers, nerds, beach-bums, and poets. They know it.
By their pure walk and practice do they eye us from their carts.[2]

The give-away is the self-indicting placement of 'poets' at the end of the
list of 'our' gods. 'We', then, are not the general populace, which hardly
worships poets nowadays, but the sorts of people who read *APR* or
contribute to it. Not for one moment does one really believe that the
speaker *fears* the Amish. Nor does the poem seriously entertain the
possibility that 'we' might really be better off if we joined the Amish;
they are a pastoral conceit, a rhetorical stick with which to beat ourselves
in a not particularly urgent act of ironic penance. It is telling that the
poem's most intense utterance, where it threatens to break free of its hip
ironic containment, displaces conviction from people to their animals:

Even their horses are thrifty and willing to starve for Christ.

The greatest irony about this poem, of which it signals no recognition I
can detect, is that, although it is 'we' who emphasize 'love for the
individual' and the Amish who will have 'everyone dressed the same',
the rhetoric throughout assumes a reader whose beliefs, aesthetic habits
and judgements are already known and close to those of the speaker.
This poem is engaging and, within its limits, quite skilfully made. But it
exploits rather than challenging the conventional responses it evokes
and, in this way, it is akin to the much cruder 'Forget It'.

Steve Orlen, elsewhere in the issue, makes a similar half-nostalgic, half-
ironic gesture in 'Modern Man Meets His Ancestor'. The speaker begins
by describing himself as 'a modern man, raised in the Age of Anxiety',
who therefore likes to

read about the young Indian boy,
He who is sent out by the elders of the tribe
Into the dark impenetrable[3]

and compares this alter-ego's rites of passage to his own struggles with a
local bully. This poem too evokes warm, fuzzy and slightly condescend-
ing feelings about a less overcivilized other, whom 'we' as enlightened
multiculturalists know better than to look down on, but cannot quite

---

[2] Robin Becker, 'Why We Fear the Amish', *American Poetry Review*, 28.1 (January/
February 1999), 4.

[3] Steve Orlen, 'Modern Man Meets His Ancestor', *American Poetry Review* 28.1 (January/
February 1999), 35–6.

confront as a challenge to 'our' habits of perception, either. The implied reader, for this poem as for Becker's, is a white educated American, troubled with cultural guilt for privilege, awash with vague good will toward the marginalized Other and hungry for contact with something a bit more primal than the classroom, the workshop, the evenings with like-minded friends or books. These are not terrible attitudes to have but, like the blind loyalties egged on by 'Forget It', they are the received habits of a social class – of 'our' social class, this time, but no less mindless for that. They are no less in need of a swift kick in the ass than those of Judd Mortimer Lewis. Or more so, since we are well-defended against Mr Lewis's brand of cant but not against the more urbane banalities that slip into the language of Becker and Orlen in their far better bred poems.

Complacency, whether of the obvious kind found in Lewis or the subtler kind found in the poems from *APR*, slips in above all when one is worried about being liked and accepted, whether by a popular reader-ship or by a literary subcommunity. True democracy, rather than a mealy-mouthed consensus rhetoric that muffles conflict, means willing-ness to ask and to subject oneself to sharp questions. So I hope those of us who most care about poetry will stubbornly insist on the terms we believe the art at its best requires, even if others reject them. I think that the faults of the poems by Orlen and Becker stem from a defensiveness about taking up an art that was, as Robert Pinsky has noted, 'reborn in European courts' within a democratic culture. So one deprecates the claims of 'the old, aristocratic authority of the form'[4] and looks anxiously over one's shoulder toward the Amish or the Indians, invoked for their superior humility, their lack of overweening pretensions, their innocence of European inequality and colonial aggression.

To be sure, if we believe in democracy, we accept that we have no more say in setting the terms of poetry than anyone else who chooses to join the discussion, but we have no less say either. If we truly believe that the courts of Europe produced no attainments that cannot be acquired within a democratic society, the test of our faith would be to hold out for poetry as it is at its most demanding, searching and rewarding, rather than dumbing it down for easier acceptance or trying to make the audience feel better about being the way it already is.

Having argued that popular poetry does not have a monopoly on being bad, I'll also insist that unpopular poetry has no monopoly on being good. It may be that the poems that brought Robert Frost a wide audience are not the ones most admired by literary critics, but his books contained both and they sold well enough to support him in his later years. Ginsberg's *Howl and Other Poems* sold hundreds of thousands of copies. Neither Frost nor Ginsberg sold as well as the late Shel Silverstein or, in

---

[4] Robert Pinsky, *Poetry and the World* (New York: Ecco, 1988), pp. 101, 122.

his heyday, Rod McKuen. Still, accessibility does not necessarily mean flattering the reader. As an example of something accessible that's also good, take Gwendolyn Brooks's well-known 'We Real Cool', which is short enough to quote in full:

> We real cool. We
> Left school. We
>
> Lurk late. We
> Strike straight. We
>
> Sing sin. We
> Thin gin. We
>
> Jazz June. We
> Die soon.[5]

The displaced line endings create two striking effects: the pronoun 'we' appears at the end of each line, as if defensively insisting on the group solidarity of the speakers, and the recurring caesura, just before 'we', followed by enjambment, induce an edgy pause before the rhyming predicate arrives. Move 'we' to the beginning of each line, put the rhymes at the end, and you significantly diminish the power of the poem. Moreover, there's a tension between the self-understanding of the speakers and the author's perception of them. Does the poet suddenly speak for them with

We

Die soon

or do the pool players themselves know and accept that fate? Are they unwittingly poetic when they say

We

Jazz June

or knowingly so? Or is the tone more aggressively sexual than lyrical, with 'Jazz' retaining its full vernacular sense and 'June' naming a woman as well as a month in spring? The poem rewards a reader who thinks about these subtleties but it also can please one who doesn't. It is not the most ambitious poem in the world; Brooks herself has written many others that demand more and give more. It's an excellent and yet

---

[5] Gwendolyn Brooks, 'We Real Cool', *Blacks* (Chicago: The David Co., 1987), p. 331.

accessible piece. On the other hand, I doubt that a wide audience is likely to appreciate Robert Pinsky's 'The Night Game', despite its marvellously evocative descriptions of night baseball and its celebration of Whitey Ford and Sandy Koufax. Baseball is a popular (and populist) subject. But this poem is after more than sports nostalgia; before baseball finally sidles in, through the mention of 'Ed Ford' in line fifteen, the reader must enter the strait gate of its opening:

> Some of us believe
> We would have conceived romantic
> Love out of our own passions
> With no precedents,
> Without songs and poetry –
> Or have invented poetry and music
> As a comb of cells for the honey.
> Shaped by ignorance,
> A succession of new worlds,
> Congruities improvised by
> Immigrants or children.[6]

You're not going to bring down the roof at a reading with lines like these, which demand alert response to their abstract diction ('precedents', 'congruities') and hypotactic sentence structure in order to yield any reward at all. Some good poetry can also be accessible but to reject poetry that isn't accessible would greatly limit the range of possibilities.

II
The Trouble with 'Language' Poetry and 'New Formalism'

Two recent 'movements' in American poetry – the inverted commas acknowledge that members of a literary movement are joined only by partial convergence of style and belief, not orthodox adherence to a manifesto – seem haunted by the marginality of poetry in relation to popular culture. They have taken different stands concerning the 'terms' in which such marginality should be addressed. One of them, New Formalism, attempts to recapture materials and forms that have been ceded to popular culture and treat them in a more inventive but still accessible way, thus winning over some of the larger audience. Polemicists for New Formalism hope to move closer to the situation of Longfellow's day, when the boundary between popular and elite versions of poetry was more permeable. The other movement, Language Poetry, sees the language of popular and elite culture alike as saturated with

---

[6] Robert Pinsky, 'The Night Game', *The Want Bone* (New York: Ecco, 1990), p. 55.

ideological manipulation and sets its task as the critique and disruption of that degraded public discourse. To defend democratic values in the larger sense, Language Poets accept marginalization as the cost of integrity. To be acceptable to all or even the many, one would have to capitulate to a discourse that is itself an instrument of their oppression, though few of them may realize it.

Though no one writer can 'speak for' all those associated with a movement, Dana Gioia's essays in *Can Poetry Matter?* and Charles Bernstein's *A Poetics* can provide a sense of what's at issue in the divergent responses of the New Formalists and the Language Poets. Gioia's much-cited title essay begins with the commonplace that poetry has become a specialized art, practised and read mainly within the academy, for an audience of writing students and their poetry-publishing instructors. He observes that other arts, such as the composition of classical music, are in a similar predicament, so it is not poetry alone that has been sealed off from what he calls 'mainstream culture'. To reclaim poetry for the 'general reader', the person who reads serious fiction and non-fictional prose, poetry must go outside the closed circuit of the academy.[7] The New Formalists, he argues, have done just that. Having come 'to maturity in the cultural disintegration of the Vietnam era', they 'looked to popular culture for perspective' and found that, there, 'the traditional genres, which the academy had discredited for ideological reasons in high art', were 'still being used'. Attending to 'what the *demos* itself actually preferred', they envisioned a poetry 'that combined 'the materials of popular art' with 'the precision, compression, and ambition of high art'. They have 'democratized literary discourse' and created a 'poetry ... accessible to nonspecialist readers'.[8]

Gioia's narrative would be heartening if true. But I agree with Vernon Shetley's observation, in *After the Death of Poetry*: 'Gioia's aim is to return poetry to the general reader, and if the general reader still existed, Gioia's program would stand every chance of success'.[9] But it is not so and has not been for a long time. Gioia is nostalgic for the days when honest, brilliant reviewers, such as Randall Jarrell, influenced public taste. But he seems to forget that, even in Jarrell's day, poetry had begun to look pretty marginal. 'The Obscurity of the Poet' – which Jarrell significantly placed first in his collection *Poetry and the Age* – broods not only on 'the fact that people don't read poetry', but on the more melancholy 'fact that most of them wouldn't understand it if they did'. And it is not just twentieth-century poetry that suffers from neglect:

[7] Dana Gioia, *Can Poetry Matter?: Essays on Poetry and American Culture* (St. Paul, MN: Graywolf Press, 1992), pp. 1–24.

[8] Ibid., pp. 252–3.

[9] Vernon Shetley, *After the Death of Poetry* (Durham and London: Duke University Press, 1993), p. 169.

When a person says accusingly that he can't understand Eliot, his tone implies that most of his happiest hours are spent at the fireside among worn copies of the *Agamemnon, Phèdre,* and the Symbolic books of William Blake ... Many a man, because Ezra Pound is too obscure for him, has shut forever the pages of *Paradise Lost*; or so one would gather, from the theory and practice such people combine.[10]

Thus spoke Jarrell in 1953, some 45 years ago.

Gioia is still seeking poets 'whose true subject is the whole of human existence', whose audience is 'the general literary community', claiming that 'this heterogeneous group cuts across lines of race, class, age, and occupation'. My own experience does not confirm the claim, at least in regard to race and class. When I go to fiction readings at bookstores, I see a white, middle-class looking crowd, unless the reader happens to be African-American or Hispanic, and, even then, it doesn't look like a cross section of the population.[11] 'The general literary community', conceived as the heterogeneous, inclusive group Gioia describes, does not exist. If it did, why would Gioia feel so embattled?

Bernstein goes in the opposite direction. He accepts the disappearance (or non-existence) of 'the general literary community' as not only bearable, but a good thing.

We have to get over, as in getting over a disease, the idea that we can 'all' speak to one another in the universal voice of poetry. History still mars our words, and we will be transparent to one another only when history itself disappears.

To the extent that there is still a public intellectual space in contemporary life, he argues, it is characterized by manipulation and erasure of conflict. Even the publicly-accepted version of pluralism too often has

the effect of transforming unresolved ideological divisions and antagonisms into packaged tours of the local color of gender, race, sexuality, ethnicity, region, nation, class, even historical period: where each group or community or period is expected to come up

[10] Randall Jarrell, *Poetry and the Age* (New York: Vintage, 1953), pp. 9–10.

[11] We need some empirical research into the actual size and constituency of literary audiences; the discussion of the audience for poetry has been hampered by impressionistic generalization in the absence of reliable evidence. I have been putting off such work for years, hoping someone else would do it; this essay includes a report on my first modest attempt to inquire for myself.

with – or have appointed for them – representative figures we all can know about.[12]

Rather than integrating itself into the mainstream of American culture, poetry should be 'evacuating or undermining the public voice'. For 'the dominant public language of our society ... has been so emptied of specific, socially refractory content that it can be easily and widely disseminated; but this is a dissemination without seed'.[13] Instead, Bernstein wishes

> to acknowledge the significance of group-identified poetries (ethnic, racial, linguistic, social, class, sexual, regional) in shattering the neoconventionalist ideal of fashioning by *masterly* artifice a neutral standard English, a common voice for all to speak ... the alternative to 'art for a few' is not one art for all, which tends to degrade and level as it comes under the sway of commercial incentives – but many arts, many poetries.[14]

Bernstein's argument seems compelling and he certainly offers a more recognizable version of American culture than Gioia's nostalgic narrative. And yet, the notion that poetry dissolves boundaries, potentially at least speaking for and to all, is very deeply ingrained. If it is a disease, it may be a congenital disease of Western culture. Orpheus, the ideal poet of myth, was not singing for Thracians only, or Greeks, or even humans: from insensate stones to gods, all orders of being responded to his song. An unrealizable ideal, of course, but one in which a great deal of Utopian longing has been invested for thousands of years. Even after the Maenads killed Orpheus,

loud
as ever, wanted or not, the bloody head
continued singing as it drifted out to sea;

only the god Apollo could finally 'shut it off'.[15] A pluralism of art and poetry would be wonderful if the many arts and poetries were familiar to each others' constituencies, with practitioners of each also forming an open-minded audience for others, sometimes accepting, sometimes rejecting, fighting with each other sometimes but also willing to learn

---

[12] Charles Bernstein, *A Poetics* (Cambridge, MA: Harvard University Press, 1992), pp. 4–5.

[13] Ibid., p. 224.

[14] Ibid., pp. 119–20.

[15] Alan Dugan, 'Orpheus', *New and Collected Poems 1961–1983* (New York: Ecco, 1983), p. 45.

from each other. If artists in one of these plural traditions were always listening for something they could use in the work of the others, if there were a significant number of people interested in and informed about the work of many and not just a few of these arts and poetries, new kinds of work would emerge constantly from the exchange. But if they were sectarian, tightly focused on their own tradition and its nearest relatives, dismissing work from other centres as beneath notice or useful only as a cautionary example, one would, indeed, expect provincialism, syco-phancy and stagnation. To a large extent, unfortunately, that is the way it is. Every time I go under the spell of Bernstein's eloquent theoriz-ing, he jolts me awake by introducing an example of its practice, as in his quotation from Bruce Andrews's *Jeopardy*, which frames each word on a separate line –

> Words/were/what/were/whole/what/wasted/
> words/want/waiting/whose/travel/there –/
> tips/threats/necessary/noise/nothing/needed/
> noise/noise/not/order ... [Bernstein's ellipsis][16]

Does such stuff, as Gioia would put it, 'matter'? Would anyone notice if a misprint had scrambled the order to: 'Words/were/what/whole/were/ wasted/waiting/words/want/travel/there/whose-/necessary/tips/noise/ needed/threats/nothing/noise/not/order/noise'? Must language behave like THAT to be purified of compromised discourse? This writing is so pure that it is puritanical, so intent on avoiding debased meaning that it is content to achieve nothing beyond that avoidance.

For Bernstein, any poetry that can succeed in what Gioia calls 'the broader culture' is likely, indeed almost certain, to be compromised. Better unread than dead, and unacknowledged legislators are the best kind:

> Poets don't have to be read, any more than trees have to be sat under, to transform poisonous societal emissions into something that can be breathed. As a poet, you affect the public sphere with each reader, with the fact of the poem, and by exercising your prerogative to choose what collective forms you will legitimate. The political power of poetry is not measured in numbers; it instructs us to count differently.[17]

Even if we allow the elided distinction between being read by few and being read by no one at all to stand, I am still bothered by Bernstein's

[16] Bernstein, *A Poetics*, pp. 76–7.
[17] Ibid., p. 226.

argument. It reminds me of Marcuse's 'one-dimensional-man' thesis: all the others are brainwashed, but fortunately you and I are here to restore them to their true consciousness, which we understand better than they do. Moreover, Bernstein's ecological twist on the venerable organic metaphor (the poem as tree) could stand some of the same deconstructive scepticism he turns on ideological opponents. What is Joyce Kilmer doing in a postmodern text like this?

To both sides, I would pose the question: what if the marginality of poetry results not from the practice of actual poets, but from circumstances beyond the domain of poetry altogether? What if it needs to be addressed not by a new kind of poetry, but by changes in education, in the distribution of wealth, in the inequities of class and race?[18] If so, we need to read Whitman's poetry as a performative utterance, calling into being that which it proclaims is so, with the implicit awareness that such Orphic power is metaphorical, not literal. We are moved by Whitman's vision of radical equality precisely because we know how far it is from the actuality of his world or ours – or perhaps any world, however socially just, where individual differences of capacity continue to exist. Will poetry ever become fully accessible to people who have been blind and deaf from birth, who are severely retarded, who are in the late stages of degenerative diseases like Alzheimer's? If not, is enjoying it a guilty pleasure?

Even if one takes Whitman's egalitarianism as a call for social rather than somatic equality, what it initiates cannot be altogether completed, and it cannot be written or declaimed into existence by sheer assertion. Bernstein's position strikes me as untenable in its empty purity, while Gioia's seems to me sentimental in its blindness to the social divisions that make his 'general literary community' as uninhabitable an abstraction as Bernstein's ideologically uncompromised but unread hermit-poet.

In this case, the middle of the road is a livelier and more dangerous place than the positions occupied by Gioia and Bernstein, who are sitting on the kerb at opposite sides of the street, gesturing toward the traffic between them. Gioia wants to believe that a mostly white, mostly upper-middle-class 'general literary community' is egalitarian. He conflates the distinction of class with the distinction that really concerns him, between academic and non-academic middle-class readers. To reach beyond the academy becomes, for him, equivalent to dissolving barriers of class, race, age and occupation. But the audiences for both New Formalist poetry and Language Poetry, if my admittedly random experience of public readings is typical, remain almost entirely white and (to judge by clothing and

---

[18] These categories usually appear with a third, gender, but, in this case, if gender comes into the equation, it does so in a reverse fashion: women, far from being excluded from poetry, are more likely to read it than men. Indeed, poetry has been consigned to the 'feminine' and, hence, to a domestic sphere removed from public discourse.

speech) middle class. Bernstein seems to think that by refusing to be a certain compromised sort of poet, one engages in a lonely but significant act of cultural resistance, even if no one is watching and even if the result is a poetry more interesting as a performance of refusal than as an alternative to what it rejects. To occupy the space between these positions is difficult. Still, I would like to believe in a poetry impure enough to engage readers inured to the compromised discourse of our sound-bite, advertising-saturated culture and principled enough to make itself difficult, disruptive, not entirely compliant to the expectations coded in the ideologies that have deformed the idiom. It has to pull the reader in but it has to challenge the reader's expectations somewhere, or it is only pandering after all.

III
Poetry in Performance: Some Crude Empirical Research

Lately, I've tried to pay attention to the audience as well as the poet when I go to readings, in the hope of learning who they – or we – are. An appearance by Robert Pinsky at the Evanston franchise of Borders Books, shortly after his appointment as laureate, drew about a hundred people. There was a mixture of student types and middle-aged professionals but I spotted just one black person and just a few Asians and Hispanics, insofar as one could tell by sight. A reading a few years earlier at an aggressively hip Chicago club, the Lower Links, featured a Chicago Language poet, Bill Fuller. The crowd, as one might expect in a venue lined with black vinyl, was younger, with more leather, pierced body parts and punk hair. But it was, like the Pinsky audience, overwhelmingly white. Its responses were tentative; there would be scattered applause until others slowly joined in. While Fuller was reading, I caught people looking around the room as if seeking guidance, in the faces of the others, to an appropriate response.

I saw something closer to Gioia's ideal audience, or Whitman's, when I attended (and briefly took part in) something called 'Nomadica', organized by a local poet and songwriter, Richard Fammerée. Moving from place to place as its name suggests, this event features poetry, music and dance. That night, Mad Bar, in Chicago's Bucktown, gave it a local habitation and a name. It so happened that the Bulls had a play-off finals game against Utah that night, shown on a large-screen television in the back of the bar. For the first half, the basketball fans were fairly quiet, and the performances in the front room went on unimpeded. There were, at peak, about seventy or eighty in the audience and fully a third of them, I would guess, were not white: there were blacks, a group of Iranians (as someone who knew them said they were), several Hispanics and Asians. One of the performers, a Haitian immigrant, had translated his poem from French; another sang Brazilian songs in the original Portuguese; and a third read her poems first in Spanish, then in English.

I wish I could honestly report that what I heard that night was wonderful or good or even interesting, but most of it wasn't. The best parts were the music and dance. Fammerée's poems had moments of compelling imagery, diluted by recycled clichés and rambling narrative; as he accompanied them with music, they sometimes transcended their unevenness in the way that good pop lyrics can. But the rest of the evening's poetry held no attractions for me. The Haitian 'poem' was a long prosaic effusion, devoid of metaphor or invention, on how marvellous Nomadica was. There were a few lineated announcements of how good it is to be a woman or an African-American or whatever one was, in thoroughly predictable language. There were poems about tensions of the streets but they treated the subject moralistically and abstractly, rather than through metaphor, keen observation or narrative.

As the Bulls dissipated their comfortable lead early in the second half, shouts and groans from the frustrated fans in the back of the bar began to impinge on the performances. Members of the Nomadica audience, including some performers who had already taken their turn, began to drift back to catch a look at the game. When Jordan's last-second shot missed, the Bulls were beaten, so the faithful stampeded out of the back room, past the Nomadica stage and out the front door. The energy had gone out of the place and the audience, already down to half its earlier size, dwindled to about fifteen people, most of them participants. And, at this point, when the event had been trying to end for at least twenty minutes, the open mic readings, in which I'd been asked to participate, began. When my turn came, I chose a poem about an incident on the New York subway that almost precipitated a fight on the station platform and another about my experiences as a young teaching assistant in the SEEK program of CUNY, Queens in 1969. Both were concerned with the themes of race and class in the city that earlier readings had raised. The drummer who had been improvising behind other poets started a tattoo as I began but gave up after about ten lines when he realized that it wasn't that sort of poetry. When the first poem was done, there was a smattering of applause and I launched into the much longer second one. About halfway through, as I tried in vain to make eye contact with someone in the audience, it occurred to me simply to stop and walk away but I brazened it out. Some of the exhausted listeners applauded faintly for three or four seconds as I left the stage. But then a young woman who had sung an hour earlier tapped my arm as I walked past her table and said, 'That was good.'

So maybe reading in 'Nomadica' was worthwhile after all, since at least one person got something out of my contribution. Maybe audiences have to be sought and created, one person at a time, rather than summoned by fiat from Whitman's 'gangs of Kosmos'. Perhaps, if more poets of the kind I take seriously persevered through events like that one, a few people on each occasion might be drawn into a kind of poetry they would otherwise not have encountered. But it is not much fun to perform with readers who would get a C in an introductory writing class.

Attempting to gather some actual facts about audiences for poetry, I threw together a questionnaire to distribute at The Green Mill, a bar that is home to Chicago's Uptown Poetry Slam. Sixty-one questionnaires did come back at the evening's end and they suggest a few tentative conclusions. I had not gone to The Green Mill intending to be a participant, but only one person had signed up for the slam. The host, Marc Smith, proposed that this contestant read against himself. Since I had some poems in my bag along with the questionnaires, I volunteered to enter. Smith put the matter to the audience, which welcomed the competition. At that point, a young woman in the back of the room spoke up and decided to give it a try as well.

The prize for winning the slam was $13.00 – ten dollars plus the number of participants. Three judges were appointed at random from the audience, then asked to introduce themselves. One was a teacher, one was an artist and one worked for Dow Chemical. Smith, whose role as MC includes ritual heckling of participants, gave him a hard time about working for the company that had manufactured napalm during the Vietnam War. Each judge was asked to hold up a score from zero to ten after each poem, as in Olympic skating or diving events. The judges' scores for each reader would be combined and the contestant with the lowest composite score dropped. The two survivors read another poem and whoever got the better score in the second round would win. Smith instructed the audience in its prerogatives. If listeners thought a poem was dragging, they were to snap their fingers softly, as if to say 'get on with it'. If a poem rhymed too predictably, they were invited to shout out the rhyme word along with the poet. And any content judged to be sexist was fair game for the 'feminist hiss'.

The woman who had signed up last was nervous, seemingly unused to performance, and, while her poem was all right by the standards of the evening, her delivery of it sealed her fate. The other contestant was a young man who had participated in a slam scene in North Carolina for poets twenty-five years old and under. His first poem was a diatribe against his poetry teacher, delivered from memory with much dramatic flair. The student, it seems, had wanted to write an erotic poem about women's legs, but (and I quote from memory)

> my PC teacher said,
> 'You are objectifying women',
> and I said, 'You are objectifying poetry'.

The instructor demanded analysis of poetry but the student thought (or felt) that poetry was all about emotion. Toward the end, the poet faced the audience and shouted:

> FEEL! FEEL! FEEL!
> LEGS! LEGS! LEGS!

There was no feminist hiss; the poem got the warmest audience response of the evening and, as I recall, the highest score. I came in second and thus survived to the final round.

Marc Smith gave me almost as much flak about being a professor as the chemist-judge got about his job with Dow. As my young opponent finished, I sat in the front row awaiting my turn and Smith said, 'The Professor's nervous now. He's doin' his yoga. He's been readin' too much Gary Snyder.' Determined to take it in good humour, I replied, 'You could do worse.' I chose a political poem, 'The Scale', published in *TriQuarterly* some years back. The typescript runs into a second page and, as I was reading, I found that I had left the second page at my table. For one moment, I paused and started to go back for it but then decided to continue from memory. One phrase was slightly garbled but no one else would ever know. When I finished, Smith heckled me a little bit about the content of the poem but then said, 'You've just seen it, folks: a reader becoming a reciter before your very eyes.' And, of course, being free of the page was an enormous advantage. A reader at a slam who hasn't memorized might as well be an actor who doesn't know his lines. Smith himself, who had recited several of his poems during the evening, is only intermittently a good poet, by my lights, but is an experienced and effective performer, making the most of inflection and gesture to hold his listeners' attention.

Then came the final round. Fortunately for me, the leg-man did not have another poem as catchy as his first so, despite his energetic performance, the response was more subdued. I chose a quiet but accessible poem, 'In a Rowboat, Once, By Night', that had appeared in *Agni*. When the smoke cleared, the professor had won the Uptown Poetry Slam by a tenth of a point. But it had been a slow night. This dubious victory does suggest, however, that kinds of poetry seemingly unsuited to a slam situation may reach some of that audience if the moment is right.

The questionnaires were modestly revealing. They showed that while it was a young crowd (forty-four per cent gave their age as twenty to twenty-nine), there were more people over thirty than under: twenty-six per cent in their thirties, eleven per cent in their forties, and eleven per cent in their fifties. (One respondent gave no age and only one confessed to being sixty.) Fifty-nine per cent of them had attended slams and poetry readings before this one; another twenty per cent had attended poetry readings but not slams; the remaining twenty-one per cent had never been to a poetry reading of any kind before. If it was a more diverse audience than Pinsky's at the suburban Borders, it was still predominantly white. Several respondents declined to give race or ethnicity, or ridiculed the question (for example, for 'Race' they wrote 'Triathlon' or 'None of your damn bidness' [sic]), thus clouding the statistical results. But only eight per cent checked African-American and three per cent identified themselves as Hispanic. Most interesting was the spread of occupations. Five per cent said they worked as clerks or waiting staff (these were in the youngest age group); twenty-three per cent worked in 'business' or 'sales'; sixteen per cent were in professions such as law or medicine, and ten per cent were engineers or technicians. Only eight per cent identified themselves as teachers and eleven per cent as students. Another eleven per cent indicated that they had careers in the arts, but only three per cent claimed to be writers. So the prevailing notion that only poets and their force-fed students attend to poetry does not hold for this audience. Whether what this audience attended to was poetry, exactly, is another question.

Questions about preferences in poetry elicited many tautological, vague or flippant answers, suggesting a defensiveness about giving reasons for likes and dislikes. The questions 'What magazines do you think publish good poetry' and 'What magazines do you think publish bad poetry' drew mostly blanks. The question 'Which poets (and/or poems) do you admire' often produced mixtures of the canonical and the popular (for example, 'Maya Angelou, Shel Silverstein, Shakespeare'; 'Shel Silverstein, Robert Frost'; 'Robert Frost, Dr Seuss'; 'Dr Seuss, Orsen [sic] Wells, Shakespeare, John Lennon'), but some lists suggested extensive reading experience (for example, 'Frank O'Hara, Robert Creeley, Allen Ginsberg, Kathleen Fraser, Galway Kinnell, Diane Wakoski, Arthur Sze, Simon Ortiz'). Shel Silverstein, Maya Angelou and Nikki Giovanni were the most often named. Ovid, Virgil and Dante received one mention each.

Most frustrating were the responses to the questions 'What qualities do you like in poems' and 'What qualities in poems turn you off'. One person liked 'good poetry' and disliked 'bad poetry' (this response came from an attorney, so the question-begging may have been quite intentional). 'Rhythm' was often cited as a good quality but what precisely the respondents meant by it is hard to guess. Some valued 'accessibility' but the question of clarity versus obscurity was less prominent than one might have expected. The only conclusion I draw from this part of the questionnaire is that soliciting reflections on aesthetics from a bunch of people in a bar is a fool's errand.

IV Coda: Arman Barnett's Front Porch

When I was a graduate student at the University of Virginia, one of my classmates was, in addition to being a PhD candidate in good standing, a marvellous traditional country fiddler. He was a northerner and had studied classical violin as a boy. But he had become interested in 'old-timey' music and could play it as idiomatically as any rural southerner. He rented a house just outside of Charlottesville and, in the summer, local musicians would gather on his porch to play. His speech identified him as a Yankee; his politics, as I recall, were typical of graduate students in English, which is to say far to the left of most rural Virginians. Most of his visitors didn't have a college degree and presumably most of them had the political and religious beliefs typical of their milieu. But once they tuned up their instruments, differences of class, ideology and regional identity were, for the time being, irrelevant. What mattered was their shared love and knowledge of the music they were playing together.

That may be about as far as democracy can go in art. If you can't play your instrument or you don't know the conventions of the genre, you simply aren't on the same terms as those who can and do. There are, to be sure, many genres. As a poet and critic, I don't claim that my front porch is the only one in town. I try to visit others, to hear what is being played there and to listen with an open mind. If I like what I hear on somebody else's porch, I'll invite the people I meet there to come to mine. And maybe I'll bring an instrument next time I visit theirs. Eventually, something new might emerge from our exchange. This analogy may not satisfy someone like Dana Gioia who believes that '[f]or the arts at least there truly is a *Zeitgeist*',[19] but for those of us who no longer discern one, something like it may have to do.

[19] Gioia, *Can Poetry Matter?*, p. 39.

9

'Where is the Nation you Promised?': American Voice in Modern Scottish and Irish Poetry

Cairns Craig

I Looping the Atlantic

Edwin Morgan's 'The Second Life', the title poem of his volume of 1968, proclaimed a new beginning for the man and a new aesthetic, one measured not by the fulfilment of a national tradition but by a deliberate displacement, a re-routing of the poet's voice – that Scottish, Glaswegian voice – through the voice of American poetry:

> But does every man feel like this at forty –
> I mean it's like Thomas Wolfe's New York, his
> heady light, the stunning plunging canyons, beauty –
> pale stars winking hazy downtown quitting-time,
> and the winter moon flooding the skyscrapers, northern –
> an aspiring place, glory of the bridges, foghorns
> are enormous messages, a looming mastery [1]

The 'I' of 'I mean' is syntactically and emotionally overwhelmed: 'it' takes place as the instrument of a 'looming mastery', which is both the mastery of American culture over the modern world and the mastery of the poet who ventriloquizes his own rebirth by discovering a voice that is appropriate to the 'aspiring place' in which he writes:

> Can it be like this, and is this what it means
> in Glasgow now, writing as the aircraft roar
> over building sites, in this warm west light
> by the daffodil banks that were never so crowded and lavish –
> green May, and the slow great blocks rising

---

[1] Edwin Morgan, 'The Second Life', *Poems of Thirty Years* (Manchester: Carcanet, 1982), pp. 162–3 (p. 162).

under yellow tower cranes, concrete and glass and steel
out of a dour rubble it was and barefoot children gone – [2]

The industrial world of Glasgow, once Second City of the Empire,
struggles towards rebirth by reflecting, like a mirror image across the
Atlantic, the styles of New York. And, just as the city reshapes itself in a
New World economy, so the American voice has become, to the poet, a
second 'eye', a second self:

and so the world is not the same,
the second eye is making again
this place, these waters and these towers,
they are rising again
as the eye stands up to the sun,
as the eye salutes the sun.[3]

Morgan's voice ventriloquizes the celebratory, incantatory lines of
American Beat poetry and 'stands up' to it – claimant of a share in a
New World that is a second 'I' within his own culture.

Morgan's salutation of the American voice was to be a significant
gesture in modern Scottish poetry. When, a few years earlier, Al Alvarez
published his influential anthology *The New Poetry*, which proclaimed
the need for British poets to follow American examples, it contained the
work of two Scottish-based poets, Norman MacCaig and Iain Crichton
Smith. In his introduction, however, Alvarez felt able to generalize about
the relationship between English and American poetry – 'My own feeling
is that a good deal of poetic talent exists in England at the moment' –
without acknowledging that some of his poets were *not* English (he
believed 'England' to be 'an island').[4] Alvarez looked for ways in which
the American and the English traditions could be 'creatively reconciled',
helping English poets get beyond 'the disease so often found in English
culture: gentility'.[5] Morgan's poem, on the other hand, refuses any
reconciliation. It is a declaration of personal and cultural independence
by the renunciation of any confusion between his voice and the poetic
voice of the English tradition, a verse statement of a new sense of cultural
filiation in which the Scottish voice can achieve liberation by adopting an
American style. In the 1960s, in Scotland, submission to American forms
was not the neo-imperialism of poetic self-oppression but an escape from
the constricting limits of a British culture to which Scotland's traditions
were increasingly marginal.

[2] Ibid., p. 162.
[3] Ibid., p. 163.
[4] Al Alvarez (ed.), *The New Poetry* (Harmondsworth: Penguin, 1962; revised 1966),
Introduction, pp. 32, 25.
[5] Alvarez, *The New Poetry*, p. 32.

The alliance between Scotland and America that Morgan exemplified was explained by Tom Leonard in 1976 in his essay 'The Locust Tree in Flower, and why it had Difficulty Flowering in Britain', which celebrated the achievements of William Carlos Williams:

> What I like about Williams is his voice. What I like about Williams is his presentation of voice as a fact, as a fact in itself and as a factor in his relationship with the world as he heard it, listened to it, spoke it. That language is not simply an instrument of possession, a means of snooping round everything that is not itself – that's what I get from Williams.[6]

Williams's 'voice' as 'fact' is, for Leonard, an assertion of the local, of language as it happens to be in a particular place. In British writing, on the other hand, what is heard is the language of class: 'There are basically two ways of speaking in Britain: one which lets the listener know that one paid for one's education, the other which lets the listener know that one didn't.' According to Leonard, William's focus on the 'voice as a fact' had little impact in Britain because British speech was riven with class meaning which made it primarily 'an instrument of possession' rather than an instrument of expression: 'the regional and the working-class languages, whatever else they're capable of, certainly aren't capable, the shoddy little things, of great Art.'[7]

Significantly, however, Leonard saw in Hugh MacDiarmid the only major British contributor to the poetry of the voice as fact, so that to follow Williams was, equally, to recognize the achievements of a Scottish writer marginalized in British poetry. For Leonard, the future possibilities of poetry required not Alvarez's confrontation with 'the forces of disintegration which destroy the old standards of civilization' but the recognition of what had happened to the very instruments of literature in modern British society:

> When you have in a society on the one hand a standardised literary grammar (standardised spelling and standardised syntax) and on the other hand a standardised mode of pronunciation, the notion tends to get embedded in the consciousness of that society, that the one is part of the essence of the other. Prescriptive grammar, in other words, becomes the sound made flesh of prescriptive pronunciation.[8]

---

[6] Tom Leonard, 'The Locust Tree in Flower and why it had Difficulty Flowering in Britain', *Intimate Voices: Selected Work 1965–1983* (Newcastle-upon-Tyne: Galloping Dog Press, 1984), pp. 95–102 (p. 95).

[7] Ibid., pp. 95, 96.

[8] Alvarez, *The New Poetry*, p. 26; Leonard, 'The Locust Tree', p. 95

To liberate the voice, poets had to follow the route of 'the largely American-initiated breakdown in prescriptive grammar', of which Carlos Williams was the progenitor, and had to resist that incorporation of the American voice into British norms which Williams's great antagonist, T. S. Eliot, had achieved: 'This was the message coming out of America. Back in Britain, the winter evening was settling down, with smell of steaks in passageways. Six o'clock. A respectable American was trying to raise Tennyson from the grave.'[9] Unlocking the poetic voice in Scotland required a loop back to the beginnings of modernism and a reversal of the Atlantic crossing made by Eliot. It is an act of negation inscribed in Leonard's imitation of Williams's 'This is Just to Say' as 'Jist ti Let Yi No':

> ahv drank
> thi speshlz
> that wurrin
> thi frij
>
> n thit
> yiwurr probbli
> hodn back
> furthi pahrti
> awright
>
> they wur great
> thaht stroang
> thaht cawld [10]

To 'know' language you have to have 'no' language in the eyes of those who 'own' language in Britain. Leonard's poem at once asserts its artfulness by its allusion to Williams's famous simplicities

> I have eaten
> the plums
> that were in
> the icebox

and challenges those notions of poetic art which, quite literally, cannot recognize meaning in vernacular speech.[11] The defamiliarization that Williams achieves by putting the most ordinary of everyday language into poetry, Leonard achieves by phonetic transcription that emphasizes

---

[9] Leonard, 'The Locust Tree', pp. 99, 102.
[10] Leonard, 'Jist ti Let Yi No', *Intimate Voices*, p. 37.
[11] William Carlos Williams, 'This is Just to Say', *Collected Poems*, A. Walton Litz and Christopher MacGowan (eds), Vol. 1: 1909–1939 (London: Paladin, 1991), p. 372.

the disjunction between the written and the spoken. Leonard's poem enacts a liberation of the Scottish voice, of the working-class voice, that can be best achieved by 'mastering' Williams's techniques for 'recognising the non-English nature of the American idiom'.[12]

Much contemporary Scottish poetry has been built on those American foundations. Liz Lochhead's 'Letter from New England' from her earliest collection, *Memo for Spring* published in 1972, presents an American world in which nothing, apparently, is happening but in a language where something distinctly American is taking place:

> I sip my coke at the counter
> of the Osterville soda-fountain
> that is also the Osterville news-stand, &
> I watch Nothing Happening
> out on mainstreet
> of this small New England town.
>
> just
> the sun &
> white clapboard houses with trees in between, &
> certain cottonclad &
> conservative spinsters nod at nodding acquaintances, &[13]

The piled litanies of the real that the Beat poets derived from Carlos Williams become the medium for 'realizing' the American world, no matter how genteel the actuality of the poet's location. Mimicry of American styles may be justified by the poem's location, but Lochhead's colloquial style, constantly searching out the significance of the commonplace and the clichéd, developed in a series of loops, both geographic and stylistic, from Scotland to America. Those loops are dramatized in Lochhead's sequence, 'Sailing Past Liberty', which begins in Manhattan, switches back to Scotland and concludes with a section in which loops of film, spliced in an editing machine, become a metaphor of a transatlantic relationship, at the level both of personal biography and of poetic style. The final section, 'In the Cutting Room', plays on the double sense of 'cutting' as both the splicing of film and as emotional hurt –

> Working together & we seem
> to love each other (but
> that too is an old story)

---

[12] Leonard, 'The Locust Tree', p. 96.

[13] Liz Lochhead, 'Letter from New England', *Dreaming Frankenstein & Collected Poems* (Edinburgh: Polygon, 1984), p. 142.

– and suggests the necessary but disruptive interaction of Scottish and American culture in which the poet is engaged:

> yet not one of those fine few skills
> (loops of language
> spliced syllables of movement) we
> have learned to curse but labour at
> together   separate

The 'liberty' of American style that the poet achieves in 'Sailing Past Liberty' is juxtaposed with the sense of irreconcilable distances; the displacement of the voice that Morgan celebrated as a resurrection has become an absence rather than a fulfilment, a sense of 'not quite accepting me on my own'.[14] The language, like the lovers, must circulate in a loop which ensures that the more it brings Scotland and America 'together' in 'spliced syllables', the more they will be 'separate', divided by the very line which unites them.

If Morgan, Leonard and Lochhead have pointed ways for Scottish poets to treat American English as a kind of displaced homeland – or their homeland as a displaced America – that 'loop' through American culture had already been taken in Ireland, both biographically and stylistically, by John Montague:

> My mother,
> my mother's memories
> of America;
> a muddy cup
> she refused to drink.
>
> His landlady didn't know
> my father was married
> so who was the woman
> landed on the doorstep
> with grown sons
>
> my elder brothers
> lonely & lost
> Father staggers back
> from the speakeasy
> for his stage entrance;

[14] Lochhead, 'Sailing Past Liberty', *Dreaming Frankenstein*, pp. 35, 33.

> the whole scene as
> played by Boucicault
> or Eugene O'Neill:[15]

Montague's childhood as an emigrant in Brooklyn becomes the justification for a voice which is 'grafted' twice over – grafted into English from its historical roots in Irish and then grafted from American back into Irish English:

> 'So this is our brightest infant?
> Where did he get that outlandish accent?
> What do you expect, with no parents,
> sent back from some American slum:
> none of you are to speak like him!'[16]

In Montague's case, having acquired an American voice is, at a personal level, a repetition of Ireland's fundamental crisis in the loss of the native language and its replacement by a foreign voice. As he puts it in 'A Grafted Tongue'

> To grow
> a second tongue, as
> harsh a humiliation
> as twice to be born.[17]

That grafted Irish tongue, however, will be liberated from English by realizing its American heritage:

> Lines of protest
>   lines of change
> a drum beating
>   across Berkeley
> all that Spring
>   invoking the new [18]

In Montague's poetry, the 'lines' have been changed: an Irish tradition (as in an American campus named after an Irish philosopher) is transformed and returns through the American voice, 'invoking the new' but also recovering what had been suppressed in itself. The American voice can be accepted and utilized because it is already, in part, an Irish voice in

---

[15] John Montague, 'A Muddy Cup', *Collected Poems* (Oldcastle, County Meath: Gallery Books, 1995), p. 166.
[16] Montague, 'A Flowering Absence', *Collected Poems*, p. 182.
[17] Montague, 'A Grafted Tongue', *Collected Poems*, p. 37.
[18] Montague, 'A New Siege', *Collected Poems*, p. 72.

exile, an Irish voice which knows its own Irishness most powerfully precisely through its displacement.

Montague's grafting of Irish and American voice is only, as Eamonn Grennan has suggested, the most prominent of many interchanges between Irish and American poetry in the twentieth century. According to Grennan, 'the importance of the American influence' for poets such as Devlin, Fallon and Kavanagh 'lies in how it helps them get beyond Yeats'.[19] So pervasive is this interaction that Grennan jokes that Irish poetry 'begins with Walt Whitman', who, for Yeats himself, points the direction from provincialism to cultural independence. Grennan believes, however, that in the rest of British poetry, 'no such deep and extended connection with America seems to exist'.[20] Clearly this is not the case in Scotland in the second half of the twentieth century and, given Whitman's influences on MacDiarmid, modern Scottish poetry might equally be assumed to begin with Whitman. For Grennan the American influence is 'synonymous with freedom', freedom from all the stifling aspects of Irish culture, its 'confining state and state of mind', and freedom from the confining effects of 'a powerful predecessor',[21] but the sheer scale of the involvement of Irish and Scottish writers with American poetry suggests something more structural than the coincidence of a variety of individuals happening to be attracted to the voice of 'liberty' – especially since, by the 1950s and 60s, the United States was a society of profound repressions as well as of potential liberation. By then, the open road offered by Whitman had become, as Louis Simpson suggested in 'Walt Whitman at Bear Mountain', something very different:

> 'Where is the Mississippi panorama
> And the girl who played the piano?
> Where are you, Walt?
> The Open Road goes to the used-car lot.

> 'Where is the nation you promised?[22]

The lost promise of the American nation was also the lost promise of the poetic nation and it was through the American experience that Irish and Scottish poets came to engage with the broken promise of their own nations.

[19] Eamonn Grennan, 'American Relations', in Theo Dorgan (ed.), *Irish Poetry Since Kavanagh* (Blackrock, C. Dublin: Four Courts Press, 1996), p. 96.

[20] Ibid., p. 95.

[21] Ibid., p. 105.

[22] Louis Simpson, 'Walt Whitman at Bear Mountain', in Donald Hall (ed.), *Contemporary American Poetry* (Harmondsworth: Penguin, 1972), pp. 119–20 (p. 119).

II Displacements

Even in this era of globalization it is assumed that the history of poetry is national and poetry the essence of the nation. Indeed, there are prevalent conceptions of the nation as 'imagined communities' which make the nation nothing more than a projection of the poetic imagination, a notion echoed in the titles of books such as Murray Pittock's *The Invention of Scotland* and Declan Kiberd's *Inventing Ireland*.[23] The intimate link between poetry and nation has been underlined in the last twenty years of the century by the proliferation of 'national' anthologies, such as Roderick Watson's *The Poetry of Scotland*, Douglas Dunn's *Faber Book of Twentieth-Century Scottish Poetry*, Donnie O'Rourke's *Dream State: The New Scottish Poets*, Gerald Dawe's *The Younger Irish Poets*, Paul Muldoon's *Faber Book of Contemporary Irish Poetry* and Peter Fallon and Derek Mahon's competing *Penguin Book of Contemporary Irish Poetry*.[24] Criticism, equally, has worked in 'national' categories – particularly in Ireland, where the issue of Ulster's poetic as well as political status has acted as a spur. Poetic lineage as a distinctively national tradition is reflected in books such as Robert F. Garratt's *Modern Irish Poetry: Tradition and Continuity from Yeats to Heaney* and Terence Brown's and Nicholas Grene's *Tradition and Influence in Anglo-Irish Poetry*.[25]

If one were writing a sociology, rather than a literary history, of modern poetry, however, a very different structure might be required – after all, some of the most prominent modern Irish poets are either full- or part-time American residents. This is not merely a matter of the Joycean 'exile and cunning': it is part of the long process of transatlantic interchange – Pound, Eliot in one direction, Auden and Gunn in the other, with Hughes and Plath as symbolic failed union – which has been fundamental to the development of poetry in English throughout the twentieth century. In November 1948, for instance, T. S. Eliot gave a lecture at the Library of Congress in Washington. In the audience were:

[23] Murray G. H. Pittock, *The Invention of Scotland: The Stuart Myth and the Scottish Identity, 1638 to the Present* (London: Routledge, 1991); Declan Kiberd, *Inventing Ireland* (London: Jonathan Cape, 1995).

[24] Roderick Watson (ed.), *The Poetry of Scotland: Gaelic, Scots and English, 1380–1980*, (Edinburgh: Edinburgh University Press, 1995); Douglas Dunn (ed.), *The Faber Book of Twentieth-Century Scottish Poetry* (London: Faber, 1992); Daniel O'Rourke (ed.), *Dream State: The New Scottish Poets* (Edinburgh: Polygon, 1994); Gerald Dawe (ed.), *The Younger Irish Poets* (Belfast: Blackstaff, 1982); Paul Muldoon (ed.), *The Faber Book of Contemporary Irish Poetry* (London: Faber, 1986); Peter Fallon and Derek Mahon (eds), *The Penguin Book of Contemporary Irish Poetry* (London: Penguin, 1990).

[25] Robert F. Garratt, *Modern Irish Poetry: Tradition and Continuity from Yeats to Heaney* (London and Berkeley: University of California Press, 1986); Terence Brown and Nicholas Grene, *Tradition and Influence in Anglo-Irish Poetry* (Basingstoke: Macmillan, 1989).

William Carlos Williams, still fuming at Eliot's betrayal of American letters; W. H. Auden, by then very much an American poet; and the young Robert Lowell, who was, at this point, the literary offspring of Eliot but was shortly to start moving in the direction of Williams's nativist style. The intertwining traditions of British and American poetry confronted one another in that encounter. Later, Lowell would discover in San Francisco, among the Beats, that his Eliotic poetry read 'like prehistoric monsters dragged down into the bog and death by their ponderous armour'.[26] He was, however, to follow in Eliot's footsteps when, in 1970, he left America for England and a post at the University of Essex. From that point onwards he spent his life translating himself back and forth across the Atlantic – with Ireland as a stopping off point. Lowell had become a displaced person: estranged from an America that could no longer be home to his poetry. Lowell continued to envy 'Whitman's huge sweep, mostly in his thirties and forties, lines pouring out, a hundred poems a year, yet with his long, idle afternoons of sauntering, chatting, at ease nearly with what the eye fell on',[27] but America was no longer the nation that Whitman had promised. In 'Words for Hart Crane' in *Life Studies*, the disjunction between the national poet and the modern poet's nation unites the voices of Lowell and Crane in fierce complaint:

> When the Pulitzer's showered on some dope
> or screw who flushed our dry mouths out with soap,
> few people would consider why I took
> to stalking sailors, and scattered Uncle Sam's
> phoney gold-plated laurels to the birds.
> Because I knew my Whitman like a book,
> stranger in America, tell my country [28]

'America' and 'my country' are now alien to one another. The book of the nation that Whitman promised has become a personal possession with no public significance. Lowell might aspire to be 'a voice for his times, a historian',[29] giving order to the modern world, but his death in a taxi, travelling from Kennedy airport, comes to seem symbolic of the world in which the poet shuttles between alternative territories, disruptively slicing national narratives into personal fragments.

For two of the leading Irish and Scottish poets of the second half of the century, Seamus Heaney and Douglas Dunn, Lowell's life and art represented the paradigmatic condition of the poet after modernism. In

[26] Paul Mariani, *Lost Puritan: A Life of Robert Lowell* (New York: W. W. Norton, 1994), p. 251.
[27] Letter to Elizabeth Bishop, 16 July 1966, quoted in Mariani, *Lost Puritan*, p. 343.
[28] Robert Lowell, 'Words for Hart Crane', *Life Studies* (London: Faber, 1959), p. 55.
[29] Mariani, *Lost Puritan*, p. 373.

his struggle to place himself – between North and South, between Ireland and Britain – Heaney adopted Lowell as the model of the poet who could turn the details of autobiography into politically significant statement. The beginnings of this relationship were comedically acknowledged in *Field Work* in 'The Skunk', in which Heaney playfully adapts to his own personal situation the image of the skunk in Lowell's 'Skunk Hour',[30] but the poetic inheritance is properly acknowledged in *The Government of the Tongue*, where Lowell is cited as the central example of the modern poet's ability to deal with the public world from a private perspective. Heaney's essay on Lowell plays on the terseness of its title – 'Lowell's Command' – to imply not only the command that Lowell has achieved over language (despite his lack of command over his own psyche), but also the command he has over other modern poets – a command that was also the command of American culture, as though the Irish (or Scottish) poets could only command their own territories if they had followed the orders of those by whom the world's, and the English language's, culture was commanded.[31]

Yet the central moment on which Heaney focuses is the moment when Lowell *refuses* the command of his nation, the moment in 1943 when he declared himself a conscientious objector. The poet's command derives directly from his refusal of the national command to enlist in the name of the nation:

> It was in this act of conscientious objection that doctrine, ancestry and politics fused themselves in one commanding stroke and Lowell succeeded in uniting the aesthetic instinct with the obligation to witness morally and significantly in the realm of action.[32]

To command (poetically) is to refuse to command (nationally); that refusal becomes a command upon other poets to command (poetically) by refusing their national traditions and routing their poetry through the American voice that is, in itself, a denial of its nation. The promise of the American voice is a promise maintained in defiance of the failure of the American nation to fulfil *its* promise.

Heaney's translation from Northern Ireland to Dublin and from there to the post that Lowell had held at Harvard was matched by shifts in his poetic style; in Dunn's case the transatlantic crossing was made early, to be followed by a long exile in Hull, where the influence of Philip Larkin defined the context of his early poetry. Such displacements produce, in a

---

[30] Seamus Heaney, 'The Skunk', *Field Work* (London: Faber, 1979), p. 52.

[31] Seamus Heaney, 'Lowell's Command', *The Government of the Tongue: The 1986 T. S. Eliot Memorial Lectures and Other Critical Writings* (London: Faber, 1988), pp. 129–48.

[32] Ibid., p. 133.

poem like Dunn's 'Renfrewshire Traveller', a tortured sense of disconnection from the narrative of the nation:

> I am Scots, a tartan tin box
> Of shortbread in a delicatessen of cheddars
>
> And southern specialities.
> I am full of poison.
> Each crumb of me is a death,
>
> Someone you never see again
> After funerals in the rain.[33]

National tradition has become corrosively destructive. In his introduction to *The Faber Book of Twentieth-Century Scottish Poetry*, Dunn comments caustically on the reception – or, rather, lack of reception – of W. S. Graham's work and notes that the defining fact is that 'he lived furth of Scotland for most of his adult life, and loved Cornwall. His relative neglect is due more to the quirk of having been not-quite-obviously-Scottish-enough; he had the cheek to live somewhere else'.[34] The living-somewhere-else, which dramatizes spiritual exile, makes Lowell, for Dunn, the exemplary poet of the modern era:

> The poems in my head were facing west,
> Towards a continental summer.
> I won't deny it. The Stars and Stripes
> On a blue autumn day is quite something.
>
> But then, so was I, in casuals,
> Fit and young, athletic, frivolous –
> As if nobody knew me then – one round year married,
> My wife in tears at having to go home so soon.
>
> I liked old villages with soldier-statued squares
> Where I could stand and feel like Robert Lowell.[35]

For Dunn, the transatlantic journey from America back to Britain becomes an exile from authenticity, an exile from that confrontation with the real in which Lowell was engaged:

[33] Douglas Dunn, 'Renfrewshire Traveller', *Selected Poems 1964–1983* (London: Faber, 1986), pp. 73–4 (p. 73).

[34] Dunn (ed,) *The Faber Book of Twentieth Century Scottish Poetry*, Introduction, p. xxxvii.

[35] Dunn, 'The Wealth', *Selected Poems*, pp. 110–13 (p. 112).

> We shipped aboard SS *United States*.
> I went home on a name
> With nothing like enough
> To live on comfortably.
>
> I felt like a Jew, at Hamburg
> On a boat bound for America,
> A Jew at Hamburg, 1939,
> And wept for laws, but not for me, civilian,
>
> Writing poetry, seasick on the North Atlantic,
> Reading *Henderson the Rain King*
> And *For the Union Dead*.
> I wanted it torpedoed, by the British.[36]

So intense is the identification with American experience that Dunn's poem wills destruction at the hands of his own culture. It is significant that the only poet who is personally memorialized in Dunn's 1979 collection, *Barbarians*, is Robert Lowell, of whose death Dunn learns from 'an *Observer*, four days out of date' while living in France:

> A radio, its non-specific song
> Far away in a leafy park ... I'm full
> Of my routine sadness. It can't be wrong
> To let these thoughts run free and overrule
>
> Tranquillity, [37]

In its very phrasing Dunn's poem echoes Lowell but, instead of a voice about to break under the pressure of its own suffering, Dunn's poem leaves its speaker hanging only on the edge of a comfortable acceptance of his alienation:

> What else can I do, feeling this way, but sit
> With my wife and my newspaper, well-fed,
> Well-wined, happy together and unfit.[38]

Lowell's experience becomes, for Dunn, a measure of the difficulties with which the poet has to struggle when he is *not* sufficiently tormented by his culture. America becomes the measure of the Scottish poet's loss of

---

[36] Ibid., p. 112–13.
[37] Dunn, 'Stranger's Grief', *Selected Poems*, pp. 132–3 (p. 132).
[38] Ibid., p. 133.

public significance – even when America is defined by the loss of its own *poetic* significance.

Dunn concludes his Introduction to the Faber anthology with the statement that, for Scottish poetry, 'the stakes have been high – the survival of a national identity'.[39] The nation on which Dunn's earlier poetry depended for its sense of public significance is, however, not the nation of Scotland. The American nation, the American experience is the authentic context of modern poetry's engagement. 'Jig of the Week No. 21' from *Northlight* recounts the childhood effort to complete a puzzle which presents a scene from the American civil war.[40] The title punningly displaces a Scottish context – a 'jig' as dance – with an American one – a 'jig' as the product of a 'jig saw'. As the picture assembles from its fragments, it seems that a shattered history is being brought back to life as the dedicated child and the reminiscent adult together

> – Put hats on heads, place heads on fallen men
> And resurrect the dead.

While Lowell, in 'For the Union Dead', witnesses the possibilities of the American past uprooted by the American present, in which

> a savage servility
> slides by on grease,[41]

Dunn is left constructing

> A reproduction of a reproduction
> Issued in multiples, mail-ordered

that negates the very scene it dramatizes:

> a wounded man waves in the paint
> A salutation from a grassy foreground

in cheery denial of the loss which he represents –

> Three hundred fragments of American
> Cardboard carnage!

[39] Dunn (ed.), *The Faber Book of Twentieth-Century Scottish Poetry*, Introduction, p. xlvi.
[40] Douglas Dunn, 'Jig of the Week No. 21', *Northlight* (London: Faber, 1988), pp. 43–4.
[41] Lowell, 'For the Union Dead', *For the Union Dead* (London: Faber, 1985), p. 72.

The completed puzzle, out of an 'old Bostonian box' that 'Crossed the Atlantic sixty years ago' brings to focus not a childhood fulfilment, but an adult loss. The republic, whose passing Lowell lamented in 'For the Union Dead', is Dunn's loss too: the quiet, suspended world of Scotland in 1949 is shaped as much by the lost ideals of the American past as it is by the commercialism of the American present:

> the missing piece
> The notional and beautiful republic.

To be at home in Scotland, for Dunn, is to be imaginatively lost in an America which has, itself, been lost to the modern world.

III The Failed Nations of Modernism

When literary history has stepped beyond the national traditions, what it finds is not the history of cultural interchange *between* the English-speaking nations but the history of 'cosmopolitanism', of a culture which is 'international' rather than 'inter-national'. In particular, modernism, in poetry as in architecture, is represented as a movement no longer determined by local conditions but based on discovering ways in which a universal 'technology' – free verse, the 'image', the unconscious – could be applied everywhere the same. The paradox of this international art, however, was that it took place in a world dominated by nationalisms, by the Versailles Treaty's principle of the 'self-determination' of peoples. Resurgent nationalisms, with their appeal to the multiplicity of autonomous cultural traditions, were the defining force of the 1920s in which literary modernism grew to maturity. In this respect, the late Romantic nationalism of W. B. Yeats, so often regarded as pre-modern, was, in fact, the herald of a poetic modernism committed to the recreation of national cultures, whether by MacDiarmid in Scotland, Carlos Williams in America or David Jones in Wales.[42]

It is in this world of recreated nationalities that the key form of modernist poetics – the 'lyrical epic' – should be understood. It is a form for which Eliot's *The Waste Land* was to provide the archetype but which had been in development in the works of Yeats and Pound throughout the First World War.[43] The inner tensions of this form – between its implied epic narrative and its limited, subjective, lyrical

---

[42] David Jones, *In Parenthesis: seinnyessit e gledyf ym penn mameu* (London: Faber, 1937), presents modern British nationality as founded upon the Welsh 'Britons' of the period at the end of the Roman Empire, but does so through a recollection and revival of Welsh culture in English.

[43] See my *Yeats, Eliot, Pound and the Politics of Poetry* (London: Croom Helm, 1982) for an account of the aesthetic origins and the development of the modernist epic.

moments of perception – made it perfectly suited to reflect the crisis of historical legitimation into which the narratives of the Western Empires had been cast by the First World War. In the 'lyrical epic', the implied order and purpose of epic narrative cannot be recovered fully from within the limited perspectives of momentary subjective consciousness: the poem is thus an 'open' or incomplete structure which demands a future closure, a closure which, in the consciousness of the appropriate reader, will generate a whole poem from the offered fragments. The future reader envisaged by such modernist techniques was – as the poet sought to be – the representative of a national consciousness conceived of as a historical continuity. The particular power of this 'crisis form' lay in the fact that it could be used both to dramatize the collapse of the West – the loss of a narrative order that connects origins to telos – and as the basis for refounding a new civilization: the reader who grasps the implicit order of the poem has become the source of a recollected nation, a resurrected nation, one born out of the power of poetry. The lyrical epics of modernism are *re-placements* of the nation, re-inscribing the nation's sense of history and of place and making anew the national identities which the First World War had set in doubt. David Jones's *In Parenthesis*, attempting to refound a British identity upon its Welsh and Celtic origins and their direct connection with the last days of the Roman Empire, enacts exactly the national project of the lyrical epic: an audience, which acquires the poem's inner logic of allusion and its system of historical parallels, will be an audience *versed* in a national imagination, an audience remade as the inheritors and future continuers of the national history of which the poet has despaired – but which the poem has, through its own fragmentary recollections, resurrected. It is in this context that Eliot's declaration of himself to be, in 1928, 'classicist in literature, royalist in politics, and anglo-catholic in religion'[44] can be seen as the necessary conclusion of a modernist aesthetics which required him to root his poetry in a national culture. If Eliot's *The Waste Land* paradigmatically enacts the loss of a historical order for modern society, his *Four Quartets* re-enacts the earlier poem's structures as a refounding of national order: 'History is now and England'.[45] The lyrical epic promised the nation as fulfilment of its own inventions and invented the nation as the completion of its own promise. Without that national context, the lyrical epic would degenerate into the endless incompletability that was Pound's *Cantos*; within it, the poet would become the creator of the very being of the nation itself. As MacDiarmid was to put it in *A Drunk Man Looks at the Thistle*:

---

[44] T. S. Eliot, *For Lancelot Andrewes* (London: Faber, 1928), p. 7.
[45] T. S. Eliot, 'Little Gidding', *Collected Poems 1909–62* (London: Faber, 1963), p. 222.

> A Scottish poet maun assume
> The burden o' his people's doom
> And dee to brak' their livin' tomb.[46]

Far from being the movement of international cosmopolitanism, poetic modernism represented a recovery of the origins of the nation, a remaking of a modern nation from the remnants of an older, and almost forgotten, history. The promise of modernism's renewed nations – and, through them, a renewed poetry – was, however, to be betrayed by the Second World War and its aftermath. By the 1950s, Louis Simpson can only imagine the nation that Whitman had promised through the absolute destruction of the nation that had come to stand in its place:

> But the man who keeps a store on a lonely road,
> And the housewife who knows she's dumb
> And the earth, are relieved.
>
> All that grave weight of America
> Cancelled! Like Greece and Rome.
> The future in ruins![47]

The nation is obstacle to, rather than vehicle of, the imagination's fulfilment: creativity can only return by its abolition, by an escape from the 'grave' of the nation. The modernist project and the modern nation fail together, their mutual promises unredeemable in the disastrous history of the mid-twentieth century.

In the absence of a resurrected nation, the innovations required by the lyrical epic become impossible to sustain. Thus the return, from Auden onwards, to a poetry of formal closures and, in an English context, to that poetry of region, of the region *as* nation, which Seamus Heaney analysed in 'Englands of the Mind':

> I believe they are afflicted with a sense of history that was once the peculiar affliction of the poets of other nations who were not themselves natives of England but spoke the English language. The poets of the mother culture, I feel, are now possessed of that defensive love of their territory which was once shared only by those poets whom we might call colonial.[48]

---

[46] Hugh MacDiarmid, 'A Drunk Man Looks at the Thistle', *Selected Poems*, Alan Riach (ed.), (Harmondsworth: Penguin, 1992), p. 112.

[47] Simpson, 'Walt Whitman at Bear Mountain', p. 120.

[48] Seamus Heaney, *Preoccupations: Selected Prose 1968–1978* (London: Faber, 1980), pp. 150–1.

Heaney might have turned his description around and declared that what afflicted English poets was the loss of history, the loss of the nation, for which the region now had to stand as surrogate, and might have said that the power and effectiveness of modern Irish – or perhaps only Northern Irish – poetry depended on the fact that the nation was still an 'open' issue. Heaney's own move to the Republic of Ireland was to discover only the banality of the modern nation, where:

> whoever is the first of us to seek
> assent and votes in a rich democracy
> will be the last of us and have killed our language.[49]

The displacement of a Lowell or a Plath within such a 'rich democracy' was to become the model, for British and Irish poets, of the modern – but non-modernist – condition. The America that had become a 'second eye', infusing itself everywhere into modern British and Irish culture, was also the America of the tortured 'I' of a poetic promise unfulfilled: the Scottish or Irish poet could resurrect him- or herself through the American voice only to discover the cultural failure with which that voice was itself afflicted.

The contemporary poet who has, perhaps, most powerfully addressed these issues is Paul Muldoon. Despite his close involvement with Northern Irish poetry, Muldoon's own poetic filiations go back to the modernist generation and, particularly, to Eliot. Muldoon's emigration to the United States in 1987 marks a moment as decisive in his career as Eliot's commitment to Englishness in 1927. In '7 Middagh Street' Muldoon ventriloquizes the voices of artist-émigrés like himself, living in a house in Brooklyn, rented in 1940 by W. H. Auden. On Thanksgiving day the seven inhabitants of the house – including Louis MacNeice and Salvador Dali – meditate on their origins:

> I left Barcelona by the back door
>
> with a portfolio of work
> for my first one-man show in New York.
>
> A starry night. The howling of dogs.
> The Anarchist taxi-driver carried two flags,
>
> Spanish and Catalan. Which side was I on?
> Not one, or both, or none.[50]

---

[49] Seamus Heaney, 'From the Land of the Unspoken', *The Haw Lantern*, p. 18.
[50] Paul Muldoon, *Meeting the British* (London: Faber, 1987), p. 129.

The displacement of the artist is driven by a dismemberment of the nation, its boundaries dissolving in a history that leaves each of us a 'one man show'.

'7 Middagh Street' sets a context for Muldoon's own emigration as a version of poetry's loss of the context of the nation in the aftermath of modernism. The first major poem of his American years, *Madoc: A Mystery*,[51] is an exploration of the origins of the America of which he is now a part, an examination of the role of poetry in national identity and a parodic commentary on the styles and significance of the lyrical epic. Its prologue ('Part One' of the volume) contains a poem – 'The Briefcase' – that has been much discussed, in part because it is dedicated to Seamus Heaney and seems to be a conscious rejoinder to the sense of a fundamentally benign transatlantic displacement that Heaney had presented in 'Beyond Sargasso'. Heaney's poem takes, as its central image, an eel which has

> drifted
> into motion half-way
> across the Atlantic,

to make its way two hundred miles inland in Ireland.[52] In Muldoon's poem the eel is a dead skin on a briefcase in Manhattan which, in a storm, threatens to come alive:

> And though it contained only the first
> inkling of this poem, I knew I daren't
> set the briefcase down
> to slap my pockets for an obol –
>
> for fear it might slink into a culvert
> and strike out along the East River
> for the sea. By which I mean the 'open' sea.[53]

The 'open sea' rather than the enclosed world of Ireland, the 'open' sea rather than the enclosed 'us' of *Sea*mus. 'The Briefcase' has an insistently closed rhyme scheme (*abcdefgfgedcba*) and yet its assertion is a desire for the 'openness' that characterized modernist aesthetics. In its fusion of fantasy, history and historical documents; in its use of elliptical allusions, with Southey's *Madoc* and the works of the major Romantic poets as intertexts; in the ironic interplay between the content of the poems and

[51] Paul Muldoon, *Madoc: A Mystery* (London: Faber, 1990).
[52] Heaney, 'Beyond Sargasso', from 'A Lough Neagh Sequence', *Door Into the Dark* (London: Faber, 1972), p. 39.
[53] Muldoon, 'The Briefcase', in *Madoc*, p. 12.

their titles (each named, in brackets, after a Western philosopher), *Madoc: A Mystery* ambitiously re-enacts the formal characteristics of the lyrical epics of high modernism. Like them it is also profoundly engaged with the relationship between poetry and the nation. In the case of *Madoc*, however, what we are given is not a resurrection of the nation through poetry but an alternative version of the national past in which poetry and history disrupt rather than fulfil each other.

   Madoc juxtaposes real events from the founding years of the United States with a fictional account of the arrival there of the poets Coleridge and Southey, tracing the lives they might have lived had they fulfilled their dream of establishing a new society – their pantisocracy – in America. *Madoc* makes a 'second eye' for America by rereading Muldoon's own emigration there back into American history, with America as the ideal place of fulfilment of the poetic imagination. The Romantic belief in the founding role of poets in the creation of a new nation is, therefore, displaced to the very nation which, if we accept Benedict Anderson's argument in *Imagined Communities*, was the source of all modern nationalisms. According to Anderson, it is the American Revolution and the establishment of the American Republic that provide the model for the European nations emerging from the aftermath of the French Revolution: 'Out of the American welter came these imagined realities: nation-states, republican institutions, common citizenships, popular sovereignty, national flags and anthems, etc.'[54] Into that American origin of the new form of the nation, Muldoon introduces Coleridge and Southey, not as the English Romantic nationalists they became but as the poet-settlers of the new America. As they struggle towards towns already named Athens and Ulster, however, what they encounter is not civilization renewed but an ancient barbarism. The Jeffersonian Republic may be new in form but, like the names of its towns, it is simply a repetition of older forms of domination, overwhelmed by the destruction of the 'Indians' and by political corruption. Classical antecedents may be sought as a means of historical justification –

> An island on the Ohio
> where Harman
> Blennerhassett
> is building a Roman
> villa
> complete with mosaics
> and frescoes
> and a modest cupola.

[54] Benedict Anderson, *Imagined Communities: Reflections on the Origin and Spread of Nationalism* (London: Verso, 1991), p. 81.

> The bog-oak
> lintel
> was unearthed
> on his god-forsaken
> family estate
> in Kerry.
> He had it shipped
> from Philadelphia
> by barge
> and bullock-cart.[55]

– but the Republic is based on the same viciousness as its classical antecedents:

> As he'd worked a broken sabre
> from temple to temple
> and under the sodden divot,
> didn't your man leap
>
> to his feet
> and begin to run
> through the bushes, balancing a caber
>
> of gore,
> and leaving behind the greater part
> of his wimple.[56]

The 'temple', the ideals of the poet-philosophers' higher truths, are founded on barbarism: the 'temple' of civilization is identical with the scalp of an Indian.

Southey's *Madoc*, to which Muldoon's poem alludes, is the account of the Welsh prince who was supposed to have sailed to America and 'colonized' it in 1169: this myth was used from the Elizabethan era as a justification of England's imperial expansion, both in Ireland and in North America. Muldoon's narrative juxtaposes the fictional experiences of Southey and Coleridge with the historical search for the descendants of those Welsh settlers – the 'Welch Indians' – that was one of the aims of the Lewis and Clark expedition that began the opening up of the West for European settlement. The poem, which appears to offer itself, therefore, as an 'origin' for Muldoon's *Madoc*, is also a poem which recounts a story which is the claimed 'origin' of Europe's settlement – and justification of

[55] Muldoon, '[Campanella]', in *Madoc*, p. 87.
[56] Muldoon, '[Rutherford]', in *Madoc*, p. 201.

its domination – of America. The national 'myth' of an earlier European origin for the settlement of America is repeated by Muldoon's poem, as it gestures to Southey's as *its* origin, but the parallel is invoked simply to show how empty such a search for origins is. Like all 'open' poems *Madoc* implies that there is a 'key' which links its individual elements to a mythic past, but Muldoon's poem parodies that search for origins, both national and poetic. Instead of a 'key' to the poem, which is also a 'key' to the nation, there is only ironic repetition of the absurdity of our search for that key:

§

And those teeny-weeny keys on their toggles of hemp?

§

And those teeny-weeny keys on their toggles of hemp?

§

Again, exactly identical.[57]

The bogus poetic claims of Southey's work (which he thought of as the best since *Paradise Lost*) are matched by the bogus claims of the history which it recounts. Poems, like nations, are founded not on the creative myths of the poetic imagination invoked by Romanticism and by high modernism but on spurious myths which are simply justifications of power.

Benedict Anderson saw, in the New World of the Americas, the deliberate creation of a 'parallel' universe – 'the aim was not to have New London succeed, overthrow, or destroy Old London, but rather to safeguard their continuing parallelism'[58] – and Muldoon, too, constructs this 'new' world as one of insistent parallels and repetitions, negating any possibility of a justifying origin or telos to the nation. The empty signifiers of this new cultural context are imaged in Jefferson's invention of a 'polygraph' to help him maintain his correspondence:

his newly-modified polygraph

will automatically
follow hand-in-glove

his copper-plate 'whippoorwill'
or 'praise' or 'love':

will run parallel to the parallel
realm to which it is itself the only clue.[59]

[57] Muldoon, '[Franklin]', in *Madoc*, p. 250.
[58] Anderson, *Imagined Communities*, p. 191.
[59] Muldoon, '[Pascal]', in *Madoc*, p. 96.

In America, instead of an innocent beginning, there is only repetition. The continuity of meaning, and the meaningful continuity, between the mind that thinks (the philosophers of the poems' titles), the hand that writes (the politicians and poets) and the hand that wields a sabre or a gun on their behalf is shattered: they inhabit parallel realms, incapable of justifying each other as the origin or purpose of historical progress. Jefferson's writing becomes the empty promise of the new nation, a mechanical reproduction which destroys, in its duplicitous duplication, the belief in any transcendental truth:

> Coleridge can no more argue from this faded blue
> turtle's splay
> above the long-house door to a universal
> idea of 'blue' or 'turtle' [60]

Muldoon's *Madoc* plays with the tactics of high modernism only to subvert them, only to reveal the unfulfilled – because unfulfillable – promise of the American nation – of any nation – as the completion of a poetic creation. Or, indeed, of the poem as the resurrection of a nation.

[60] Muldoon, '[Hobbes]', in *Madoc*, p. 92.

10

Contemporary Poetry and the Great War

Jonathan Allison

And somewhere in the nervous system of each survivor the under-
world of perpetual Somme rages on unabated. (Ted Hughes)[1]

I

The Great War won't go away and, no doubt, it shouldn't. Most of the
veterans are dead but are ritually remembered each November. Their
stories are told in many ways, and the war to end all wars continues to
exercise greater power over the imagination than any other modern
conflict. Lyn McDonald recently wrote:

> It never ceases to amaze me that interest in that momentous conflict,
> far from diminishing as time goes on, actually appears to increase –
> and with it the passions it arouses ... the pale ghosts of the 'Great
> War' ... still haunt the popular mind three generations on, inspiring
> pity – even anger.[2]

The very idea of war poetry brings with it certain expectations and
conceptions of value. War poetry (particularly of the 1914–18 war) is
seen in the United Kingdom as part of British nationalist culture, memory
and self-definition; it honours those who fought for their country, representing in personal terms the experience of the Front, but remembers too
the vast scene of national bereavement witnessed in those years. (In the
Republic of Ireland the memory of the Great War is more complicated
than that, for obvious reasons. In Northern Ireland, it is tied intimately to
contemporary debates about Unionism, loyalty and British military

[1] Ted Hughes, *Winter Pollen: Occasional Prose*, ed. William Scammell (New York:
Picador, 1995), pp. 70–1.
[2] Lyn McDonald, 'Preface', *Anthem for Doomed Youth: Poets of the Great War* (London:
Folio Society, 2000), p. xvii.

history. In the USA, where I teach, many students, in my experience, value this body of work for a variety of reasons, but it is fair to say that the Great War figures less large in American history than it does in the national histories of European countries.) Of course, World War One poetry protests against the horrid conditions of the war and the military bungling or indifference of the 'donkey' Generals who led the men to slaughter. In many ways, World War One poetry is seen as – at its best – *anti-war* poetry, bestowing upon it immense philosophical and political value. Formally, this poetry made the English pastoral absorb experiences unlike anything before, and part of the pleasure of these texts lies in the uneasy marriage, as Paul Fussell and others have shown, of pastoralism with the diction and imagery of industrialised slaughter. Not modernist, but absorbing the shocks of modernity at their most immediate and extreme, World War One poetry looks back uneasily to long-established traditions and forward, often despairingly, into the nightmare of the Somme.

Much of it is elegiac and every culture needs elegies, no matter how lacking in consolation those poems may appear to be. But the value of the elegiac war poem lies not only in the brilliance of individual poets (though that can never be ignored) but also in society's need for elegy which, at its best, does not lose its poignancy and power with time. Indeed, such poems will always have power as long as nations go to war. Furthermore, World War One poetry has been 'pre-evaluated for us', in Barbara Herrnstein Smith's terms, both as war poetry and as elegy:

> Although our experience of the value – in the sense here of positive effects – of literary works is not a simple product of 'social forces' or 'cultural influences', nevertheless texts, like all the other objects we engage with, bear the marks and signs of their prior valuings and evaluations by our fellow creatures and are thus, we might say, always to some extent pre-evaluated for us. *Classification* is itself a form of pre-evaluation, for the labels under which we encounter objects are very significant in shaping our experience of their value, often foregrounding certain of their possible effects and operating as signs – in effect, as culturally certified endorsements – of their performance of certain functions.[3]

It makes sense and is not tautologous to say that British war poems are valued because they perform their function well, in Smith's terms (they are valued according to 'their performance of certain functions'). And

---

[3] Barbara Herrnstein Smith, 'Value/Evaluation', in *Critical Terms for Literary Study*, Frank Lentricchia and Thomas McLaughlin (eds), (Chicago: University of Chicago Press, 1990), pp. 177–85 (p. 182).

when Philip Larkin in 1960 completed a poem about the Great War, he perhaps struggled with the fact that the experience of that war in national memory had been precisely 'pre-evaluated' for his generation. Perhaps we value originality exactly because, at its most original, it seems to escape such pre-evaluation.

Larkin wrote 'MCMXIV' between late 1958 and 1960.[4] Wistful, nostalgic, the poem laments the loss of national innocence in England in the war, focussing on the seemingly idyllic peace of the summer of 1914, when thousands of men queued up at recruitment stations, smiling for the camera as if it were just 'An August Bank Holiday lark'.[5] Written in four, tidy stanzas, with unrhymed trimeter lines, it has a gentle, muted power, and the steady build-up of imagery (old coinage, children named after English monarchs, advertisements for Cocoa, rural place names, wheat fields) conveys a cumulative elegiac effect of national proportions. The poem evokes a culture fundamentally rooted in English traditions going back to the Norman Conquest and, in so doing, it betrays nostalgia for the hierarchies and imperial power that the Great War undermined and that certainly has ended by the date of composition.

Of course, this meditation on the mythic summer of 1914 says more about the poet in 1960 than it does about England in 1914. This is nothing new. Poetry tends to express contemporary anxieties, and post-war poetry about World War One tends, often (as Blake Morrison has shown), to construct a myth of fallen, postlapsarian nature, that war's awful legacy.[6] There is poignancy in the risky repetition of 'never' in Larkin's last few lines and in the climactic, if rather conventional, phrase, 'Never such innocence again'.[7] This emotion is increased by the irony of men tidying their gardens before they depart (as though leaving for a brief interlude), those gardens which represent a dignified personal sphere and also national virtues of domestic order, self-sufficiency and civic pride. Idealizing a stable past that never existed, the poem is a kind of pastoral, particularly in its evocation of

> The place-names all hazed over
> With flowering grasses

---

[4] Andrew Motion, *Philip Larkin: A Writer's Life* (New York: Farrar Straus & Giroux, 1991), p. 300.

[5] Philip Larkin, 'MCMXIV', *Collected Poems*, ed. Anthony Thwaite (London: Faber, 1988), pp. 127–8.

[6] Blake Morrison examines this poem in light of a tradition of poems that portray nostalgically the summer of 1914, after which everything changed. See *The Movement: English Poetry and Fiction of the 1950s* (London: Methuen, 1986), p. 199.

[7] Larkin, 'MCMXIV', p. 128.

and the suggestion of 'Domesday lines' under the wheat fields. At once a personal expression of regret for a lost stability and a meditation on Englishness, the poem suggests a mythic point of origins for the modern malaise. As such, the poet, despite his famous remark about hating modernist poets' 'common myth-kitty', is reiterating a common myth about how the Great War ended England's greatness.[8] (Morrison even goes so far as to compare the poem to Eliot's statement that 'dissociation of sensibility' set in during the English civil war.)[9]

Foreshadowing a wave of national interest, during the 1960s, in the First World War and its literature, 'MCMXIV' anticipates the work of a number of poets who focussed on the war as a crucial moment of cultural definition. The poem illustrates the kind of lyric that Al Alvarez, in his anthology *The New Poetry* (1962), associated with English 'gentility', which he contrasted with the poems of Ted Hughes and others.[10] Yet, Alvarez shares with Larkin a sense that the Great War was a moment of national fracturing: '[England] is, literally, insulated from the rest of the world. But since the First World War, that insulation has slowly broken down.'[11] He proceeds to discuss the 'forces of disintegration which destroy the old standards of civilisation', manifest in two world wars and in the threat of nuclear Armageddon, forces which all poets should recognize and address in their work. It might be said that Larkin's Great War poem does exactly that – face up to disintegration which changed English society – but Alvarez clearly admires poetry which registers that violence in the form of the language itself. It is the 'violent, impending presence' of Hughes's horses he values and the forceful language that expresses it. Larkin's tidy stanzas, with his measured nostalgia, don't do the trick.[12]

II

Hughes wrote two review essays in the mid-1960s concerning the Great War, as well as a number of important poems on the subject.[13] Something in the air in the 60s (perhaps the emergence of CND, concomitant fears of a nuclear arms race, the 50th anniversaries of the war, perhaps all three) brought the Great War into the historical limelight. Many history books

[8] Philip Larkin, 'Statement' (1955), *Required Writing: Miscellaneous Pieces 1955–1982* (New York: Farrar, Straus & Giroux), p. 79.

[9] Morrison, *The Movement*, p. 195

[10] Al Alvarez, 'The New Poetry, or Beyond the Gentility Principle', in *The New Poetry* (Harmondsworth: Penguin, 1962), pp. 21–32.

[11] Ibid., p. 25.

[12] Ibid., p. 31.

[13] 'Unfinished Business', *New York Times Book Review*, April 1964 rpt. in *Winter Pollen*, pp. 42–4; 'National Ghost', *The Listener*, 5 August 1965, rpt. in *Winter Pollen*, pp. 70–2.

were published, their revisionist conclusions echoed in Joan Littlewood's *Oh What a Lovely War* and elsewhere.[14] War memoirs from the 1920s were brought back into print, scholarly studies of the war poets appeared and new anthologies of war poetry provided the means by which the war poets would be read by a new generation.[15] The rhetoric of historians and editors at the time communicated a sense of urgency, which they all seemed to share and which made claims for the continuing relevance of the Great War. A. J. P Taylor wrote, in 1963: 'The First World War cut deep into the consciousness of modern man ... Its memorials stand in every town and village. Half a century afterwards the experiences of it are not stilled.'[16] This suggests something of the atmosphere in which Hughes's essays were written.[17]

In his 1964 essay on Wilfred Owen, the subject elicits a visceral response from Hughes, whose father was a veteran of Gallipoli.[18] The war is not over, he claims, and survives in the British political unconscious. He praises Owen's 'genius for immersing himself in and somehow absorbing that unprecedented experience of ghastliness, the reality of that huge mass of dumb, disillusioned, trapped, dying men'.[19] He was impressed by Owen's ability to find a language to express the 'unprecedented experience' of modern war and, while most men were inarticulate about the experience, he was able to speak for them. The idea of finding a voice to express the fears of combat has enormous personal significance for Hughes, whose father was silent about his own wartime experience. Hughes criticizes the 'unshaken imperial arrogance' of those on the Home

---

[14] See Derek Paget, 'Popularising popular history: "Oh What A Lovely War" and the sixties', in *Critical Survey* 2.2 (1990), pp. 117–27. Paget lists the three most important revisionist histories for the writing of *Oh What A Lovely War!* – Leon Wolff's *In Flanders Fields* (1959), Alan Clark's *The Donkeys* (1961) and Barbara Tuchman's *August 1914* (1962). See Claire Tylee's useful account of writing on the Great War during the 1960s in her *The Great War and Women's Consciousness* (Iowa City: University of Iowa Press, 1990), pp. 1–17.

[15] Robert Graves, *Goodbye to All That* (London: Cassell, 1957), Siegfried Sassoon, *Memoirs of an Infantry Officer* (London: Faber, 1965), Edmund Blunden, *Undertones of War* (Oxford: Oxford University Press, 1956). Critical studies published in the sixties include Bernard Bergonzi, *Heroes' Twilight* (London: Constable, 1965) and John H. Johnson, *English Poetry of the First World War* (Princeton: Princeton University Press, 1964). Anthologies include Brian Gardner, *Up the Line to Death* (New York: Clarkson N. Potter, 1964), I. M. Parsons, *Men Who March Away* (London: Chatto & Windus, 1965), Maurice Hussey, *Poetry of the First World War* (London: Methuen, 1967).

[16] A. J. P. Taylor, *Illustrated History of the First World War* (London: Hamish Hamilton, 1963; London: Penguin, 1966), p. 11.

[17] Editors of poetry anthologies made equally strong claims for the continuing significance of the war and the poetry. For example, Maurice Hussey: 'Fifty years on from World War I, the events still refuse to bury themselves in oblivion' (Preface, p. 1).

[18] Hughes, 'Unfinished Business'.

[19] Ibid., p. 44.

Front, the 'tyranny of jingoism' that led to slaughter. Indeed, the gap between experiences at Home and at the Front, as Hughes understands it, constituted a split of catastrophic proportions:

> For England, the Great War was, in fact, a kind of civil war (still unfinished – which helps to explain its meaning for modern England, its hold on our feelings, and why Owen's poetry is still so relevant). His poems had to be weapons.[20]

This argument highlights the contrast between Larkin's melancholic sense that the war marked the end of a long idyll and Hughes's belief that it was the moment when modern class war gained dramatic expression.[21] For Larkin, the war spelled the end of greatness; for Hughes, it was a moment of radical unmasking, leading to social disintegration at the profoundest levels, 'where suddenly and for the first time Adam's descendants found themselves meaningless'.[22]

Early and late in his poetry, the Great War boils under the surface of the language, sometimes appearing explicitly, sometimes merely hinted at. In 'Ghost Crabs' (*Wodwo*, 1967), the ominous crabs stare inland 'like a packed trench of helmets'.[23] The seaside jawbone, in 'Relic' (*Lupercal*, 1960), is compared to 'a cenotaph' and there is the satirical pricking of the pompous bubble of British chauvinism in 'Wilfred Owen's Photographs' (*Lupercal*), clearly echoing the hatred of jingoism in the early essays.[24] In 'The Retired Colonel', from *Lupercal*, Hughes caricatures the sort of chauvinistic brass-hat that features in so much war literature. For Sassoon and Graves, such men were a scourge but, for Hughes, a comic anachronism.[25] In 'Out' (*Wodwo*), which foreshadows the 1980s war poems, his father's oppressive influence dominated the speaker's childhood, as he sat

> recovering
> From the four-year mastication by gunfire and mud.[26]

Deprived of agency, he sits submerged in memories of the dead and the carnage ('recovering' is used with a certain irony). As the father suffers

[20] Ibid., p. 43.
[21] 'The First World war goes on getting stronger – our number one national ghost ... An English social revolution was fought out in the trenches.' Hughes, 'National Ghost', p. 70.
[22] Ibid., p. 72.
[23] Hughes, *New Selected Poems* (New York: Harper & Row, 1982), p. 57.
[24] Ibid., pp. 41, 30.
[25] Ibid., p. 38.
[26] Ibid., p. 87.

passively, so the son, doomed to absorb his example, is a four-year-old *doppelganger*, the father's 'luckless double'. The father is 'wordless' and we may presume that such inarticulacy is, for a poet, a fatal sign of emasculation. In the poem's surreal second section, the father is dead, buried in a cave, then a broken but reconstructed automaton ('The reassembled infantryman').[27] He was killed but resurrected – an image to which Hughes will return in another poem twenty years later, 'Dust As We Are' (*Wolfwatching*).[28] Hughes's Great War poems are not all raging or satirical; one of his earliest forays in the genre, the ekphrastic 'Six Young Men' (*Hawk in the Rain*, 1956), voices awe-struck intimations of mortality, in the course of discussing a photograph of six Yorkshiremen killed in the trenches.[29] In 'Scapegoats and Rabies' (*Wodwo*), while much of the poet's anger is indeed focused on the much-demonized figure of the First World War General, the poem has gentler moments in which military and pastoral images are juxtaposed ironically, in a manner Paul Fussell found typical of war poetry:

> The soldiers go singing down the deep lane
> Wraiths into the bombardment of afternoon sunlight.[30]

In the final section of 'Out', entitled 'Remembrance Day', the traditional image of the poppy appears not as a conventional emblem of noble sacrifice, but as something sinister:

> The poppy is a wound, the poppy is the mouth
> Of the grave ...[31]

Womblike grave, the poppy and all it stands for must be dispensed with. No dignified flower of grievance, it represents a memory of catastrophe that absorbed the speaker and his father. Grandly (as though in ritual exorcism), he bids it farewell:

> Goodbye to all the remaindered charms of my father's survival.
> Let England close. Let the green sea-anemone close.[32]

Beginning with a personal statement about the father's memories, the poem concludes with the majestic pronouncement (spell-like, charm-like)

---

[27] Ibid., p. 88.

[28] Hughes, 'Dust As We Are,' *Wolfwatching* (New York: Noonday, 1992), pp. 13–14.

[29] Hughes, *New Selected Poems*, pp. 19–20.

[30] Paul Fussell, *The Great War and Modern Memory* (Oxford and New York: Oxford University Press, 1975, 2000), pp. 231–69. Hughes, *New Selected Poems*, p. 73.

[31] Hughes, *New Selected Poems*, p. 88.

[32] Ibid., p. 89.

about nothing less than the nation.[33] An ambiguous finale, with echoes of John of Gaunt's speech and of Blake's 'Jerusalem', one wonders whether he is dismissing English nationalism in general or the conception of imperialism that made the First World War inevitable.[34] Furthermore, in the image of the closing anemone, does he envisage the end of imperial ambitions only – the anemone, with its 'charming' tentacles, which kills all it touches – or a meditative turning inward of national consciousness? Either way, it seems likely the sea anemone will re-open, as they tend to do.[35]

Fussell wrote: 'One did not have to be a lunatic or a particularly despondent visionary to conceive quite seriously that the war would literally never end and would become the permanent condition of mankind.'[36] The 'Neverendians' were proved wrong but unpleasant memories haunted many veterans all their lives, not excepting Hughes senior. The poet returns to the war in *Wolfwatching*: we might say the anemone re-opened. The title of the poem 'Dust As We Are' overlays Biblical imagery upon Rupert Brooke's idealized 'richer dust' and on the dust on Isaac Rosenberg's poppy ('Break of Day in the Trenches'). It revisits the domestic No Man's Land of 'Out':

> His lonely sittings
> Mangled me, in secret – like TV
> Watched too long, my nerves lasered.[37]

In this re-writing of 'Out', the father listens to the past, the son to the father. The father was 'masticated', the son 'mangled'; the father was wounded, the son 'lasered'. The visionary effects of 'Out' are replaced by more realistic effects, harking back as much to the language of Owen as to early Hughes. He imagines his father's horrible visions: 'Swampquakes of the slime of puddled soldiers.'[38] (Hughes observed in 1964 that Owen's language was Keatsian and sensuous but also weapon-like and shocking. His own language, forged not in battle but in the oppressive domestic sphere dominated by his father, tries to live up to that intensity.) The

---

[33] Note that he says 'England' not Britain. As Neil Roberts argues, in his later Laureate poems he refers to 'Britain' not 'England'. See 'Hughes, the Laureateship and National Identity', in *Q/W/E/R/T/Y: arts, littératures & civilisations du monde*, volume 9 (October 1999), pp. 203–9.

[34] Roberts, 'Hughes', p. 206.

[35] See Hughes's verse on the sea anemone in his comic sequence in the *New Statesman & Society*, 26 August 1994, p. 4: 'None can resist my grace. / All fall for my charms.'

[36] Fussell, *The Great War*, p. 71.

[37] Hughes, 'Dust'. Rupert Brooke, 'The Soldier' in Jon Silkin (ed.), *Penguin Book of First World War Poetry* (London: Penguin, 1979), p. 81. Isaac Rosenberg, 'Break of Day in the Trenches', in Silkin, *Penguin Book*, p. 219.

[38] Hughes, 'Dust As We Are', p. 13.

anti-heroic father turns the home into a mausoleum in which he has been resuscitated. Both zombie and marble bust, he recalls the 'reassembled' soldier of the earlier poem, with overtones of Plath's 'Lady Lazarus' thrown in:

> His muscles very white – marble white.
> He had been heavily killed. But we had revived him.[39]

But he has no message to give, no prophecy. He has nothing to say whatsoever.

The title of 'For the Duration' (*Wolfwatching*) suggests the never-ending war, perhaps, but also the duration of the paternal silence about the war.[40] The poem's self-revelatory tone, bitter and compassionate, is conveyed through short lines and blunt sentences:

> I felt a strange fear when the war-talk,
> Like a creeping barrage, approached you.[41]

Although his father never divulged details, he had won the DCM for carrying in wounded men, under intense enemy fire, and was hit by shrapnel while doing so. On another occasion, he narrowly escaped death when a dud shell landed beside him and, in an incident referred to in several poems, he escaped death from shrapnel because of a book in his pocket. All other male veterans of his father's acquaintance told their tale, with the son present, but not the father:

> But what alarmed me most
> Was your silence.[42]

This silence seems to betoken some trauma, hence the boy feels 'fear' – what ghastly isolation must the father be enduring? Yet he feels frustrated: is the father being over-indulgent with his hoarded memories? Amongst the garrulous fraternity of veterans, the boy was embarrassed:

> Why was your war so much more unbearable
> Than anybody else's?[43]

Hearing him from his bedroom, the boy feels helpless in the face of the father's nightmares:

[39] Ibid., p. 13.
[40] Hughes, 'For the Duration', *Wolfwatching*, pp. 26–7.
[41] Ibid., p. 26.
[42] Ibid., p. 26.
[43] Ibid., p. 27.

> No man's land still crying and burning
> Inside our house ... [44]

The lines supply an eerie juxtaposition of the domestic with the unspeakable horror of combat – home without refuge. The phrase 'still going on' suggests 'Neverendian' continuity, hinted at in the poem's title; it has been internalized, the border between past and present broken down. Yet the poem's closure suggests the father, no mere zombie, will somehow 'rescue' his family. Partly this is pathetic, suggesting a delusional state, but it has a warmth absent elsewhere in the poem. As elegy, the poem posits the continuity of family unity in the face of trauma, though the whole attempt at such unity is undermined by this unnerving silence.

While defending himself against the charge that his poetry is despicably violent, Hughes made a distinction between positive and negative kinds of violence, claiming his poetry (particularly his animal poetry) is more interested in the former. The Biblical conversion from Saul to Paul he thinks of as a positive sort of violence, whereas the graphic description of mere destruction would clearly be negative. 'This radical, negative, strong sense of the word violence seems to be its primary one. That's the meaning we use when we call Hitler's gang "men of violence".'[45] His animal poems, often viewed as negatively violent, are, in his opinion, very positive, since the animals are obeying their natures and are beyond ethical codes. His hawks and sharks, following the laws of their nature, 'are innocent, obedient, and their energy reaffirms the divine law that created them as they are'.[46] In these terms, how do we read the war poems? They are elegies for a casualty of 'negative' violence. What he hoarded in memory was absorbed by the speaker, whose painful second-hand knowledge has been an immense burden, as has the knowledge of his father's isolation. Animals' violence exists on a different scale of value, for Hughes, as implied by his 'Tiger Psalm' (from *Earth Numb*), in which the tiger's Blakean energies are contrasted with the ruthless, post-Enlightenment rationalism of the mechanical age and the gun:

> The machine guns shake their heads,
> They go on chattering statistics.
> The tiger kills by thunderbolt. [47]

What is valuable in Hughes's war poems is the power and range of the language, the ability to express the force that fell upon the father and, in

[44] Ibid., p. 27.
[45] Hughes, 'Poetry and Violence', *London Magazine*, January 1971. In *Winter Pollen*, p. 254.
[46] Hughes, 'Poetry and Violence', p. 259.
[47] Hughes, *New Selected*, p. 229.

turn, falls upon the son and the insidious, destructive power of the father's silences. This gives witness to and expresses violence but achieves critical distance from it. At the same time, Hughes's language is rich enough to suggest not merely individual pathology, but a general condition of which this case is a representative. As such, the bleak, heartbreak house of Hughes replicates the experience of a generation and, like Larkin's poem, Hughes's poem attempts to portray a national crisis embodied in the individual.

In a note about a poem a reader had found 'incomprehensible', Hughes attempted to explain himself, to readers of the *Weekend Telegraph*, as son of a war veteran. The poem in question

> defines the outlook of an offspring of that war, one for whom it was virtually the Creation Story, and such a shattering, all-inclusive, grievous catastrophe that it was felt as a national *defeat*, though victory had somehow been pinned on to it as a consolation medal.[48]

For Alvarez and Larkin, the war was a watershed in European history and English (or British) culture. For Hughes, it was 'virtually the Creation Story', a myth of beginnings, rendering life apparently meaningless for its survivors. Out of that shattered world he builds non-consolatory elegies, as he refuses the wreathes and poppies that continue to wound and never heal.

III

Michael Longley is also the son of a veteran, and his Great War poems also focus on his father's memories. He tells the story in different ways, but the following account is representative:

> At the age of seventeen he had enlisted in 1914, one of thousands queuing up outside Buckingham Palace. He joined the London-Scottish by mistake and went into battle wearing an unwarranted kilt. A Lady from Hell. Like so many survivors he seldom talked about his experiences, reluctant to relive the nightmare. But not long before he died, we sat up late one night and he reminisced.[49]

As with Hughes, he notes the lifetime paternal reluctance to talk but Longley senior finally opened up. Formally traditional, measured in tone, Longley's poems, at first sight, may seem close to the Alvarez model of

---

[48] Cited in Roberts, 'Hughes', p. 207.
[49] Michael Longley, *Tuppenny Stung: Autobiographical Chapters* (Belfast: Lagan Press, 1994), p. 18.

'gentility' – they lack the bleakness of Hughes's work and the sense of enormous violence haunting the speaker and his subject. They focus on the battlefield and its memories (there is no Larkinesque pre-war idyll), but there is nothing akin to Hughes's extravagantly alliterative depiction of 'the slime of puddled soldiers'. But, just as Hughes returned, in his fifties, to a theme he explored as a younger man (to attempt the elegiac consolation that had earlier escaped him, or to pay tribute to a father whose ripe age he had now reached), Longley also returned in the 1980s to the paternal theme attempted in the 1960s.

Written in five iambic pentameter stanzas, 'In Memoriam' begins with the prayer that the speaker's language will not misrepresent the memory of the father:

> let no similes eclipse
> Where crosses like some forest ... .[50]

The caveat is balanced by the confident commitment to a formal narrative, though he's unafraid of risky but satisfying half-rhymes ('in the face'/'the Palace') and humorous rhyming juxtapositions ('none the wiser'/'kibosh on the Kaiser'; 'future spill'/'testicle'). The poem is written to record, primarily, the father's experience but also those of other soldiers –

> Let yours
> And other heartbreaks play into my hands.

Explicitly, the speaker takes on the role of medium for their grief. Almost castrated, wounded in the testicle, the father survived and later had twin sons, including the speaker:

> That instant I, your most unlikely son,
> In No Man's Land was surely left for dead.

The link with the father is made intimate by the sense of having accompanied him into battle, inside that testicle. Pre-embryonic, he too was wounded and, hence, can sympathize with the father. Held 'secure' in the father's body, the son returns the compliment by holding his father's voice in his mind.

This account contrasts markedly with the sense of filial embarrassment in Hughes's poem. Despite the father's near-castration, he remained potent and sexually active. The poem almost celebrates this fact in the account of the father's postwar womanizing in France and the final lines

[50] Longley, *No Continuing City* (London: Macmillan, 1969), pp. 41–2.

recall those pre-marital intimacies, imagining a final, ghostly sexual encounter. The dead soldier's spiritual mistress comes to him: her final skirt-lifting gesture blends Joycean prostitute with the Scottish soldier, whose kilt is historically the focus of all those old jokes.

> Now those lost wives as recreated brides
> Take shape before me, materialise.

The poem remembers the wound but affirms the persistence of hetero-sexual passion, despite it. The father's wartime experience is a triumph for his libido, as much as anything else, and the poet's myth of himself seems to revolve around the ideas of fortunate escape and the inheritance of qualities that make of one a lucky, sexually potent survivor. Behind this lie the historic associations between potency and poetic power.

Longley revisits the landscape of the Western Front in later poems, such as 'Edward Thomas's War Diary' (*Man Lying on a Wall*, 1976), 'The Third Light' (*Selected Poems 1963–1980*, 1981) and 'Bog Cotton' (*The Echo Gate*, 1979), but his most famous poem on the subject was 'Wounds' (*An Exploded View*, 1972).[51] Written in the early 1970s, it is a group elegy for the speaker's father, a veteran of the Somme, and for the 36th (Ulster) Division, which lost 5,500 men on 1 July 1916 and many more thereafter.[52] It also remembers three teenage British soldiers, killed in action in Belfast in 1970, and an innocent Belfast bus conductor, murdered by paramilitaries, in front of his family. The poem skilfully combines the deaths in a general lamentation, also a satire, which (not unlike Hughes's elegies) undermines elegiac convention in offering ambiguous consolatory prayers. The poem comprises two long blank-verse stanzas, beginning with the conceit of entering into the father's memory by way of two pictures from his head.

If Hughes criticizes English or British imperialism in his war elegies, Longley, as a Belfast Protestant of English parentage, son of a British Army veteran (Englishman in a Scottish regiment), has a somewhat more complex relationship with the history of British nationalism. In

---

[51] 'Edward Thomas's War Diary', from *Man Lying on a Wall*, 1976, is printed in Michael Longley, *Selected Poems 1963–1980* (Winston-Salem, NC: Wake Forest University Press, 1981), p. 42; 'The Third Light' (*Selected*, p. 63); 'Wounds' (*Selected*, pp. 18–19). 'Bog Cotton' was printed in *The Echo Gate* (London: Secker & Warburg, 1979), p. 33.

[52] The Battle of the Somme is central to Ulster Protestant mythology, sometimes seen by Loyalists as a re-enactment of the Battle of the Boyne. Annual Orange processions in July at Drumcree, Portadown, are nominally commemorations of the Somme. An interesting literary treatment of the Somme myth can be found in Frank McGuinness's play *Observe the Sons of Ulster Marching Towards the Somme* (London: Faber, 1986). For discussion of the Somme in Belfast street murals, see Bill Rolston, 'From King Billy to Cu Chulainn: Loyalist and Republican Murals, Past, Present and Future' in *Eire-Ireland* 32.4 and 33.1–2 (Winter/Spring 1997–8), pp. 6–28.

'Wounds', he pays tribute to the ferocity of Ulster Loyalists going into battle at Thiepval (Northern France), seemingly without condoning or condemning their point of view explicitly

> 'No Surrender!': a boy about to die,
> Screaming 'Give 'em one for the Shankill!'[53]

While not a didactic poem, it is finally a de-idealizing of violence and conveys a sense of the aimless casualness of political murder in contemporary Ulster, depicted in mock-heroic contrast to the savage patriotism of the Somme's doomed combatants. The IRA assassin is a 'shivering boy' who apologizes to the victim's family:

> To the children, to a bewildered wife,
> I think 'Sorry Missus' was what he said.[54]

Longley has described his elegies as 'wreathes' offered modestly in the face of present violence.[55] There is a greater effort in his elegies than in Hughes's to honour the dead and to resort to traditional consolatory emblems – the burial of the dead, flowers, poppies. In 'Wounds', despite the devastating bathos of the final lines, in which the assassin skulks away, there is a surreal effort at traditional ritual. He buries his father 'with military honours of a kind', alongside the three soldiers and the bus conductor's uniform, mingling civilian uniform with military, the war veteran's medals with the recent dead. The 'Sacred Heart of Jesus', however, is 'paralysed', as the anti-elegiac vies with the conventionally elegiac, in this modern, understated, unillusioned attempt at remembrance.[56]

Crucial to Hughes's depiction of his father is the embarrassment he feels in the face of his father's silence and the poet feels he is the inheritor of disability and silence (though, ironically, it is that very silence that gives him a subject for poetry). As such, Hughes's later elegies involve anxiety about paternal competence. Similarly, in Longley's first elegy, there is a preoccupation with his kilt-wearing father's near-castration and his continued potency after the war; in 'Wounds' he is cancer-ridden, dying, 'a belated casualty'. In an early, unpublished draft of the poem, however, the earlier preoccupation with the paternal genitalia, anxiety about manhood and inheritance are painfully obvious:

[53] Longley, 'Wounds'.
[54] Ibid.
[55] 'An Interview with Michael Longley, conducted by Dermot Healey,' *Southern Review* 31.3 (Summer 1995), p. 560.
[56] Longley, 'Wounds'.

I sit down to pee now like a woman.
I have a penis and two testicles
But for all the use they are, to me
Might as well hang them up as a door-knocker.[57]

The anxiety about masculinity displayed in the father's words harks back to the near-castration in 'In Memoriam' and the compensatory focus on postwar heterosexual passion. The impotency of the old man manifests a disability latent in the earlier poem, but triumphantly defeated. The speakers in Longley's and Hughes's poems are concerned about their personal inheritances. In Hughes's case, the 'luckless double' absorbs the 'negative violence' suffered by the father. In Longley's case, the early draft, with its stark confession of paternal impotency, is a discarded stage in a process of thinking about filial inheritance. Had it remained in the poem, it would have detracted from the dignity of the dying man; it would also distract attention from the communal burial of soldiers with old veteran with bus conductor. Also, the feminized father might, therefore, resemble the assassin, as drawn in the first draft, who, also feminized, is

a youth who wore a woman's stocking
Over his face.[58]

Hughes and Longley are rightly protective of their weakened fathers, seeing in each an image of what they might become – silent or decrepit.

Like some anxious Hughesian return, in *Ghost Orchid* (1995), Longley revisits the father's war and, in a book rich with meditations on the role of violence in culture, evocation of the Western Front (as in the short, deft stanzas of 'The Kilt' and 'A Pat of Butter, After Hugo Claus') is not inappropriate.[59] However, I want to consider, in closing, a recent war elegy with a much wider explicit focus, 'The War Graves'.[60] In 1997, Longley published an article in the *Belfast Telegraph* during a very tense period in Northern Ireland, after the Orangemen's violent protest march at Drumcree in early July and the traditional Orange parades held on the twelfth of that month.[61] He recalls a recent visit to the 36th (Ulster) Division war cemetery at Thiepval, close to where 5,500 Ulster men fell,

---

[57] Early draft of 'Wounds'. Michael Longley archive, Box 23, item 51. Special Collections, Robert W. Woodruff Library, Emory University, Atlanta.

[58] Early draft of 'Wounds'.

[59] Michael Longley, *The Ghost Orchid* (London: Cape, 1995), pp. 35, 36.

[60] Longley, 'The War Graves', *The Guardian*, Friday, 3 March 2000. Reprinted in *The Weather in Japan* (London: Cape, 2000), pp. 23–4.

[61] Michael Longley, 'A monument to bad taste', *Belfast Telegraph*, 16th July, 1997, p. 11. Reprinted in *The Twelfth: What It Means To Me* (Belfast: Ulster Society, 1997).

on the first day of the Battle of the Somme. He admires the layout of the cemetery and the tidiness of the gardens: 'Immaculately mown lawns and dainty flowerbeds add to the feeling that these sorrowful vistas were laid out only yesterday by some omnipresent gardener from a British suburb.' In particular, he praises the Lutyens-designed Memorial tower (a facsimile of the Clandeboye tower in County Down) – 'every detail is simple and clear-cut, without a hint of jingoism or triumphalism' – but he finds fault with the obelisk erected in memory of Orangemen who died in the war: 'Aesthetically a disaster, an ugly lump of prose that detracts from the poetry of its setting ... a monument to bad taste ... a failure of the imagination.' He criticizes the Orange Order's behaviour at Drumcree two weeks earlier and implies that, by their behaviour, they are 'trampling on the graves' of the dead in France. It was a courageous article and he makes it clear that he resents the appropriation of the memory of the Somme by the Orange Order. Inevitably, Longley's article suggests what political values we feel entitled to attribute to his poetry, in poems where those values are not explicit. The essay politicizes other things Longley has written about the subject of the war and its commemoration, providing a set of arguments we may always assume to be implicit. It has a bearing on how we read 'The War Graves', first published in *The Guardian* on 3 March 2000, a poem evidently based upon the experience in France outlined in the newspaper article. *The Guardian* published several poems by Tom Paulin a few weeks earlier – 'Drumcree Four' (4 February) and 'Decommissioning' (11 February). These poems, which evince virulent anti-Unionist sentiment, stylistically and in other ways provide a stark contrast to Longley's elegy. Clearly, they provide one element in the background against which we read 'The War Graves' and, coming in their wake, a 'war' poem, by a poet renowned for writing about the Troubles, raises certain readerly expectations. The poem also gains resonance in light of the unusual 1998 commemorations at Messines of all Irishmen (Protestant and Catholic) who died in the Great War, an event that saw the unprecedented appearance of the Queen with the President of Ireland. Something of the energy of that event lies behind this poem.[62] Furthermore, a poem thus titled, published in March, 2000, is likely to suggest the widely-publicized graves of those who were murdered in Ireland in the 1970s that the IRA had promised to find, so that victims' families could finally come to terms with their loss. Their unsuccessful efforts to do so in 1998–9 were widely publicized. Another, related text that forms part of the interpretative network of this poem is *Lost Lives*, published in September 1999, a stark catalogue of

---

[62] Andy Pollak, 'Two traditions united at last on Belgian battlefield', *Irish Times*, 12 November 1998; Mary McAleese, 'Peace Park invites all to remember differently,' *Irish Times*, 12 November 1998.

murders in Northern Ireland, that gives further denotation to the public act of commemorating the dead in the poem.[63] These background texts provide a dynamic context in which the Longley poem has meaning and value; and, alongside its considerable aesthetic satisfactions, it gains power from its timely integration with these other events and texts. Indeed, its aesthetic value is intimately tied to its social power.

'The War Graves' is written in twelve unrhymed quatrains, each stanza a conversational, end-stopped sentence. Beginning with the 'exhausted cathedral' (barely recovered from its wartime shelling), it ends in Wilfred Owen's graveyard, where the speaker and his partner symbolically pick from a bed of nettles '[O]ne celandine each, the flower that outwits winter'. 'There will be no end to clearing up after the war,' he writes (a remark with considerable resonance in the year 2000, when the Stormont assembly was stalled on the issue of the decommissioning of IRA weapons). Again, the elegiac effects of the poem are powerful because the utterance has double duty to serve as a Great War poem and a Northern Irish elegy. It has something of the stateliness and the sense of tired tragedy found in Longley's poem 'Ceasefire', which also had a public hearing before its publication in the collection *The Ghost Orchid*, appearing in both *The Irish Times* and *The New Yorker*. Published after the IRA ceasefire of 1995, the power of that poem – its social and political value, inseparable from its aesthetic power – is suggested by a recent letter to *The Irish Times* from Irish Senator Mary Henry. The author quotes the final lines of the poem ('And kiss Achilles' hand, the killer of my son'), adding: 'No matter what our views on the Orange marches, the process of reconciliation and the development of a tolerant Irish society has to take place here as well as in Northern Ireland.'[64] The Irishness of Longley's Achilles was guaranteed upon publication.

'The War Graves' includes elements of traditional pastoral elegy: the garden's pruned roses and planted sweet william are reminiscent of the tidied gardens of 'MCMXIV', and the violets and wild flowers, along with woodpigeons, finches and blackbirds, participate in Nature's lament. There is a Longleyesque catalogue of names ('Rifleman Parfitt, Corporal Vance ...') and the allusions to Sorley, Thomas and Owen locate the poem in a tradition of poets whose wartime, poetic conventions

---

[63] *Lost Lives* by David McKittrick, Seamus Kelters, Brian Feeney, Chris Thornton (Edinburgh: Mainstream Publishing, 1999), provided a record of every single victim of the Troubles. Nell McCafferty wrote in review: 'It is majestic and consoling. It is the first book of its kind, the only one ever, anywhere in the world, to document every single person to die in a specific conflict. This book is an act of redemption.' Retrieved 8 February 2002 from the World Wide Web: http://www.amazon.co.uk/exec/obidos/tg/stores/detail/-/books/184018504X/reviews/026-6122993-1969261#184018504x4500.

[64] Mary Henry, 'Orange March in Dublin', Letters, *Irish Times*, 29 March 2000. 'Ceasefire' was published in *The New Yorker* on 15 May 1995.

are remembered by Longley's pastoral quatrains.[65] Longley has been called a conservative or traditionalist poet, labels that do not do justice to the elements of surrealism and brilliant surprise within his work, but here is a poem that self-consciously and with mild irony offers consolation in familiar terms in the face of the 'unendurably moving'.[66] The interpretative context of post-ceasefire Ulster provides added burden to lament and console and confers particular value on that enterprise.

Again, we don't experience the value of such poems as either 'purely' aesthetic or 'purely' socio-political (the very idea rests on a fallacious distinction between form and content); we don't experience the value as (Herrnstein Smith again) 'a simple product of social forces or cultural influences'. However, it is true that 'The War Graves' has been 'pre-evaluated' for us as a sort of belated World War One elegy, with the enormous emotional pull that that entails. Its double duty as a Northern Irish 'Troubles' poem bestows added power to the utterance, doubling the tears shed and doubling the thirst for consolation. As long as the 'Troubles' have been in progress, there have been expectations that indigenous poets would respond feelingly. The way that Ulster poetry gets evaluated is linked to the question of how well it functions under the special burdens of duress to which it is, in many cases, a response and to the readerly expectations of the poetry of that place. It is probably true that, as Smith implies, poetry's value is always dependent upon what culture expects it to perform. When Yeats, long indebted to notions of heroic will, dismissed Wilfred Owen's poetry on the grounds that 'passive suffering' was not a fit subject for poetry, he was delimiting the functions he expected poetry to perform.[67] However, that so-called 'passive suffering' is possibly at the core of Hughes's portraits of his father and those poems are recognizable as powerful and valuable performances.

[65] See John Lyon, 'Michael Longley's Lists', *English*, 45.183 (Autumn 1996), pp. 228–46, and Fran Brearton, 'Michael Longley: Poet in No Man's Land', *Critical Survey* 10.1 (1998), pp. 75–6. A revised version of the latter essay was published in Brearton's splendid study, *The Great War in Irish Poetry: W. B. Yeats to Michael Longley* (Oxford: Oxford University Press, 2000).

[66] 'We found it unendurably moving.' Longley, 'A monument to bad taste', p. 11.

[67] W. B. Yeats, Introduction to *Oxford Book of Modern Verse* (Oxford: Oxford University Press, 1936).

Notes on Contributors

Jonathan Allison is Associate Professor of English at the University of Kentucky and was formerly Associate Director of the International W. B. Yeats Summer School in Sligo, Ireland. He has edited *Yeats's Political Identities* (University of Michigan Press, 1996), *Patrick Kavanagh: A Reference Guide* (G. K. Hall, 1996) and *Poetry for Young People: William Butler Yeats* (Sterling, 2002). He was general editor of the series 'Irish Literature, History and Culture', published by the University Press of Kentucky.

Vicki Bertram is Senior Lecturer at Nottingham Trent University. She edited *Kicking Daffodils: Twentieth-Century Women Poets* (Edinburgh University Press, 1997) and has published articles on poetry and feminism. She is currently completing *Gendered Poetics: Contemporary Poetry, Culture And Sexual Politics* (Pandora, 2002)

Paul Breslin is the author of *The Psycho-Political Muse: American Poetry Since the Fifties* (Chicago, 1987), *Nobody's Nation: Reading Derek Walcott* (Chicago, 2000) and a collection of poems, *You Are Here* (TriQuarterly Books, 2000). With Robert Hamner, he will be co-editing a special issue of *Callaloo* on Derek Walcott, planned for late 2004. He is a Professor of English at Northwestern University.

Cairns Craig is the author of *Yeats, Eliot, Pound and the Politics of Poetry* (Croom Helm, 1981), *Out of History: Narrative Paradigms in Scottish and English Culture* (Polygon, 1996) and *The Modern Scottish Novel* (Edinburgh University Press, 1999). He was General Editor of the four-volume *History of Scottish Literature* (Aberdeen University Press, 1987–9) and is an editor of the Canongate Classics series of Scottish texts. He is Director of the Centre for the History of Ideas in Scotland at the University of Edinburgh, where he has also been Chair of the English Literature Department.

Robert Crawford's most recent collection of poetry is *Spirit Machines* (Cape, 1999). A selection of his poems appears in *Penguin Modern Poets 9* (1996) and, with Mick Imlah, he edited *The New Penguin Book Of Scottish Verse* (2000). His critical books include *The Savage and the City in the Work of T. S. Eliot* (Clarendon Press, 1987), *Devolving English Literature* (2nd edn, Edinburgh University Press, 2000) and *The Modern Poet* (Oxford University Press, 2001). He is Professor of Modern Scottish Literature at the University of St Andrews.

Lilias Fraser is a postgraduate in the School of English at the University of St Andrews. She is completing a thesis on commercial production and critical values in contemporary Scottish poetry.

Alan Golding is Professor of English at the University of Louisville. He is the author of *From Outlaw to Classic: Canons in American Poetry* (University of Wisconsin Press, 1995), a CHOICE Best Academic Book award winner, and of numerous essays on writing in the Objectivist, Black Mountain and post-New American Poetry traditions. He is currently writing a book on experimental poetics and/as pedagogy from modernism to the present. He also co-edits the Contemporary North American Poetry Series for the University of Wisconsin Press.

Romana Huk is Associate Professor of English at the University of Notre Dame. Her publications include *Contemporary British Poetry: Essays in Theory and Criticism* (edited with James Acheson; State University of New York Press, 1996), *Assembling Alternatives: Reading Postmodern Poetries Transitionally* (Wesleyan University Press, 2003) and *Stevie Smith: Between the Lines* (Palgrave, 2003). Her new work, begun while on fellowship at Oxford Brookes University's Centre for Modern and Contemporary Poetry, is on postmodern theology and avant-garde poetics.

Marjorie Perloff's most recent books are *21st-Century Modernism* (Blackwell, 2001), *Poetry On & Off The Page* (Northwestern, 1998) and *Wittgenstein's Ladder: Poetic Language and the Strangeness of the Ordinary* (Chicago, 1996). She is Sadie Dernham Patek Professor Emerita at Stanford University.

Andrew Michael Roberts is Senior Lecturer in English at the University of Dundee. His publications include *Conrad and Masculinity* (Macmillan, 2000), edited volumes on *The Novel* (Bloomsbury, 1993) and *Conrad and Gender* (Rodopi, 1993) and articles on twentieth-century fiction and poetry. He is currently completing a book on the work of Geoffrey Hill (Northcote House, 2002).

Index